UNITED METHODIST DOCTRINE

D1468240

UNITED
METHODIST
DOCTRINE

The Extreme Center

Scott J. Jones

Abingdon Press
Nashville

UNITED METHODIST DOCTRINE: THE EXTREME CENTER

Copyright © 2002 by Abingdon Press

All rights reserved.
No part of this work may be reproduced or transmitted in any form or by any means, electronic or mechanical, including photocopying and recording, or by any information storage or retrieval system, except as may be expressly permitted by the 1976 Copyright Act or in writing from the publisher. Requests for permission should be addressed to Abingdon Press, P.O. Box 801, 201 Eighth Avenue South, Nashville, TN 37202-0801.

This book is printed on acid-free, recycled, elemental-chlorine-free paper.

Library of Congress Cataloging-in-Publication Data

Jones, Scott J.
    United Methodist doctrine : the extreme center / Scott J. Jones.
       p. cm.
Includes bibliographical references and index.
    ISBN 0-687-03485-X (pbk. : alk. paper)
    1. United Methodist Church (U.S.)—Doctrines. 1. Title.
    BX8382.2.Z5 J66 2002
    230'.76—dc21

                                                                    2002003684

All Scripture quotations, unless otherwise noted, are from The New Revised Standard Version of the Bible copyright © 1989, by the Division of Christian Education of the National Council of the Churches of Christ in the United States of America. Used by permission.

Those noted KJV are from the King James Version.

"Here I Am Lord," © 1981, Daniel L. Schutte and New Dawn, Music, 5536 NE Hassalo, Portland, OR 97213. All rights reserved. Used with permission.

"God of Many Names" by Brian Wren, © 1986 Hope Publishing Co. Used by permission.

"Come, All of You," "In Christ There Is No East or West" (St. 3, Laurence Hull Stookey), and "Wash, O God, Our Sons and Daughters," © 1989 The United Methodist Publishing House. (Administered by The Copyright Company c/o The Copyright Company, Nashville, TN). All rights reserved. International Copyright secured. Used by permission.

06 07 08 09 10 11—10 9 8 7

MANUFACTURED IN THE UNITED STATES OF AMERICA

To Richard Heitzenrater and to the memories of Jameson Jones, Albert Outler, John Deschner, and John Wesley, the teachers and theological friends who have most influenced my thought

THE SECOND POINT TO BE CONSIDERED IS, WHAT IS REAL, GENUINE CHRISTIANITY? WHETHER WE SPEAK OF IT AS A PRINCIPLE IN THE SOUL, OR AS A SCHEME OR SYSTEM OF DOCTRINE. CHRISTIANITY, TAKEN IN THE LATTER SENSE, IS THAT SYSTEM OF DOCTRINE WHICH DESCRIBES THE CHARACTER ABOVE RECITED, WHICH PROMISES, IT SHALL BE MINE, (PROVIDED I WILL NOT REST TILL I ATTAIN,) AND WHICH TELLS ME HOW I MAY ATTAIN IT.

LETTER TO CONYERS MIDDLETON,
WORKS, (J) 10:72

CONTENTS

Part II The Teaching of The United Methodist Church

Chapter 3 The Triune God   99

Chapter 4 Scripture Alone . . . Yet Never Alone   127

Chapter 5 Creation, Sin, Law, Grace, and Repentance   145

Chapter 9 Means of Grace

PART III THE GOAL OF DOCTRINE

Chapter 10 Preaching and Maintaining United Methodist Doctrine

ACKNOWLEDGMENTS

This book has been long in the making. I taught a course in United Methodist doctrine for the first time at Perkins School of Theology in June, 1984. Over the last seventeen years I have had innumerable conversations with persons who have shaped my thought. The dedication acknowledges five of the most important of these persons, some of whom would disagree strongly with the views I have come to hold. Yet, without their influence this book would never have been written by me.

Ted Campbell and I were fellow students studying with Richard Heitzenrater, John Deschner, Albert Outler, and the rest of the faculty at Southern Methodist University. He and I talked about our similar projects on this subject, and I was pleased his *Methodist Doctrine: The Essentials* came out in 1999. I have learned much from him.

I am also grateful to my colleagues at the Perkins School of Theology with whom I have shared many conversations around this topic. Directly affecting the research behind this book, William Abraham, William Babcock, Alyce McKenzie, Rebekah Miles, Joerg Rieger, Mark Stamm, and Charles Wood have helped me grow as a scholar. My Dean, Robin Lovin, has provided many forms of encouragement and helped create a supportive environment in which to work. Serving on the Perkins faculty has been a privilege without which this book would not have been finished at all.

Several persons have read portions of this book in manuscript form at various stages of its development. I am indebted to Leslie Conn, Richard Heitzenrater, Greg Jones, James Logan, Randy Maddox, Alyce McKenzie, Rebekah Miles, Mark Powell, Mary Lou Reece, Mark Stamm, Carole Walker, Robert Williams, and Charles

Wood for their suggestions. Carolyn Herring helped compile the index. Any remaining mistakes, infelicitous phrases, or confused expressions are, of course, my responsibility.

I must again thank my family for their support during the difficult time of finishing this book. My wife, Mary Lou Reece, supported and encouraged me continually. She also read the manuscript and helped with its final preparations. My children, Jameson, Arthur, and Marynell, believed in me and my work. They did not mind too much when the book interfered with family events. To all of them, I say thanks for sharing in my ministry.

Scott Jones
Dallas, Texas
October 15, 2001

Introduction

A renewed interest in Christian doctrine has arisen in part because churches are being challenged in at least two contrasting if not contradictory ways. On the one hand, persons within churches, both lay and clergy, refuse to acknowledge the binding authority of official doctrine, whether denominational teaching, episcopal pronouncements, or pastoral statements. Official teaching is greeted by the church's own members and clergy with a variety of reactions and is frequently ignored altogether.

On the other hand, some persons, both within and outside the church, experience a diverse marketplace of ideas and ask for greater clarity and definition of what teachings truly belong to each church. Laypersons ask, "What do we believe?" Those thinking about joining the church often inquire about its teaching before deciding to join.

While doctrinal considerations and controversies have always been part of the life of the church, in times of cultural change they become particularly pointed; now is one of those times. For example, as congregations experiment with new and old forms of worship, music, and preaching, the doctrinal concerns are (or should be) brought to bear on liturgical and homiletical decisions being made. In some places and times in United States history, a Protestant cultural consensus could carry the weight of Christian teaching so that congregations paid little or no attention to the basic teachings of the faith. While such cultural islands still exist, they grow smaller and more isolated with each new subscription to cable television.

The renewed interest in doctrine also arises from the evangelistic and spiritual formation ministries of congregations. As they seek to proclaim the gospel to unchurched and non-Christian persons, they must ask questions about the content of the message. What is the gospel? How is it best and most effectively communicated? In the process of spiritual formation, what is the goal of the Christian life? What does a mature Christian look like? How do we know if progress is being made? Christian doctrine gives answers to those questions for particular communities of faith; as more attention is being paid to them in ministries like the Walk to Emmaus, Disciple Bible Study, Christian Believer, Alpha and Sunday school classes, questions about their adequacy and truthfulness come to the fore.

Renewed interest in doctrine also stems from the current conflicts over ethical issues. Christian doctrine also includes the church's teaching in these areas. Whether it is the perils of nuclear war, the difficulties and opportunities of multicultural communities, the demands of environmental justice, the complexities of bioethics in an age of increasingly sophisticated technological possibilities, or the ethics of revenge and retaliation in international war, people look for answers. What does the church have to say? Is its teaching credible? Is it clear and cogent? The quality of its teaching has immense implications for all of its ministries. The quality of its social action and its ministries of social justice depend, at least in part, on the credibility, clarity, and cogency of its doctrine.

In addition, there are two enduring problems in white, Protestant Christianity in the United States to which I think United Methodism can make some contribution. For too long, many of those churches have been internally divided into factions variously labeled fundamentalists and modernists, evangelicals and proponents of the social gospel, conservatives and liberals. In the words of Jean Miller Schmidt's important study, it is a conflict between the competing concerns for souls and the social order. She describes the existence of two Protestantisms which grew out of nineteenth-century evangelicalism. I am persuaded by her analysis, including her own revision, that her work is most valuable in describing certain segments of white, Protestant Christianity in the United States.[1] Furthermore, it is more accurate to say that various segments of both parties held views about how the social order ought to be Christianized, they simply held different ideas about which issues and which policies Christians should support.

Nevertheless, by 1912 two parties were well formed, and since that time they have hardened their positions.[2] She says in her conclusion:

> Predictions are not the task of the historian. But it is difficult not to be profoundly concerned about the outcome of this schism, which may well be the most crucial problem still facing the Protestant churches. The dispute over social versus individual, public versus private Protestantism runs through every denomination. It has occasioned deep division between clergy and laity, and, as this study shows, among the clergy themselves. Those who insist on the social involvement of the church are committed to change for the sake of a more just and more Christian social order. Those who want to maintain a privatized religion resist this kind of change, some in an attempt to defend what they see as the central doctrines of the faith; others for the sake of preserving the familiar religion that offers them comfort and meaning in a troubled and unstable world.[3]

One of the strengths of United Methodist doctrine is its potential for answering Schmidt's question, "what are the 'possibilities for accommodation and reconciliation' between these two parties within the institutional structures of American Protestantism?"[4] At its best, United Methodist doctrine holds together a number of concerns in dynamic and mutually reinforcing tension. On the theological spectrum Wesley occupies the extreme center, and his approach has shaped the church's doctrine. Greater clarity about the importance of and interrelations between worship and social action, evangelism and justice ministries, spiritual formation and political involvement could be a contribution to healing a blight on the souls of all these churches.

The division of the one church of Jesus Christ into many different denominations, each claiming to be *the* church, is an ongoing problem. The ecumenical movement of the twentieth century was one of the major contributions of that era to Christianity. It takes many forms in the world, including grassroots cooperation between congregations, the migration of members from one church to another, and joint action for social justice on the national and international level. The movement also fosters official dialogue between churches that seek to overcome centuries of estrangement so that visible communion might be possible. It may be that those working for that kind of unity will not see it in their lifetime. Edward Cardinal Cassidy, who recently retired as President of the Vatican's Pontifical Council for Promoting Christian Unity, said that such dialogues are really opening up possibilities for our grandchildren.[5] Authentic dialogue requires partners who are able to describe themselves accurately to each other. Attention to authoritative doctrine is a way for churches to understand each other better and thus begin to overcome the barriers to closer communion. In such dialogues each church frequently comes to understand itself better as well.

For these reasons, it is important, at least to United Methodists, to inquire about the implications of and answers to the question *What are our doctrines?* This study is an attempt at such an inquiry and the formulation of one such answer.

The word "doctrine" can be used in many ways. This book examines authoritative doctrine, in the same sense of the word used by George Lindbeck in *The Nature of Doctrine:* "Church doctrines are communally authoritative teachings regarding beliefs and practices that are considered essential to the identity or welfare of the group in question."[6] This is how the United Methodist Church uses the word in the process of ordaining persons to the clergy. By long-standing tradition, every elder in full connection with an annual conference of the Church has been asked the following questions:

> Do you know the General Rules of our Church?
> Will you keep them?
> Have you studied the doctrines of The United Methodist Church?
> After full examination, do you believe that our doctrines are in harmony with the Holy Scriptures?
> Will you preach and maintain them?[7]

While other issues are addressed in a variety of ways, these questions are addressed to the candidates in front of their brother and sister clergy. The bishop usually asks them, along with fourteen other questions, in the presence of all those who are already ordained immediately prior to the conference's vote on whether or not the candidates are worthy of ordination.

This practice raises four important questions:

What are "our doctrines" and how do they relate to the General
  Rules?
How are the doctrines of the United Methodist Church best under-
  stood?
Are these doctrines in harmony with the Holy Scriptures?
How does one best preach and maintain these doctrines?

This book seeks to provide an answer to these questions. Part 1
will answer the first question by discussing the shape and nature
of United Methodist doctrine. Before examining the content of
what the United Methodist Church teaches, we must first analyze
what the term "our doctrines" means and how it is delimited. This
question raises the prior questions of what is Christian doctrine in
general and how United Methodist doctrine is related to it. A full-
scale discussion of Christian doctrine is beyond the scope of this
book, but some analysis is necessary in order to set the proper context for discussing the methods and the sources of United
Methodist doctrine. The proper starting point for determining
what are "our doctrines" is to determine which texts constitute the
teachings of the church. It is the argument of part 1 that there are
ten different doctrinal texts ranked in three different levels of
authority which constitute the authoritative doctrine of the United
Methodist Church.

Part 2 will answer the second and third questions by discussing
the content of United Methodist doctrine. A comprehensive understanding of "our doctrines" is best done not by reviewing each of
the ten texts in turn, but by seeking a holistic understanding of
what they say together. Each chapter will thus draw on several, if
not all, of the texts.

The third question is the most complicated of all because of the
many ways in which the phrase "in harmony with the Holy
Scriptures" can be construed and the various criteria different
scholars would cite to answer it. The claim that there is a unified
teaching of the whole canon or even a self-consistent theology of
either testament has been challenged. Such an argument that
would take all of these positions into account is well beyond the
scope of this study. Rather, it must suffice for this study to indicate
some of the biblical texts to which Wesley and the other authors of
our doctrinal statements have appealed or might have appealed as

warrants for their teaching. More important, attention to the reading of Scripture that informs United Methodist doctrine will show how the Church understands its doctrine to be in harmony with the Bible's teaching.

Part 3, constituted by chapter 10, will discuss the purpose of United Methodist doctrine, thereby offering some answers to the question of how to preach and maintain it. It is a characteristic of United Methodist teaching that, all other things being equal, orthodoxy is not the goal of the Christian life; orthodoxy can be and should be an important instrument in reaching the goal. Thus, the final section of this book will treat the goal of all doctrine as understood by The United Methodist Church, which is the making of disciples of Jesus Christ through faithful and effective evangelism, worship, education, and works of mercy. The United Methodist Church believes that the goal of the Christian life is not orthodoxy, or right opinions, but holiness of heart and life. It is hoped that Christian doctrine is in fact good for us, and that a deeper understanding of The United Methodist Church's witness of faith will bring about an increase of "the holiness without which no one will see the Lord."[8]

CHARACTERISTICS OF THIS STUDY

Three characteristics of this study should be made clear at this point. First, it will focus on the denomination's authoritative doctrine. "Doctrine" can refer to the teaching of the church in all of its forms. Sermons are often, if not always, teaching moments in the lives of congregations. Sunday school classes, youth fellowship meetings, confirmation classes, retreats, and television advertisements all are forms of teaching whereby the church seeks to convey its message to an audience, either internally or externally. Wesley's preface described his 1780 *Collection of Hymns for the Use of the People Called Methodist* as "a little body of experimental and practical divinity."[9] In a similar way, Ted Campbell suggests, *The United Methodist Hymnal* is a form of doctrine.[10]

Jaroslav Pelikan began his magisterial history of Christian doctrine with a description of his subject: "What the church of Jesus Christ believes, teaches and confesses on the basis of the word of

God: this is Christian doctrine."[11] In his usage, "believes" refers to "the form of Christian doctrine present in the modalities of devotion, spirituality and worship." "Teaches" refers to "the content of the word of God extracted by exegesis from the witness of the Bible and communicated to the people of the church through proclamation, instruction, and churchly theology." By "confesses" he means "the testimony of the church, both against false teaching from within and against attacks from without, articulated in polemics and in apologetics, in creed and in dogma."[12] Clearly the relation between believing, teaching, and confessing is complicated and has shifted over time. A history of doctrine should pay attention to the various ways in which the devotion of individual Christians, the artistic expression of their faith in church buildings, the writings of bishops and theologians, and other forms of teaching all interact with the normative doctrinal statements that Pelikan calls creeds and dogmas.

This book is not a history of United Methodist doctrine. While the history of doctrine and the history of theology are both important areas of study, in this work comments on historical developments will be placed in the notes unless they are directly pertinent to the subject of this study. Rather, it is focused on interpreting the current teaching of the United Methodist Church in its authoritative form.[13] "Authoritative form" means that to which the church itself looks when asking about the norms of its preaching, worship, teaching, and witness. Insofar as there is doctrinal discipline within the church, these texts are the ones to which appeal is made when difficult questions are to be decided. This is the purpose behind the questions asked of those being admitted to the Conference in full connection and ordained as deacons and elders in the denomination. The Church asks them if they know the doctrines, believe them to be scriptural, and are committed to communicating them to others. A candidate who answered no would then not be accepted into the Conference or ordained as an elder in the Church.

Commitment to the Church's doctrine is also expected from those already in the Church. For both clergy and laity the "dissemination of doctrines contrary to the established standards of doctrine of The United Methodist Church" is a chargeable offense that could lead to expulsion from the ministry or from membership in the denomination.[14] Thus doctrine functions as a way in which the

Church defines its identity, and the discipline of its clergy and members has reference to specific, official doctrinal texts.

Those outside the Church who wish to know what the whole United Methodist Church teaches are directed to its authoritative texts. In ecumenical dialogue, for example, persons from other denominations of the Christian church, having read the authoritative texts as the official statement of the whole United Methodist Church, can understand its official position therefrom. Similarly, these texts can be construed as the denomination's apologetic activity to explain the gospel to those outside. Clearly, the forms these texts typically take are not conducive to effective witness to outsiders, but they serve as the norms by which all authentically United Methodist evangelistic witness should be measured. Serious inquirers into the United Methodist witness to the Christian faith are able to read the authoritative texts and understand that this is how United Methodists understand their own teaching.

This raises the question of whether such outsiders will actually find the regular, local teaching of a particular United Methodist congregation congruent with the doctrinal statements of the whole denomination. One might ask whether the sermon at a particular United Methodist church on any given Sunday would be in agreement with, contrary to, or have any recognizable relationship at all to the denomination's doctrine.

This is an empirical question that would require a sociological study of what individual United Methodist clergy and laity believe and teach. While such a study would be very interesting and informative, it would not be, however, a study of authoritative doctrine. When candidates for ordination are asked the questions about doctrine, it is not the intent of the denomination to ask whether they will "preach and maintain" the doctrines of a particular congregation or region or faction of the Church. Rather, they are being asked about the doctrines of the whole Church. No empirical study can answer that question. It is only the Church's official teaching that can answer that. This study inquires into the teaching of the whole United Methodist Church. The doctrines of the whole Church can be studied only by examining its official teaching. Within the category of official teaching, however, another distinction is important. Some teaching is official because it is done on behalf of the Church. Whether it is authoritative official teaching is determined by whether disputes are referred to it as an arbiter of what truly belongs to the church's teaching. Sunday school curricula and pronouncements of General Boards are examples of teaching that is official without being authoritative.

The second characteristic of this study is that it is an interpretation of its subject matter. It is neither a defense nor an extrapolation of United Methodist doctrine. At several points in the analysis significant problems as well as opportunities for further development will be briefly noted. However, the goal of this book is to present a comprehensive understanding of the Church's teaching, which could then enable and enhance doctrinal reflection and development.

The word "interpretation" also indicates that only the texts can speak for themselves. A desire for faithfulness to the texts is limited by the reality that any attempt at a comprehensive reading of them inevitably involves an interpretation that could conceivably be different. Persons from other perspectives will perhaps wish to present different readings of these texts, even if they agree on the methodological arguments presented in part 1. Such a dialogue about how the doctrines of the United Methodist Church should best be read is a necessary part of both the Church's life and witness and the academic study of United Methodist doctrine as well. Once someone begins explaining the texts, or comparing the texts to each other, or asking how the texts should function in the church today, the task of interpretation has begun. Further, my social location—I am a white, male, forty-seven-year-old ordained United Methodist elder in the United States with a Ph.D. in the history of Christianity, a previously published book on Wesley and Scripture and an appointment on the faculty of a United Methodist university—will clearly influence my interpretation. Others with different backgrounds—whether of ethnicity, gender, level of education, status of ordination, country, age, or any other characteristic—may well write different books interpreting the texts in different ways. Such books will, presumably, be recognizably interpretations of the same texts. It is my goal to be as faithful to the texts as possible and to set them as the limits of the subject matter. Our common witness and our disagreements ought to be based on our various interpretations of the agreed-upon texts. The way we discern, preach, and maintain the truth in service to the church of Jesus Christ is through having a common base on which to analyze our different interpretations.

This method not only fosters faithfulness, but also helps the texts speak for themselves. At some points this means exhibiting a set of connections between various parts of the texts that might not be evident to the casual reader. However, the discernment of such connections is always open to argument based on various legitimate interpretations.

The third characteristic of this study is its distinction from and yet dependence upon other academic disciplines including Wesley studies and the histories of Methodism, the Evangelical Association, and the United Brethren in Christ. While the study of United Methodist doctrine is not the same as studying the histories of these predecessor Churches or the life and thought of John and Charles Wesley, the work of historians is important to the task. For example, the Bicentennial Edition of Wesley's works is an indispensable contribution to United Methodist doctrine. The historical material contained in *The Book of Discipline* reflects the contributions of many historians, most notably Albert Outler and Richard Heitzenrater. However, the distinction between the two disciplines is important as well. For example, the study of Wesley's theology needs to concern itself with the whole of his thought as expressed in all of his writings, not just a body of sermons and his commentary on the New Testament. Further, it must look at the development of his thought over time and the social and cultural context in which his thoughts developed. The roles played by personal events such as his experience at Aldersgate and his visit to the Moravians at Herrnhut may loom large in such analyses. The interplay between his theological development and key events of the revival might take on a prominent role. Because our study is not about Wesley directly but about a selected group of his writings, that is, those which have been adopted as constitutional standards of The United Methodist Church, all of those writings not so adopted must serve as no more than background. Thus his journal, letters, polemical writings, and even his doctrinal writings other than the *Sermons* and *Notes* will be used only as necessary to explain and interpret those of his writings that are authoritative United Methodist doctrine. Similarly, the theological and ecclesiological developments of the last two centuries have left their mark on other texts, but they will be considered only as necessary to interpret them in their context.

Specifically, the relation of this study to several recent studies of Wesley's theology needs to be made clear. Albert Outler's monumental edition of Wesley's sermons in the Bicentennial Edition has marked a turning point in Wesley scholarship. Since 1984 a number of significant studies have been published that seek to describe and evaluate Wesley's theology as a whole. *Responsible Grace* by Randy Maddox stands out as the most thorough and well-documented study published in this period. Books by many persons including Richard Heitzenrater, Ted Campbell, John Cobb, Kenneth Collins, Stephen Gunter, Theodore Jennings, Henry Knight, Manfred Marquardt, Theodore Runyon, and Donald Thorsen have added to the scholarship on the subject. Many other books, articles, and dissertations have made their mark.

The aim of this study differs from those in at least four ways. First, it limits the Wesleyan source material to the General Rules, *Sermons*, and *Notes*. Journals, letters, other sermons, *The Explanatory Notes Upon the Old Testament*, and all of Wesley's other writings are excluded on principle. Where Wesley treats a topic that he does not address in the standards, it is ignored. Second, it considers additional material such as the Articles, Confession, contemporary doctrinal statements, and the liturgical material. Some of these have various connections to Wesley, but none were written by him. Third, as a study of Church doctrine, the study focuses on the content and meaning of the authoritative texts as they currently stand. Thus, questions of historical development are of importance only when needed to account for difficulties in interpreting the text. With regard to all of these texts, it is presumed that The United Methodist Church has decided to speak all of these things at one time and that it means what it says. How these texts came to be authoritative or to have the specific content they have is a very important question that belongs to the history of United Methodism and the history of Christian doctrine. This is a study of what The United Methodist Church professes to teach today. Thus, many of the excellent studies of Wesley's theology focus on the development of his thought, comparing and contrasting the works produced during the early, middle, and late periods of his life. This present study avoids such questions on principle, assuming that when Wesley published the *Sermons* and *Notes* he intended them to stand as a unit and as standards of Methodist teaching, and that United Methodism continues to make that judgment today with certain additions. Fourth, several of these scholars, notably Jennings, Cobb, and Runyon, have brought Wesley's theology to bear on contemporary issues, in effect suggesting trajectories for how Wesleyans might think and act in the future. This is the proper function of theological reflection. In a sense that same issue of what United Methodists should do with their Wesleyan doctrine is addressed every four years by the General Conference. This study will not extrapolate from United Methodist doctrine to new issues. It seeks to show how the various documents of its present authoritative teachings are best understood.

The work of these studies in Wesley's theology is useful and important, as are the various studies in the history of United Methodism, including the history of Methodist theology. However, one should be careful of making assumptions about equating what Wesley thought with what United Methodist doctrine teaches. The conclusion that Wesley held a particular position may or may not apply to United Methodist doctrine. For example, many of Wesley's late sermons have interesting and helpful positions on topics that are not part of the Church's teaching because they are not contained in the authoritative texts. The same can be said for his polemical writings and his private letters. Thus, the evidence that would properly lead to one conclusion in a study of Wesley's theology may in fact not be relevant in understanding United Methodist doctrine. However, on many points there is considerable overlap, and the reading of studies of Wesley's theology will greatly enrich one's understanding.

In the same way, this is not a study in systematic theology. The critical evaluation of the church's doctrine is one important task of the theologian. However, critical evaluation depends in part on careful exposition. It would be hard to evaluate the adequacy of United Methodist doctrine without first inquiring into what it is. It is intended that this study's interpretation of authoritative United Methodist doctrine will serve theologians in their critical evaluation of it and their proposals for its reformulation. The vitality of the Church's witness depends on the clarity of the Church's teaching seen as distinct from the theologians' critical reflection upon that teaching.

Notes

1. Schmidt, xvii-xxxiii.

2. Schmidt, 197.

3. Schmidt, 220.

4. Schmidt, 221. The quote is from Jeffry K. Hadden, *The Gathering Storm in the Churches* (Garden City, N.Y.: Doubleday, 1969).

5. Presentation to seminar "Common Faith, Common Witness," World Methodist Conference, 27 July, 2001, Brighton, England.

6. Lindbeck 1984, 74.

7. Discipline 214, ¶327. See also p. 204, ¶321d for a slightly different text used with deacons in full connection. For the presumed universal use of these questions for elders and since 1996 for deacons as well, see footnote 10 on p. 214.

8. Heb. 12:14.

9. §4, *Works* 7:74.

10. Ted Campbell 1999, 24-26. This helpful book focuses on those aspects of doctrine common to the four main branches of episcopal Methodism in the United States: African Methodist Episcopal, African Methodist Episcopal Zion, Christian Methodist Episcopal, and United Methodist Church. I am in substantial agreement with Campbell's views and regard the argument of this study as differing primarily in focus and scope from his, whatever minor disagreements or differences in emphasis we might have.

11. Pelikan, 1.

12. Pelikan, 4.

13. Ted Campbell 1999, 17 defines "Methodist doctrine" as "that which Methodists have agreed to teach." While he goes on to mention "consensus" as well as "agreement," I think the word "authoritative" is stronger because it defines the subject as those teachings agreed upon in official ways by the denomination, whether there is any church-wide consensus or not.

14. Discipline 696-97, ¶2702.1(f).

PART I

UNITED METHODIST DOCTRINE AS CHRISTIAN DOCTRINE

CHAPTER ONE

THE SHAPE OF UNITED METHODIST DOCTRINE

TEACHING IN THE UNITED METHODIST CHURCH

Discerning the structure of United Methodist teaching requires taking statements from a variety of official sources and inquiring about the internal relationships between them. While the structure genuinely shapes the Church's teaching, it is not explicit. It must be elucidated from a careful reading of the relevant sources.

As noted in the introduction, "doctrine" can be used in a variety of different ways. In its broadest meaning, it encompasses all of the teaching that the church does in all of its forms. Within that broad category, one can distinguish official teachings that are the activities leaders of the church undertake to instruct others. They exercise their offices as teachers, pastors, catechists, deacons, bishops, synods, councils, and conferences to convey the content of the Christian faith. It is possible to use this kind of meaning to refer to either the activity of teaching or the content that is conveyed.

A yet more narrow distinction can be made. Within the category of official teaching, there are some teachings that are authoritative official teaching. This is the sense of Lindbeck's use of the word "doctrine," where certain teachings are agreed upon by the community as essential to their identity or welfare.[1] When any teaching, whether official or unofficial, is called into question, it is authoritative teaching that resolves the dispute. Authoritative doctrine is that body of teaching to which all other doctrines refer for their validity.

Since the beginnings of Methodism in the United States, the Conference has been the primary source of authoritative teaching in the Church. This is true for the Methodist Episcopal traditions as well as for the United Brethren and the Evangelical Association. At the same time, however, each of these traditions had bishops who played significant roles both formally and informally in the doctrinal activity of their denominations.[2]

Today there are five levels of conferences that guide the life of the denomination: local church, district, annual, jurisdictional or central conference, and General Conference.[3] While each of these bodies carries on a teaching function as it guides the mission and ministry of its part of the denomination, it is only the General Conference that speaks for the whole denomination.[4]

We will consider the discernment and teaching functions as two ways in which the General Conference functions as doctrinal authority, and then consider the role bishops are understood to play. One of the purposes of the General Conference is to discern the will of God for the Church. In 1744 John Wesley and the preachers who were in connection with him held the first conference. According to the minutes, they asked three questions: "What to teach? How to teach? What to do?"[5]

While the Conference has evolved in many ways since its beginning, there is still a sense in which these questions are the business of the General Conference. Part of the Conference's discernment process takes place in the formation of study committees or through requests for study made to one or more of the general agencies of the denomination. Frequently these groups spend four years looking at a particular set of issues. Their intense study facilitates the discernment process during the General Conference session. In the area of doctrine, the work of the doctrinal study committees chaired by Albert C. Outler (1968–72) and by Bishop Earl Hunt (1984–88) was crucial to the process of reformulating the doctrinal statements of the United Methodist Church at the General Conferences of 1972 and 1988 respectively.[6] Sometimes the Conference makes doctrinal changes in response to petitions sent by general agencies, individual church members, congregations, or groups in the Church.

In considering the future of the Church, many months of preparation are spent by the approximately one thousand delegates to the Conference. Delegates are encouraged to pray and converse with their colleagues in seeking God's will for the future. Occasionally, official groups such as study commissions, general boards, and other agencies send in reports that have a direct bearing on doctrine. Often unofficial groups do similar work and offer their understandings to the whole Conference. When the Conference convenes, a great deal of time is first spent in worship and prayer. The Conference then spends a week of its time in legislative committees where the task of discernment is carried out often with great care. Clearly the discernment process works better on those petitions where significant time for their consideration and refinement is built into the agenda. Other petitions are barely considered at all.

Sometimes these proceedings are described as primarily political, reflecting the human side of the process. There is an inevitably political side of conferencing because of the human composition of the group. Human groups making decisions together are by definition engaging in a political process. However, there is a theological conviction that God also uses conferencing as a means of grace.[7] If the church is understood to be a sacramental entity, then one trusts that the Holy Spirit is present in this process. It follows then, that despite human sinfulness, God uses these Conferences.

With regard to doctrine, the work of legislative committees has been significant in recent years. In 1988 the Legislative Committee on Faith and Mission was formed to examine the recommendations of two study committees that had worked during the previous quadrennium. One had examined the Church's doctrine and the other its mission. Each brought petitions that were referred to a newly formed legislative committee. Concerning this Conference, Langford says:

> The Legislative Committee on Faith and Mission of the 1988 General Conference was constituted to engage in theology. . . . These people understood themselves to be engaged in theological activity as a church and for the church. They were challenged to model how The United Methodist Church actually does its

35

theological work. They were reminded that this was a new legislative committee and, therefore, they were part of a new venture. They were commissioned to seek truth and serve the church; the spirit and quality of their work would leave its mark. [8]

In 2000 there was a Legislative Committee on Faith and Order to deal with doctrinal issues before the Conference.

Another purpose of the General Conference is to teach what it has discerned. Some may argue that this is the same as the discernment process, but there have been many occasions where the Conference has debated significant issues and then declined to produce a statement.[9] When the General Conference chooses to make a doctrinal statement, it usually does so by amending one of the existing texts that embody the Church's teaching. These statements serve as the Church's teaching until another General Conference chooses to amend what has been said. The resolutions of the General Conference lose their status after eight years unless explicitly reaffirmed.

JUDICIAL COUNCIL

The Church's Judicial Council has the responsibility, in part, "to determine the constitutionality of any act of the General Conference upon an appeal of a majority of the Council of Bishops or one-fifth of the members of the General Conference." It also reviews the decisions of law made by bishops in annual conference sessions.[10]

Conceivably, the Judicial Council could then determine whether a doctrinal statement of the General Conference violated the Restrictive Rules and was thus unconstitutional. In one case, it invalidated the action of a Central Conference that violated the Church's commitment to infant baptism on the basis of the First Restrictive Rule.[11] In four other decisions, however, the Judicial Council has kept its approach to doctrine very narrow in focus. It has not allowed the Church to alter the wording of the doctrinal standards, but has also refused to interpret them. In 1948 it said, "It is the opinion of the Judicial Council that the Judicial Council was not set up as an interpreter of doctrine but as an interpreter of law from the strictly legal standpoint."[12] This language was reaffirmed in decision 86 in 1952, and again in decision 358 in 1972.[13] In the 1972 decision, the Judicial Council offers a narrowly construed version of the question before it, and says that the report of the Theological Study Commission does not change the doctrinal standards and thus does not violate the Restrictive Rules. It says "We find no recommended substantive changes or additions to the documents themselves."[14] In a crucial paragraph it then says,

> The broader question of whether or not changes in paragraphs of historical and theological interpretation in Part II of the Discipline make changes in these protected documents we do not decide. The Judicial Council, historically, and we think properly, has refused jurisdiction over questions which demand of it theological interpretations. (Decisions No. 59 and 86) We believe the General Conference is competent to make this decision.[15]

More recently, the Judicial Council refused to answer a broad request on the status of the Social Principles, instead narrowly deciding the meaning of a particular sentence based on its legislative history.[16] Thus, the Judicial Council's role in the determination of United Methodist doctrine has been limited.

NONAUTHORITATIVE OFFICIAL TEACHING FOR THE WHOLE CHURCH

The *Book of Discipline* gives to bishops the task of doctrinal teaching in the whole denomination. Section IV of chapter 3 of the Discipline is titled "Specific Responsibilities of Bishops." Paragraph 414 is labeled "Leadership—Spiritual and Temporal," referring to the Constitution's provision that the bishops be responsible for "the general oversight and promotion of the temporal and spiritual interests of the entire Church."[17] Subparagraph 3 gives them the responsibility "to guard, transmit, teach, and proclaim, corporately and individually, the apostolic faith as it is expressed in Scripture and tradition, and, as they are led and endowed by the Spirit, to interpret that faith evangelically and prophetically."[18] In a similar way, paragraph 427.2 says, "The Church expects the Council of Bishops to speak to the Church and from the Church to the world and to give leadership in the quest for Christian unity and interreligious relationships."[19]

Bishops, as United Methodist elders, are expected to "preach and maintain" United Methodist doctrines. But paragraphs 414.3 and 427.2 give them added responsibilities of guarding and transmitting that doctrine and speaking to the Church and from the Church to the world. In addition, as a corporate body of leaders in the church, they have opportunities for fulfilling these functions in ways not open to anyone else.

There is a clear tension between the teaching roles of the General Conference and the office of bishop.[20] Francis Asbury had a teaching role in the early days of the Methodist Episcopal Church through his itinerant preaching and his editing of the Discipline. In 1812 the General Conference gave to the bishops control over the course of study followed by candidates for the ministry. Jim Kirby says, "This was a first in the history of the church and a new responsibility for the bishops. They were now established officially in the traditional episcopal function of being the teachers of the church."[21] Over time their leadership has diminished in favor of the power of the General Conference. Now the Discipline formally acknowledges the teaching role that the bishops have played in Methodism from the beginning. They exercise their role corporately by issuing statements from time to time. In 1986 they issued "In Defense of Creation," in 1990 they issued "Vital Congregations, Faithful Disciples," and in 1996 they published "Children and Poverty: An Episcopal Initiative." However, the authoritative status of these documents is clear. They are teachings of the bishops of the United Methodist Church, but not teachings of the denomination. Kirby says:

> Richey is correct in regarding these pronouncements as representing the attempt of the bishops "in a united fashion" to give "theological leadership to the Church." But they carry nothing like the historic weight of pronouncements from the bishop of Rome to the Catholic Church. At most, these comments of United Methodist bishops have only the force that respect for their opinions and the power of their arguments may have among their constituents. There is little evidence that they have influence outside of Methodism. Finding the most effective way to exercise the teaching office remains a challenge for the Council of Bishops as the church enters the next century.[22]

Other parts of the United Methodist Church engage in this sort of teaching from time to time. For over one hundred years Methodism published official catechisms intended to instruct children and youth about correct doctrine.[23] Annual Conferences and local congregations publish resolutions. Some general agencies, such as the General Board of Church and Society, are given the responsibility of engaging in witness and addressing the Church and the world.[24] The General Board of Discipleship publishes tracts and books bearing the denomination's name, which would lead some to believe that they are part of the Church's official teaching. The United Methodist Publishing House publishes curricula that is official Church teaching, as overseen by the denomination's Curriculum Resources Committee. In the first part of the new millennium, television is the most powerful medium of communication. It is not the deepest or most well-argued approach. It clearly reaches the most people and has great impact. Thus, in designing television advertisements bearing the name of the Church, United Methodist Communications may exercise the most influential official teaching activity in the whole connection.

In sum, all of these other activities are teaching by official bodies acting in their various areas of ministry. However, they are not authoritative teaching because in each of these cases, including the pronouncements of the bishops both individually and as a Council, the content of such teaching is to be measured finally against what the General Conference of the Church teaches.

THE FORMAL SHAPE OF UNITED METHODIST DOCTRINE

An answer to the question *What is authoritative United Methodist doctrine?* must begin with the question, *What are the documents that embody the doctrine and how do they relate to one another?* The authoritative doctrine of the United Methodist Church is determined by the General Conference. This body of lay and clergy representatives elected by the annual conferences has been given "full legislative power over all matters distinctively connectional."[25] A later paragraph interprets this to mean that "no person, no paper, no organization, has the authority to speak officially for The United

Methodist Church, this right having been reserved exclusively to the General Conference under the Constitution."[26]

Thus, what is sometimes called the magisterium of the Church is located, for the United Methodist Church, in its General Conference. This view of how teaching authority is located is deeply rooted in the history of the Church and its predecessor denominations. In 1744 John Wesley met with some of those who were in connection with him to discuss the state of the revival. They began by considering three issues, "1. What to teach; 2. How to teach; and, 3. What to do; that is, how to regulate our doctrine, discipline, and practice."[27] When Methodism became independent in the United States, its conference of preachers was the supreme authority in all matters, including the election of bishops. As time went on, the conference of all the preachers or the General Conference was held every four years largely as a matter of convenience. In 1808 the decision was made to create a delegated General Conference to allow for more balanced representation among the different regions of the country. However, restrictions were placed upon what the General Conference could do without seeking the consent of all the preachers. These Restrictive Rules have changed slightly over the years, but still limit the power of the General Conference to make major changes without approval of the members of annual conferences. These rules restricting the freedom of the General Conference to change the most basic features of United Methodist doctrine and polity are an expression of the basic nature of the Church's polity, that the annual conference is the fundamental body of the Church.[28] Similar patterns developed in the Evangelical Association and the United Brethren. In all these denominations decisions were made to add laypersons as members of the conferences in equal proportion to the clergy members.[29]

The claim that the source of authoritative teaching in the United Methodist Church is located in the General Conference can be challenged on several grounds. First, there is the claim that functionally there is a great deal of teaching going on and that, particularly, bishops have a teaching role that they have always fulfilled in the life of the Church. This argument does not dispute that authoritative teaching exists, but argues that the focus should be placed on doctrine construed in a broader fashion. Indeed, it must be admitted that the vast bulk of what Charles Wood calls "active teaching" is not authoritative. Persons do not typically read Wesley's Sermons or the Confession of Faith on a regular basis. Rather, teaching happens in a great variety of ways, ranging from Sunday school curricula to the sermons given in United Methodist pulpits. Jaroslav Pelikan's definition of doctrine as "what the church of Jesus Christ believes, teaches and confesses on the basis of the word of God"[30] seems much better suited to a holistic investigation.

While Pelikan's definition is admirably suited to an investigation of the *history* of Christian doctrine, it does not describe the status of authoritative doctrine today. In particular, when candidates for ordination are asked, "Have you studied our doctrines?" they are not being asked, "Do you have a grasp of the range of different ideas being taught in our congregations?" Rather, they are being asked if they have studied the teachings that are essential to the identity and well-being of the community into which they are being ordained as leaders.

Second, one might argue that no Protestant church can even have a magisterium. One might argue that Article V and Confession IV[31] mean that only Scripture is authoritative and that any one person's judgment about its interpretation is just as authoritative as the pronouncements of the General Conference. If *sola Scriptura* is the watchword of Protestantism, and United Methodism is a Protestant denomination, then any attempt to claim authority is a usurpation of the individual's rights to read and interpret Scripture for him or herself.

The confusion in this argument rests with the meaning of the word "authority." The General Conference has the authority to define the doctrine of the United Methodist Church. Individuals who disagree with its teachings can choose either to seek to change the Church's teaching or leave the denomination. That United Methodist doctrine is binding on or authoritative for all human beings is well beyond the meaning of "authority." The General Conference is the appropriate body to define what it means to be a United Methodist, including in that definition the body of beliefs that the Church holds.

Third, one might argue that the basic tenets of Christianity are such that United Methodism cannot alter them. Such a claim is absurd because of the great variety in Christian teachings among the many denominations, which all claim to belong to the same faith. However, two more subtle forms of this third claim might be put forward. First, one might define "basic" narrowly enough to suggest that something like the Nicene Creed and the Chalcedonian Definition must determine the faith. On this view, United Methodism cannot alter its teaching that "the Son, who is the Word of the Father, the very and eternal God, of one substance with the Father, took man's nature in the womb of the blessed Virgin."[32] Whatever the Discipline says about altering the constitutional standards, some of them are unalterable because they are basic to the faith. A second version of this argument is to treat the claim as having analytic status, leading to the proposition that a necessary condition of being Christian is confessing truths contained in the Nicene Creed. To alter the conviction that the Son is of one substance with the Father is to cease to be Christian by the simple definition of the term "Christian."

This third argument in both of its subtle forms has much to commend it. Yet, two problems diminish its force. First, the definition of "basic" is vague. Even identifying the Nicene Creed and Chalcedonian Definition as the sole content of "basic" would exclude a number of persons and denominations one might otherwise wish to see included. Second, the point made by McGrath about faithfulness to the intent of the formulation is significant. How can one confess the faith of the Nicene Creed in words that are intelligible and meaningful today? Also, has not the Holy Spirit over time revealed to the church deeper meanings in the gospel, so that some interpretations have improved over time? The Christian witness against slavery in the last three hundred years is deeply biblical and faithful despite those New Testament passages that seem to permit it.

Fourth, one might argue that the General Conference is not capable of carrying out its duties well. People who have attended the General Conference have observed that it is not well suited for careful theological deliberation, dialogue, and the writing of precisely worded doctrinal texts. Few of the delegates are specialists, and there is a shortage of time in which to do high-quality work.

Such an argument does not touch the claim that, for better or worse, the United Methodist Church has chosen to place its doctrinal authority in the General Conference. Whatever truth there is in the argument really points either to revising the way in which the General Conference does its business (for example, by lengthening the sessions) or to adopting a different magisterial structure. Consideration of how bishops hold this authority in the Roman Catholic Church or how congregations hold it in Baptist churches would lead to helpful comparisons. That United Methodists teach authoritatively through the General Conference is clear. Whether this is the best way for Christians to teach is debatable; dialogue about how United Methodists might teach better is urgently needed.

Given that the General Conference makes these doctrinal statements, how should one read them? One might begin with a presumption of wholeness—that in publishing these texts as its teaching, the United Methodist Church believes that it is offering a coherent body of teaching that also aims at consistency. The latter is more difficult to achieve than the former, because over time inconsistencies are very likely to occur as new ideas are added and old ones are not adjusted. However, maintaining coherence is possible if there is a general tenor that binds all of the texts together to function in the same way. Discerning the wholeness of the body of material, however, requires finding that general tenor that holds it all together.

Yet, conflicts do appear and differing points of emphasis do show up among the texts. How does one adjudicate among them? Are some of the texts more central to the Church's teaching than others? If so, which texts take precedence? These questions are answered in two ways. Formally, the pronouncements themselves give clues about those which are more important and which are less so. Materially, the general tenor of the texts gives a key for interpreting all of them in accordance with their main theme and purpose.

TEN TEXTS IN THREE LEVELS

Formally, the key to the relative significance of the texts lies in the relative difficulty in altering them. While the General Conference is the only voice of the Church that can teach normatively, there are six rules that restrict its activities. The First, Second, and Fifth Restrictive Rules prevent it from changing the doctrinal standards of the Church without a three-fourths approving vote of the aggregate number of annual conference members.[33] The Constitution and the General Rules cannot be changed without a two-thirds approving vote of the annual conference members. In the traditions stemming from the Methodist Episcopal Church, which first instituted these rules in 1808, there has never been a vote to override them. Thus, in any conceivable conflict between the constitutionally protected doctrinal standards, and any text passed by a General Conference, the standards would have to prevail. Hence, the Constitution, the doctrinal standards, and the General Rules occupy the highest level of authority. To treat them as a group we shall use the term "constitutional standards." In many ways these texts are different from each other and treating them as one group must not be taken as suggesting they are all alike. They do, however, share this level of authority as the most permanent expression of United Methodist teaching.

Within the doctrinal statements of the General Conference, the intent of the Conference is the other criterion used to evaluate relative authority of the texts. The question becomes, to what extent did the General Conference intend each of these documents to be teaching the Christian faith?

The structure of the *Book of Discipline* is of first importance here. The Discipline has five major divisions called "Parts." After the Constitution come Parts II, III, and IV, labeled "Doctrinal Standards and Our Theological Task," "The Ministry of All Christians," and "Social Principles," respectively. They, along with the *Book of Resolutions*, are clearly intended to be doctrinal statements. Most of the relevant material will be found there. However, the General Conference is often not very consistent about where it places doctrinal statements. There are also explicitly doctrinal statements embedded in various places in Part V of the Discipline titled "Organization and Administration." All together they are treated as contemporary doctrinal statements of the Church. Their secondary level of authority is constituted by the fact that a majority vote of any General Conference can alter what was said previously.

Resolutions are valid for only eight years unless they are explicitly readopted.[34] One could argue that they are of lesser authority than the Social Principles and other statements in the Discipline because the General Conference intends for them to lose their status after a period of time. However, several resolutions bearing on the Church's doctrine have been continually renewed since their first passage.[35]

However, a curious phrase in the preface to the Social Principles raises questions about the authority of this text in relation to other statements. It says:

> The Social Principles are a prayerful and thoughtful effort on the part of the General Conference to speak to the human issues in the contemporary world from a sound biblical and theological foundation as historically demonstrated in United Methodist traditions. They are intended to be instructive and persuasive in the best of the prophetic spirit. The Social Principles are a call to all members of The United Methodist Church to a prayerful, studied dialogue of faith and practice. (*See* ¶ 509.)[36]

Does this paragraph mean they are not binding on United Methodists in the same way as our understanding of the four sources and criteria of theology is binding? Does the intention to be "instructive and persuasive" mean that the church is not teaching authoritatively? Does the Principles' character as a "call" to "prayerful, studied dialogue" mean they are simply an agenda for conversation and not a body of teaching to be received? Finally, what does the parenthetical reference to ¶509 mean?

Three arguments seem decisive in interpreting the Social Principles as having the same authority as other statements of the General Conference. First, the parenthetical comment refers to the right of the General Conference to speak for the church. Second, another parenthetical comment at the end of the Social Principles recommends that they be "continually available to United Methodist Christians" and "emphasized regularly in every congregation."[37] Third, many of the resolutions contained in the BOR refer to the Social Principles as an authority.[38] It would be odd to attribute to the Social Principles a lower level of authority than exists for the Resolutions. Yet, the ambiguity in the preface to the document is disturbing.

The lowest level of authoritative doctrine is liturgy, including the church's hymnody, which is contained in the *United Methodist*

Hymnal and *Book of Worship.* While the authoritative status of these texts is lower than the constitutional standards and contemporary statements of doctrine, their power to shape the life of the functional church is usually much higher. There are clearly doctrinal implications to both of these texts. When the General Conference authorizes a liturgy such as the ones for Holy Communion, ordination, and baptism, statements of faith with clear doctrinal implications are being made. Further, when it approves hymns for congregational singing the texts carry theological messages. The table of contents of the UMH carries headings that could serve as an outline of the Church's doctrine. While it is possible to pray and sing these words as praise to God, in United Methodism they can be used to teach the faith as a form of active doctrine. At the very least they are implicitly doctrinal, and often they are used to instruct people in the faith. They are thus doctrinal statements. However, it is not clear that the General Conference regards these as binding in the same way as it does the texts on the other two levels of authority.[39]

There are still other ways of construing the relationships among these various texts. There are those who wish to discount the constitutional standards as historical texts with no authority for today. One might take the reverse chronological order as signifying the greatest authority—the most recent statements are most authoritative and the oldest have the least authority. However, a careful reading of the Church's constitution prevents such a misunderstanding. It is the constitutional standards that take precedence. The General Conference can teach for the Church so long as it does not violate the Restrictive Rules. Any doctrinal statement that violates those standards would be invalid. The analogy between these texts and the relationship between the Constitution and the laws of the United States is clear. In both cases the more recent does not take precedence. Rather, the constitutional standards take precedence over even the most recently approved law or statement.

There are those who wish to discount all expressions of the General Conference as competing with the standards of doctrine and thus violating the Restrictive Rules. In particular, the existence of sections 1, 2, and 4 of Part II of the Discipline are sometimes viewed as unconstitutional because they were passed by the General Conference without following the procedures for amending the Constitution. However, the first Restrictive Rule does not prohibit the General Conference from adding to the denomination's doctrinal standards. It says, "The General Conference shall not revoke, alter, or change our Articles of Religion or establish any new standards or rules of doctrine contrary to our present existing and established standards of doctrine."[40] Thus, the General Conference has deemed that its contemporary doctrinal statements are not contrary to its constitutional standards.

There are those who wish to argue that the best judgment of contemporary scholarship should be followed in doctrinal matters, whether it is the interpretation of the Restrictive Rules or language used in reference to God or contemporary versions of the doctrine of Christian perfection. The relationship between the United Methodist Church's leadership—bishops, General Conference, general boards and agencies, and others—and its scholars deserves significant attention. There have been scholars who have held leadership roles in the shaping of United Methodist doctrine.[41] However, it is not the task of scholarship to determine the church's teaching. Rather, it is the task of the Church's authorized leaders to make those determinations, and of both scholars and leaders to develop the kind of working relationships that will foster the best possible results.

In summary, the shape of United Methodist doctrine is that of ten texts occupying three different levels of authority:

1. Constitutional standards: Constitution, Articles of Religion, Confession of Faith, Standard Sermons, *Explanatory Notes Upon the New Testament*, and General Rules.

2. Contemporary statements: *Book of Discipline* (nonconstitutional sections) and *Book of Resolutions*.

3. Liturgy: *The United Methodist Hymnal* and *United Methodist Book of Worship*.

Constitutional Standards

First, there are doctrinal texts protected by the Restrictive Rules and other provisions of the Constitution. The most obvious of these is the Constitution itself, which makes a number of doctrinal claims that should not be overlooked. Three texts—the Articles of Religion, the Confession of Faith, and the General Rules—are mentioned specifically. The first Restrictive Rule also refers to "our present existing and established standards of doctrine," the interpretation of which is disputed. It will be argued that it covers Wesley's Standard Sermons and his *Explanatory Notes Upon the New Testament*.

The Articles of Religion have remained substantially unchanged (with one interesting exception) since the Christmas Conference of 1784, which founded the Methodist Episcopal Church. When John Wesley revised the Thirty-nine Articles of the Church of England he deleted fifteen articles completely.[42] He altered the text of nine articles, usually by deletion and sometimes with great significance.[43] One was changed by the Methodist Episcopal Church prior to 1808.[44] Fourteen are identical in wording.[45] One article was added by the 1784 Conference.

The reasons for Wesley's editing are not easily ascertained. In his publishing activity he abridged many different texts and frequently did so for one of three reasons. On some occasions, he did not agree with the author's views and excised statements that he did not want to reprint. In other cases, he regarded the content as important but thought it could be said more cogently. In still other cases, he regarded the material as superfluous and thought it did not need to be reprinted for the intended audience, even though he did not object to it. Thus, for example, Wesley's removal of the article "Of the Three Creeds" could indicate any of these three reasons. Without clear evidence, it is impossible to say why he removed the articles he did or made the changes he made.

One of the changes made to the Articles after Wesley's editing came in the Discipline of 1788. In the Thirty-nine Articles the first article, "Of Faith in the Holy Trinity," says that God does not have "body, parts or passions."[46] The American version of the article deletes the word "passions" and says, "There is but one living and true God, everlasting, without body or parts, of infinite power, wisdom, and goodness; the maker and preserver of all things, both visible and invisible."[47] There is no evidence to show who made this change, on what basis (if any) they were authorized to do so, or why the change was made. Possible reasons include editorial mistake, a judgment that the word was more confusing than helpful, and deep theological convictions about the nature of God's interactions with the world. Lacking more historical evidence, it is impossible to draw a valid conclusion.

An additional Article, which was numbered XXIII, concerned the rulers of the United States of America. It made clear that this new Church recognized the independence of the United States. Further, it aligned the denomination with the new political philosophy that governments are "delegates of the people." Given the difficulties facing Methodist preachers during the War of Independence because of their British connections and allegiances, as well as Mr. Wesley's pamphlet condemning the revolution, this article made clear they were loyal Americans.

The Confession of Faith was composed by the board of Bishops of the Evangelical United Brethren Church. For sixteen years the EUB Discipline carried in it both the Articles of Religion of the Evangelical Association (last substantively revised in 1839) and the Confession of Faith of the United Brethren in Christ (approved in 1889).[48] Steven O'Malley describes the various influences leading up to the new Confession in his article "The Distinctive Witness of the Evangelical United Brethren Confession of Faith in Comparison with the Methodist Articles of Religion." In it he makes an important point about the general tone of the 1814 version of the Confession in comparison with the Articles. He says:

> Whereas this early CF [Confession of Faith] of the United Brethren was terse, less technical, and earthy in its expressions, the AR [Articles of Religion] was formal, more reflective of the technical language of the ecumenical creeds, and less capable of being understood by the lay folk who would constitute the heart of the M.E. Church. The CF was appropriate for a movement of awakening that did not at first aspire to attain a full-blown ecclesiastical status. The AR, as abridged by John Wesley from the 39 Anglican Articles of Religion, was intended for a movement that was about to become a church, and an "Episcopal" one at that! In addition, the CF was written in the first person plural, indicating that it was a normative statement, commanding personal loyalty at the heart of their faith. The AR, written in the more impersonal third person, was intended to define the outer perimeters within which faith and order and life and work could proceed.[49]

O'Malley gives an interesting and well-documented history of the steps that led to the 1962 Confession of Faith. In his discussion of the origins of the Evangelical Association's "Articles of Faith," he notes that its author, George Miller, adapted the Methodist Articles of Religion, reducing them from twenty-five to nineteen articles, with some changes in terminology.[50] In these predecessor documents O'Malley finds traces of the irenic Reformed theology of the *Heidelberg Catechism*, the special interests of Reformed Pietism, Anabaptist theology, the ethos of German-American revivalism, the Anglican Thirty-nine Articles, and Wesley's theology.

In 1958 the Evangelical United Brethren General Conference asked the Board of Bishops to combine the two statements. O'Malley says:

> It was on this basis [the authority of the General Conference to determine doctrine] that the 1958 General Conference authorized the Board of Bishops "to conduct a study of the respective confession of faith of the two former communions, with a view to combining both statements into a unified creedal statement of belief." This action was predicated on the assumption that the former communions "were American born with their origins in a rebirth of spirit and not in a theological revolt" and that "In all the basic and enduring elements of faith and ecclesiastical organization they are alike." The authors of the revised CF [Confession of Faith] were charged not to alter the content of either of the preceding doctrinal standards. They were to represent its content in an integrated manner, restated in contemporary language. It was further decided to continue the first person plural, confessional format of the United Brethren CF.[51]

O'Malley suggests that United Methodists have overlooked the EUB Confession of Faith in discussion of doctrinal standards and that this has been shortsighted with the result that "it has not enabled them to recognize the broader (i.e., continental Reformation and Pietist) traditions in which United Methodism was shaped."[52] Without seeking further to review the complicated processes that led to their current formulation, we will explore in later chapters the different nuances of perspective that the Articles and Confession bring to the discussion of the relevant topics of United Methodist doctrine.

The General Rules were written by Wesley after he expelled sixty-four persons from the Newcastle society in February of 1743. Joining the society required only that persons have "a desire to flee from the wrath to come, and to be saved from their sins."[53] Continuing in the society meant exhibiting behavior that showed one's desire was sincere. The three rules were simple: do no harm, do good, and attend upon all the ordinances of God. Richard Heitzenrater says,

> Although Wesley had often said that these three prerequisites were not the whole of true religion, they now became the minimum expectations for a person to manifest the sincerity of his or her desire for salvation. They represented the antithesis to antinomianism, which represented one of the biggest threats to the Wesleyan program at this point.[54]

The Discipline notes that these rules were "a way of discipleship."[55] The General Rules have largely been unaltered through the years. At various points in early American history the rule prohibiting slaveholding and the buying and selling of slaves was not printed in Methodist Episcopal Disciplines.

The other texts that are included in the first level of church teaching are placed there by a less direct claim. Wesley's *Sermons* and *Notes* are included on the basis of a vague phrase in the first Restrictive Rule. The correct interpretation of "our present existing and established standards of doctrine" has been the subject of heated debate, with Richard Heitzenrater and Tom Oden being two of the key protagonists.[56] However, only the General Conference can authoritatively interpret this phrase, and it has done so. While the interpretation is not as clear as one would expect, it points to their inclusion. In the section "Doctrinal Standards in American Methodism" the Discipline adopts Heitzenrater's argument by saying:

> The Articles of Religion, however, did not guarantee adequate Methodist preaching; they lacked several Wesleyan emphases, such as assurance and Christian perfection. Wesley's Sermons and Notes, therefore, continued to function as the traditional standard exposition of distinctive Methodist teaching.
>
> The General Conference of 1808, which provided the first Constitution of The Methodist Episcopal Church, established the Articles of Religion as the Church's explicit doctrinal standards. The first Restrictive Rule of the Constitution prohibited any change, alteration, or addition to the Articles themselves, and it stipulated that no new standards or rules of doctrine could be adopted that were contrary to the "present existing and established standards of doctrine."

> Within the Wesleyan tradition, then as now, the *Sermons* and
> *Notes* furnished models of doctrinal exposition. Other documents
> have also served American Methodism as vital expressions of
> Methodist teaching and preaching. Lists of recommended doctri-
> nal resources vary from generation to generation but generally
> acknowledge the importance of the hymnbook, the ecumenical
> creeds, and the General Rules. Lists of such writings in the early
> nineteenth century usually included John Fletcher's *Checks
> Against Antinomianism* and Richard Watson's *Theological Institutes*.
> The doctrinal emphases of these statements were carried for-
> ward by the weight of tradition rather than the force of law. They
> became part of the heritage of American Methodism to the degree
> that they remained useful to continuing generations.[57]

This narrative suggests that the phrase "present existing and established standards of doctrine" should be interpreted to cover the
Articles of Religion. Heitzenrater has persuasively argued that this
was the intention of the 1808 General Conference. The other texts
mentioned have the same status as Wesley's *Sermons* and *Notes*,
carrying the "weight of tradition." This historical analysis is important, but not decisive for the current interpretation of the phrase.

The decisive indicator of the current position of The United
Methodist Church is in the Discipline under the heading
"Doctrinal Standards in the United Methodist Church":

> In the Plan of Union for The United Methodist Church, the pref-
> ace to the Methodist Articles of Religion and the Evangelical
> United Brethren Confession of Faith explains that both were
> accepted as doctrinal standards for the new Church. Additionally,
> it stated that although the language of the first Restrictive Rule
> never has been formally defined, Wesley's *Sermons* and *Notes*
> were understood specifically to be included in our present exist-
> ing and established standards of doctrine.[58]

Immediately following the Confession of Faith are bibliographical
notes dealing with "The Standard Sermons of Wesley," "The
Explanatory Notes Upon the New Testament," and "The General
Rules of the Methodist Church."

The historical argument between Heitzenrater, Oden, Ogletree,
and others is important, primarily because it underlies the final
text in the Discipline. It is the text approved by the General

Conference that is decisive, because only that body has the authority to interpret the ambiguous phrase. As noted above, the Judicial Council has consistently refused to make doctrinal interpretations, arguing that the General Conference is competent to make such decisions. While the relevant passages from the Discipline are not entirely clear, they do indicate that Wesley's *Sermons* and *Notes* are covered under the ambiguous phrase in the first Restrictive Rule.

Once it is agreed that Wesley's *Sermons* are part of the authoritative doctrine of the Church, a further complication arises. Which sermons are included in *Sermons*? No clear answer is given in the Discipline. "Our Doctrinal History" notes the origin of using sermons as doctrinal standards in the Model Deed of 1763, which referred to "four volumes of Sermons." The American Conference before independence accepted the British standards of Minutes, *Sermons* and *Notes*. Under the Heading "The Standard Sermons of Wesley" is a bibliographical note referring the reader to the Bicentennial Edition of *The Works of John Wesley* for the critical edition of the sermons. Within Wesley's lifetime, his *Sermons on Several Occasions* were published in three editions. The first four volumes included forty-three, fifty-three, and forty-four sermons respectively. The British Methodist Conference has determined that the standards are forty-four in number.[59]

Two arguments would suggest that fifty-three is the appropriate number to use. First, when the Methodists in the United States became independent, the four volumes most recently printed in England had fifty-three sermons in them. Originally the sermons had been published as separate volumes in 1746, 1748, 1750, and 1760.[60] Together these had forty-three sermons. However, a second edition of volume three has an extra sermon added for a total of forty-four. Hence, when the Model Deed was issued in 1763, one could assume that forty-four sermons were meant.

In 1771 Wesley issued his *Works*. The first four volumes of this set, sometimes called the Pine edition because of its printer, were the sermons. They had all forty-four of the previously published sermons from the four volumes of *Sermons on Several Occasions* but also included nine additional sermons. These additional ones are "The Witness of the Spirit, II," "Sin in Believers," "Repentance of

Believers," "The Great Assize," "The Lord Our Righteousness," "The Scripture Way of Salvation," "The Good Steward," "The Reformation of Manners," and "On the Death of Mr. Whitefield." In 1783, an American edition of the four volumes of sermons was published in Philadelphia. Based on the Pine edition, it had fifty-three sermons. Another complication arises from the 1788 edition of his sermons, where the four volumes include forty-four sermons.[61] However, if one is concerned with the status in 1784, the later editions are not relevant. In the edition of Wesley's works most current at the time of the formation of the Methodist Episcopal Church as a separate body in the United States, the phrase "four volumes of sermons" most obviously refers to fifty-three sermons.

If there is a tradition of understanding the phrase "present existing established standards of doctrine" to include *Sermons*, one might argue that the time of separation from England is the time at which to fix the meaning of the phrase. However, one might equally well argue that 1808 is the time when the phrase was first used in this context, and some other edition of Wesley's sermons might have been the best referent.

The second argument is much less legalistic and perhaps of less influence. One might seek to interpret the phrase in the first Restrictive Rule as broadly as possible in order to include as much of Wesley's work as possible. If historical considerations suggest no more than fifty-three sermons, then a concern for the content of these "extra" nine sermons would encourage as broad an interpretation as possible. "The Use of Money" is one of those additional sermons whose content is important to include. Tom Oden agrees with this count while others have come to different conclusions.[62] However, given that the General Conference is the only authorized interpreter of these matters and that the Discipline is silent on the subject, a number of different, reasonable choices regarding how many of Wesley's sermons are "standard" is possible. Indeed, on the "broadest possible interpretation" argument, one might treat all of Wesley's sermons as authoritative. Such an approach completely cuts off the meaning of the phrase "four volumes of *Sermons*," and yet it includes some of Wesley's most interesting sermons. When the Model Deed was drawn up, there were only four volumes of sermons. Was Wesley's editorial work in later editions explicitly done with regard to which of his sermons were to be standards of doctrine? Was the failure to alter the terms of the Model Deed due to legal considerations or oversight? It seems clear that many of Wesley's sermons not included in the fifty-three are among his most speculative and therefore theologically interesting. But for that very reason one might suppose that they do not belong in a collection of doctrinal standards. At the same time, using all of the sermons would result in the inclusion of the sermon "Free Grace," which he published separately in the heat of controversy with George Whitefield, but never subsequently included in his collected works.

Whatever the answers to these intriguing historical questions, the General Conference has left the matter unclear. Based on the status of the "four volumes of sermons" in 1784, this study will rely on the first fifty-three in the Bicentennial Edition of the *Works*.

Contemporary Statements

The second level of doctrine is composed of those statements of the General Conference intended to be doctrinal in nature but which are not covered by the Restrictive Rules. Thus, they can be changed by a majority vote at any General Conference session. Primarily, these are sections 1, 2, and 4 of Part II of the Discipline, labeled "Our Doctrinal Heritage," "Our Doctrinal History," and "Our Theological Task" respectively; Part III, "The Ministry of All Christians"; Part IV "Social Principles"; and the *Book of Resolutions*.

However, there are doctrinal statements embedded in many places in the Discipline. For example, there is teaching about the nature of the church placed at significant points throughout Part V. There is a relatively long discussion of connectionalism and mission at the beginning of chapter 5, "Administrative Order."[63] Paragraph 1301 makes a statement about the mission of the church.[64] Each of these doctrinal statements, regardless of its placement in the Discipline, should be treated with the same regard as those statements in Parts II through IV that are not constitutionally protected.

Liturgy

The third level is composed of those officially sanctioned documents that are not explicitly intended to be doctrine but that clearly have doctrinal functions: *The United Methodist Book of Worship* and *The United Methodist Hymnal*. Many scholars distinguish between first-order religious speech and second-order speech. They often relegate doctrinal pronouncements to the latter category as a kind of grammar for guiding first-order speech. However, such a distinction does not inhere in the texts themselves as much as in how the texts are used. For United Methodists, hymnody and liturgy have been used to teach the faith, and so function as both first-order and second-order speech.[65]

The shape of United Methodist doctrine provides for a number of problems as well as possibilities. The presence of so many different types of texts, from articles to narrative to sermons to notes to hymns, means that a variety of interpretations are possible. But the ranking of different levels of authority provides an order to the ways in which different views are reconciled within the variety of sources that have a claim to being authoritative United Methodist doctrine.

QUESTIONS ARISING FROM THE FORMAL SHAPE OF UNITED METHODIST DOCTRINE

What does it mean that United Methodism counts sermons, exegetical notes, and rules of behavior as parts of its fundamental doctrinal statements? One answer lies in the distinction between causative and normative authority discussed below. While all of the different literary forms can serve in either capacity, these forms are better adapted to convincing persons about the truth of a position than setting a legally enforceable standard. Propositions such as those contained in the Articles and Confession better serve that latter purpose. Their presence makes The United Methodist Church a confessional Church. But the other texts show the practical side of the Church's doctrine because their form is more readily suited to the transformation of individuals than are traditional creeds and confessions. On such an understanding, it is appropriate to create doctrinal standards that are in sermonic form. If sermons, exegeses, and rules are among the chief ways in which the word of God is applied to the contemporary lives of persons, then putting doctrinal matters in these forms emphasizes the practical end of the doctrinal activity.

What function do the General Rules play in doctrine? They illustrate the way in which Christian teaching is transformative and builds character. Seen in the light of the teachings about establishing the law, Christian perfection, salvation by grace through faith, and the means of grace, these rules provide a practical framework by which individuals could work out their own salvation. The General Rules are transformative and thus practical. The Discipline says that they are a way of discipleship and that Wesley "rejected undue reliance upon these rules."[66] However, "undue reliance" did not mean one was allowed to break them. Instead, one was to rely on God's grace and see the ways in which grace was working through them. They were not church law before 1784, but they were the law of the Methodist societies. These rules were a means of grace by which people who feared God and sought salvation could find it.

What does it mean that United Methodism is unclear and vague about important points in its doctrinal standards? Two answers can be given here. First, the denomination ought to give more attention to the clarity of its teaching. There is a sense in which such unanswered questions are problematic if the Church really does believe its doctrine is important. Thus, clarifying the status of the *Sermons* and *Notes* and which sermons are included would be helpful. Students are now required to take courses in United Methodist doctrine, and they should know precisely what it is they are studying. In a larger context, as the United States becomes more culturally diverse and different religious groups become more direct competitors for the hearts and minds of the people, many persons will ask what it is the United Methodist Church believes. Giving the best possible answer empowers the Church's witness. Filling these holes would improve the denomination's proclamation.

The second answer qualifies the urgency of the first. United Methodist doctrine is practical, and its vagueness at some points is simply another sign of this. Unless and until these problematic points actually affect the preaching, teaching, and serving in local congregations, there will be little incentive for United Methodists to fix them. United Methodists tend to do ministry first and reflect about it later, and are willing to give only that amount of time for reflection that is necessary to keep on ministering. Doctrinal reflection takes time and resources, and the burden of proof is on those who wish to commit that time and those resources to show that the ministry of the Church will be enhanced by it later.

The Church has devoted too little of its time for such doctrinal reflection, and it lacks the necessary structures to foster the "doctrinal reinvigoration" in which it says it believes. The General Commission on Christian Unity and Interreligious Concerns invited a diverse group of United Methodist leaders to dialogue about the controversies around homosexual practice, feminist images for God, and other matters that have threatened to divide the Church. They met in 1997 and 1998 and concluded that these conflicts have deeper roots in differing understandings of Christology, ecclesiology, and the authority of Scripture.[67] Their first recommendation was that the Council of Bishops create a Committee on Theological Dialogue.[68] There is an urgent need for the Church to give more attention to its authoritative doctrine.

What kinds of authority do these texts have? In his essay "Scripture, Authenticity, and Truth," Charles Wood makes use of resources from Protestant theologians of the seventeenth century and two twentieth-century philosophers to clarify the meaning of the authority of Scripture. He says:

> The first, called "causative authority" by such Lutherans as David Hollaz, and known by other names (sometimes simply as "divine authority") among the Reformed theologians, was (to follow Hollaz) that "by which scripture generates and confirms in the human mind assent to the things to be believed." It is the "illuminating power" that begets faith by bringing the reader or hearer to understanding; it is Scripture's capacity to teach, to convey the knowledge of God. . . .
>
> The second kind of authority, called "normative authority" or "canonical authority" by these writers, is displayed in the use of the Bible in the church as the norm or judge of doctrine. The church appeals to Scripture, as the rule of faith and morals, to resolve controversies or to measure the adequacy of a statement.[69]

Wood then discusses the work of Richard De George, a philosopher who has written about authority. His first conclusion is that we should "expect Scripture's authority to be complex, and to ask, not 'What kind?' but 'What kinds? In what contexts? For what purposes?'"[70] Wood goes on to argue that normative authority "determines what the church shall hold to be true. It determines whether a given teaching is to be considered a teaching of the church."[71] Wood argues that normative authority presumes that a doctrine is true. It is causative authority which ascertains truth. In the reverse direction, causative authority sometimes requires the assistance of normative authority so that it can become a condition of learning. He says, "It is the normative authority of Scripture—the fact that it is definitive of the community's identity and purpose—that, so to speak, sends the members of the Christian community back to check their own perceptions of the truth against what is mediated afresh through Scripture."[72] Thus, Wood helps us see that two different kinds of authority are at work in Scripture's relationship to the church, and that they interact with each other in complex ways.

This same distinction for the authority of Scripture can also be applied to the authority of doctrine. United Methodist doctrine carries causative authority in the ways in which it commends itself as true and becomes a way in which the gospel of Jesus Christ is grasped by persons. Some of the denomination's doctrinal texts particularly lend themselves to this function. It will be argued below that Wesley's *Sermons* and *Notes* are particularly well adapted to this type of authority. At the same time, the Articles and Confession can be seen as better adapted to the normative function of authority.[73] However, it will be argued that all of the denomination's doctrinal texts fulfill both functions.

THE MATERIAL SHAPE OF UNITED METHODIST DOCTRINE

The formal shape of authoritative United Methodist doctrine consists of three levels: constitutional standards, contemporary statements, and liturgy. The doctrinal texts of United Methodism are a complex body of material as we have seen. To construe them as a whole requires discerning a pattern that renders a main theme. David Kelsey, looking at the wholeness of Scripture, calls this a "discrimen" that allows the interpreter to discern the wholeness of the text.[74] This process inevitably gives priority to some texts and then interprets others in light of their leading role. The formal shape of United Methodist doctrine points to that pattern by giving priority to the Constitution, Articles, Confession, General Rules, *Sermons*, and *Notes*.

SAVING DOCTRINE

With these texts as the most important, it is clear that the heart of United Methodist doctrine is soteriology. Doctrines of God (including Christology and pneumatology) and Scripture are its necessary prolegomena and constant presupposition; doctrines about heaven, hell, and the second coming of Christ are the de-emphasized conclusion. Instead, this body of teaching focuses on what Wesley called the way of salvation, the progress of individuals, and thus also of societies, from creation and sin through repentance and justification to entire sanctification as the goal of human life. The church as the bearer of the means of grace is the inescapable locus of God's saving activity in this process. Chapters 2 through 9 of this book argue this thesis. There are three sections to this argument. First, United Methodist doctrine bears witness to the reality of the triune God who is Father, Son, and Holy Spirit. The Articles of Religion and Confession of Faith both begin with this confession.

The great bulk of United Methodist teaching focuses on the way of salvation. The "Distinctive Wesleyan Emphases"[75] discussed in Part II of the Discipline summarize the bulk of the *Sermons*, *Notes*, Social Principles, and Resolutions. Seven key words summarize the main sections of this teaching: creation, sin, repentance, justification, new birth, assurance, and sanctification provide a framework for how these doctrines fit together. These words summarize different stages in God's dealing with human beings. For each there is a different aspect of saving grace: prevenient, convincing, justifying, and sanctifying. Ecclesiology is typically treated by United Methodist doctrine under the heading of the means of grace. A focus on United Methodist ecclesiology is crucial to knowing how God's grace is conveyed to people. This discussion of the means of grace, the nature of the church, and the mission of the church are all central to knowing how United Methodist doctrine teaches that persons are to make progress in the way of salvation.

BIBLICAL DOCTRINE

Second, United Methodist doctrine is not self-generating, but is under the authority of Holy Scripture. While the doctrinal standards are clear about biblical authority, they are also clear about what kind of authority the Scripture should have. Doctrinal statements have further clarified that position in their discussion of how Scripture is interpreted by and has authority over reason, tradition, and experience.

PRACTICAL DOCTRINE

Third, the goal of United Methodist doctrine is a life of Christian discipleship. It teaches the religion of the heart. Thus, one should always keep in mind that the end of doctrine as making disciples of Jesus Christ should always be kept in mind. This also means that doctrine is shaped by practice. Philip Meadows suggests that

> in the Wesleyan tradition, faithfulness to doctrine has always been connected to disciplined discipleship; and those qualified to teach have been those who have learned the faith, whose theological lives commended their judgment as spiritual leaders. The recovery of authentic Christian fellowship, accountable to Methodist doctrine, must be a core practice for the apprenticeship of learning the faith in any authentic account of Wesleyan theological reflection.[76]

QUESTIONS ARISING FROM THE MATERIAL SHAPE OF UNITED METHODIST DOCTRINE

Is United Methodist doctrine coherent? United Methodist doctrine is coherent but not completely consistent. Consistency is a higher standard that means there are no internal conflicts. Coherence is compatible with such conflicts if the overall content forms an intelligible whole.

There are some places, particularly within the *Notes*, that appear to be in conflict with more recent statements of the church or that are otherwise problematic. Charles Yrigoyen draws attention to a number of these places.[77] Perhaps one of the most glaring, however, is the timetable in the *Notes* at Revelation 17:10. It says there,

Perhaps the times hitherto mentioned might be fixed thus—

1058 Wings are given to the woman.
1077 The beast ascends out of the sea.
1143 The forty-two months begin.
1810 The forty-two months end.
1832 The beast ascends out of the bottomless pit.
1836 The beast finally overthrown.[78]

The note on the following verse explains part of the calculation, that "the whole succession of Popes from Gregory VII are undoubtedly anti-christ."[79] Mitigating the force of this passage is the preface to his notes on Revelation where Wesley says:

The following notes are mostly those of that excellent man [Johann Albrecht Bengel]; . . . Every part of this I do not undertake to defend. But none should condemn him without reading his proofs at large. . . .

Yet I by no means pretend to understand or explain all that is contained in this mysterious book. I only offer what help I can to the serious inquirer, and shall rejoice if any be moved thereby more carefully to read and more deeply to consider the words of this prophecy. Blessed is he that does this with a single eye. His labour shall not be in vain.[80]

In addition to Wesley's disclaimer, the note before the chronology says that the dates "might be fixed thus," which is a less than full commitment to this interpretation. However, the *Notes* clearly identify the antichrist with the papacy. What is the force of this exegetical approach for United Methodist doctrine?

In another example, Wesley's note on 1 Corinthians 14:34-35 says:

Let your women be silent in the churches—Unless they are under an extraordinary impulse of the Spirit. *For,* in other cases, *it is not*

permitted them to speak—By way of teaching in public assemblies.
But to be in subjection—To the man whose proper office it is to lead
and to instruct the congregation.

And even *if they desire to learn anything*—Still they are not to
speak in public, but to *ask their own husbands at home*—That is the
place, and those the persons to inquire of.

Given the argument that the *Notes* are a constitutional standard of
doctrine, what force does this exegesis have? It is true that Wesley's
exception—a woman is allowed to speak if under an "extraordinary" gift of the Spirit—led him to permit a few women to preach
in Methodism during his time. Viewed historically, he was pro-
gressive for his time and place. However, as a standard of United
Methodist doctrine this conflicts with the denomination's policy
of treating men and women equally for all positions of church
leadership.

**How does the denomination deal with such problematic pas-
sages?** Again, there are holes in the framework of United
Methodist doctrine. The most explicit answer comes in relation to
the interpretation of Articles XIV, XV, XVI, XVIII, XIX, XX, and XXI.
In a resolution first passed in 1970 and subsequently reaffirmed,
the General Conference did not repudiate these articles but committed the denomination to interpreting them "in consonance with
our best ecumenical insights and judgment."[81] One could easily
imagine the denomination making the same statement about various problematic texts in the *Notes*, including the section on end-
time chronology in Revelation, the passages on subordination of
women, and slavery. In such a resolution, the Church might suggest that Wesley's *Notes* are to be interpreted in the light of the best
contemporary scholarship about the Bible. In fact, something similar to this is said in the section on Scripture in "Our Theological
Task."[82]

But another argument might be made as well. In interpreting
Scripture, Wesley said about the analogy of faith, "Every article
therefore concerning which there is any question should be determined by this rule: every doubtful scripture interpreted according
to the grand truths which run through the whole."[83] In a similar
way, problematic texts should be referred to the general tenor of
United Methodist doctrine. Just as verses about women being
silent have been judged less central to the faith than those texts

about there being neither male nor female in Christ, and just as texts about slavery were judged to be less central than God's desire for the dignity and fulfillment of all persons, so passages in the *Notes* about end-time chronology, the status of women, and the papacy should be judged in the light of the message of salvation carried by the whole body of teaching. These answers are not definitive and lack sufficient evidence to say that they are the teaching of the Church. Yet, they account for how the denomination does in fact carry these conflicting teachings at the same time.

It is significant that this description of the shape of United Methodist doctrine is not drawn from a coherent statement about doctrinal authority written in the Discipline. Rather, they are gleaned from a number of places where the underlying structure of United Methodist doctrine is referred to, often obliquely. This illustrates the essentially practical character of United Methodist doctrine. The United Methodist Church has always poured more energy and resources into accomplishing its mission than refining its doctrinal statements. Nevertheless, the doctrinal structure has been there since the beginnings of its predecessor denominations. Making such a structure clear highlights the shape of the United Methodist ethos even if that ethos has sometimes been obscured.

Notes

1. Lindbeck 1984, 74.

2. See Richey 1995 and Kirby 2000.

3. Jurisdictional and Central Conferences are roughly equivalent but not overlapping. Thus together they constitute one level despite important differences between them.

4. Discipline 299, ¶509. The paragraph refers to the General Conference's "full legislative power over all matters distinctively connectional," ¶15 of the Constitution.

5. *Works* (J) 8:275.

6. The work of these two study committees is described in Outler 1991 and Heitzenrater 1991b.

7. Richey 1996, 199-204.

8. Langford 1991b, 176.

9. The General Conferences of 1984, 1988, and 1992 considered the orders of ministry on the basis of study commissions it had appointed or asked to be appointed. Only in 1996 did the conference take action. In 1984 it received the report of a task force to study homosexuality and recommended the Church study the task force's report, but did not adopt it.

10. Discipline 38.

11. Judicial Council decision 142, http://www.umc.org/judicial/100/142.html.

12. Judicial Council decision 59, http://www.umc.org/judicial/1/59.html.

13. Judicial Council decision 86, http://www.umc.org/judicial/1/86.html, decision 358, http://www.umc.org/judicial/300/358.html.

14. Decision 358, http://www.umc.org/judicial/300/358.html.

15. Decision 358, http://www.umc.org/judicial/300/358.html.

16. Decision 833, http://www.umc.org/judicial/800/833.html.

17. Discipline 35, ¶45.

18. Discipline 280, ¶414.3.

19. Discipline 287-88, ¶427.2.

20. Richey 1995.

21. Kirby, 84-85.

22. Kirby, 244-45. The quotation is from Richey 1995, 165.

23. Kirby, Richey, and Rowe, 168-70, 234-35.

24. Discipline 490-91, ¶1004.

25. Discipline 25, ¶15 of the Constitution.

26. Discipline 299, ¶509.

27. *Works* (J) 8:275. See also Heitzenrater 1995, 142-46.

28. Discipline 24, ¶10 of the Constitution.

29. Richey 1996, passim.

30. Pelikan, 1.

31. Discipline, 60, 67.

32. Discipline 60, Article II.

33. Discipline, 27, 39.

34. Discipline 300, ¶510.2a.

35. For example, see "Health and Wholeness," BOR 263-68, "Guidelines: The United Methodist Church and the Charismatic Movement," BOR 818-33, and "Resolution of Intent—With a View to Unity," BOR 236-38.

36. Discipline, 95.

37. Discipline, 122.

38. See BOR, 65, 167, and 436 as examples.

39. Interestingly, Wesley did not feel bound by the theology of all of the hymns in the 1780 hymnal. He said, "Though there are some expressions in my brother's Hymns which I do not use, as being very liable to be misconstrued; yet I am fully satisfied, that, in the whole tenor of them, they thoroughly agree with mine, and with the Bible," *Works* (J), 10:426.

40. Discipline 27, ¶16.

41. One thinks of Albert Outler, Richard Heitzenrater, John Cobb, Tom Langford, and Tom Oden as such leaders since 1968. Many of the United Methodist authors whose books appear in the selected bibliography are making their contributions currently.

42. Specifically, he omitted the following articles:

3. Of the Going Down of Christ Into Hell

8. Of the Three Creeds

13. Of Works Before Justification

15. Christ Alone Without Sin

17. Of Predestination and Election

18. Of obtaining eternal salvation, only by the name of Christ

20. Of the Authority of the Church

21. Of the Authority of General Councils

23. Of ministering in the Congregation

26. Of the unworthiness of the ministers, which hinder not the effect of the Sacraments

29. Of the Wicked, which do not eat the Body of Christ in the use of the Lord's Supper

33. Of excommunicate persons, how they are to be avoided

35. Of homilies

36. Of consecration of bishops and ministers

37. Of civil magistrates

43. Using the numbering of the MEC Articles of Religion, the following articles were altered by Wesley from the wording of corresponding Church of England articles: 2, 5, 7, 12, 13, 16, 17, 21, and 22.

44. Article I had the word "passions" deleted.

45. Using the number of the present Articles of Religion, the following articles are substantially the same as their corresponding Church of England articles: 3, 4, 6, 8, 9, 10, 11, 14, 15, 18, 19, 20, 24, and 25.

46. *Book of Common Prayer.*

47. Discipline, 59.

48. See "Doctrinal Traditions in The Evangelical Church and The United Brethren Church," Discipline, 55-58.

49. O'Malley 1999, 60. See also Behney and Eller, 358.

50. O'Malley 1999, 69.

51. O'Malley 1999, 73-74.

52. O'Malley 1999, 76.

53. Discipline, 72.

54. Heitzenrater 1995, 139.

55. Discipline, 48.

56. See Heitzenrater 1991a, Oden 1991, and Oden 1988. Wheeler, 26 refers to "the fifty-three sermons which are among the standards of doctrine in Methodism." A historical study of how the Restrictive Rule has been construed in the history of Methodism would perhaps be helpful to a General Conference seeking to revise its present interpretation. However, this is not relevant to the current question of what does the Discipline currently say. Frank, 130-33, and Yrigoyen reach the same conclusion as I have about the status of the *Sermons* and *Notes*. Oden 1988 affirms the inclusion of the sermons without taking a clear position on the question of how many. He acknowledges the "general agreement that at least forty-four are indisputably doctrinal standards" (94). Then he notes that British Methodists usually say forty-four while Americans are more likely to say fifty-two. He then proceeds to give titles and summaries of fifty-three sermons (97).

57. Discipline, 53-54.

58. Discipline, 58. However, Ogletree, D&T, 174 notes that this part of the Plan of Union was for information only and not constitutionally binding on the new

denomination. He says, "In short, the Plan of Union can be said to have stipulated that the *Sermons* and *Notes* are covered by the First Restrictive Rule only in the sense that the General Conference of the two uniting churches accepted a particular historical judgment about what might have been the original reference of the First Restrictive Rule. Like any critical reconstruction of past events, this judgment remains open to historical review. Further, the action which included this stipulation in the Plan of Union had the status only of General Conference legislation. It simply cannot be described as a constitutional matter." My claim is precisely this, that the General Conference of 1988 (and subsequent sessions that have left the relevant words unchanged) has authoritatively interpreted the Restrictive Rule to include the *Sermons* and *Notes*. A future General Conference could change the interpretation by majority vote.

59. For an accounting of the decision made by the British Conference, see Sugden 2:331-40.

60. Outler, "Introduction," *Works* 1:38-49.

61. The attorney's opinion, which was accepted as the proper interpretation by the British Conference, was that the Model Deed applies to this edition, and thus they count forty-four sermons as standard. See Sugden, 2:340.

62. Oden 1988, 93-94, 97.

63. Discipline, 426.

64. Discipline, 524.

65. Ted Campbell 1999.

66. Discipline, 48.

67. See *In Search of Unity*.

68. A petition creating such a committee was passed by the 1996 General Conference without funding and so was never created.

69. Wood 1996, 190. He is using his own translation of Hollaz as quoted in Heinrich Schmid, *Die Dogmatik der evangelisch-lutherischen Kirche dargestellt und aus den Quellen belegt*, 10th ed., ed. Horst Georg Pöhlmann (Gütersloh: Gütersloher Verlagshaus Gerd Mohn, 1983), p. 48. A published English translation of this book is *The Doctrinal Theology of the Evangelical Lutheran Church*, 3rd ed., trans. Charles A. Hay and Henry E. Jacobs (Minneapolis: Augsburg, 1961), p. 104.

70. Wood 1996, 199.

71. Wood 1996, 203.

72. Wood 1996, 204.

73. I am indebted to Charles Wood for this insight.

74. Kelsey 1975, 100-106.

75. Discipline, 45.

76. Meadows, 84. Meadows unfortunately regards the Wesleyan Quadrilateral as a chief culprit in blocking this kind of practical doctrine. Like Abraham in *Waking from Doctrinal Amnesia*, he argues against the way the Quadrilateral has been misused rather than considering arguments for how it might properly be used. For another helpful discussion on the issue of practical doctrine, see Knight and Saliers.

77. Yrigoyen 2001.

78. *Notes* Rev. 17:10.

79. *Notes* Rev. 17:11.
80. *Notes*, Preface to Revelation.
81. BOR, 238.
82. Discipline, 78.
83. *Notes* Rom. 12:6.

CHAPTER TWO

THE NATURE OF UNITED METHODIST DOCTRINE

United Methodist doctrine is the historic Christian faith in God taught by that part of the body of Christ called The United Methodist Church. Five theses drawn from its doctrinal statements illustrate how the denomination understands its own doctrinal activity.

UNITED METHODIST DOCTRINE IS CHRISTIAN DOCTRINE

United Methodist doctrine is Christian doctrine as understood by one part of the body of Christ.[1] While saying that United Methodist doctrine is Christian doctrine may appear redundant, it serves to locate that body of teaching in two ways. Diachronically it is located in the Christian tradition, bearing the historic faith in continuity with the teaching of the apostles. As a living tradition, United Methodist doctrine understands that it must adapt the witness to new circumstances that arise over the course of time. In a very deep sense, however, United Methodists understand themselves as proclaiming the same gospel that true Christians have always and everywhere proclaimed. They are the heirs of a particular part of that Christian church, coming down through the English Reformation, the Evangelical Revival, the Second Great

Awakening in the United States, and now serving God around the world.

Synchronically, it is an authentic part, but only one part of the whole body of Christ. When it teaches about the word of God it is not teaching United Methodism as a religion distinct from other forms of Christianity. It teaches the United Methodist understanding of the apostolic faith that is authentically one, yet tragically divided.

ECUMENICAL

Because it is Christian doctrine, United Methodist doctrine must take account of other expressions of Christian doctrine both in terms of what others have to offer and what United Methodists can give to others. The denomination's constitution shows the depth of its commitment to Christian unity:

> The United Methodist Church is part of the church universal, which is one Body in Christ. . . .
> *Article V. Ecumenical Relations*—As part of the church universal, The United Methodist Church believes that the Lord of the church is calling Christians everywhere to strive toward unity; and therefore it will seek, and work for, unity at all levels of church life: through world relationships with other Methodist churches and united churches related to The Methodist Church or The Evangelical United Brethren Church, through councils of churches, and through plans of union and covenantal relationships with churches of Methodist or other denominational traditions.[2]

One essential part of that unity is doctrinal agreement, which would then enable the united churches to confess the Christian faith together. During the twentieth century The United Methodist Church and others made numerous ecumenical efforts toward doctrinal convergence.[3] A presupposition of such efforts is that each participating church must know where it stands before genuine dialogue can occur. A frequent result of genuine dialogue is that each church better understands its own doctrinal position.

Such an encounter is both a challenge and an opportunity. On one hand, the existence of other expressions of Christian doctrine confronts the church with several questions. Why is the doctrine of the other church different? Is one right and the other wrong? Are the two versions of Christian doctrine actually compatible or equivalent expressions of the same truth? If there is mutual recognition of each other as Christians and if there is commitment to a coherent understanding of truth, then existing doctrinal differences challenge a United Methodist understanding of the gospel.

At the same time, such differences represent an opportunity for the specific insights of one's own denomination to be considered by others. Just as the United Methodist understanding of ecclesiology could be informed by insights, for example, from Roman Catholics and the Orthodox, so those churches might need to encounter what United Methodists believe about the priesthood of all believers and the participation of the laity in decision-making meetings. The Church states, "The heart of our task is to reclaim and renew the distinctive United Methodist doctrinal heritage, which rightly belongs to our common heritage as Christians, for the life and mission of the whole church today."[4]

UNITED METHODIST DOCTRINE IS PRACTICAL

United Methodism understands Christian doctrine to be characteristically practical. Perhaps all Christian doctrine is, or should be, practical in the ways in which United Methodism understands it to be. One may reasonably assume that, by describing the Christian faith in the ways that it does, this denomination is making certain claims, either implicitly or explicitly, about Christian doctrine generally. Whatever is the case with other understandings of Christian doctrine, its United Methodist version is practical.

United Methodist doctrine is practical. Clearly, the use of "practical" needs clarification in this context. Sometimes "practical" is seen as the opposite of "theoretical." For many years theological education has divided its disciplines into biblical, historical, systematic, and practical. This has led many to think of systematic theology as a theoretical inquiry, which is then put into practice through activities such as preaching, worship, Christian education, pastoral care, and evangelism. Charles Wood in his *Vision and Discernment* says, "The conventional and centuries-old division of the theological disciplines into the theoretical and the practical is seriously misleading. It implicitly denies the properly theoretical aspects of practical theology, and it exaggerates the extent to which the other disciplines are themselves theoretical enterprises."[5] Wood warns that several different versions of the problem of how to relate theory and practice all mask and compound the real problem. Instead, we should think of vision as the effort to grasp the wholeness of Christian witness, and discernment as the attempt to understand the particular. He says,

> *Both* vision and discernment are informed by, and in turn inform, practice, as we shall later see. At the same time, vision and discernment *together*—and not vision (or "theory") alone—are constitutive of theological reflection. Theology is not simply "theory"; nor is it "theory and practice" together (except in the sense in which any reflective activity is a practice); it *is* theory (in the "vision" sense) and discernment.[6]

Thus, all of theology has a strong relationship to Christian witness. At its best, all Christian theology is practical, both informing and being informed by Christian witness. Theology answers questions arising out of Christian practice and should inform that practice by helping it better achieve its own goals. There is thus a dialectical relationship between all of Christian theology (practical, historical, and systematic) and the practice of the Christian faith. Wood is clearly aware that many theological works have obscured this relationship and thus become less helpful to their aim than originally intended. In an analogous way, one might argue that Christian doctrine should be practical but has not always been so. At its best, it exhibits three characteristics.

First, both the origin of doctrine and its goal is in the practice of the Christian faith. Alister McGrath presents a sophisticated argument about the origins of Christian doctrine. He suggests that even in New Testament times, the Christian community was formulating confessions to summarize and communicate why Jesus of Nazareth was important. As the gospel spread, simply repeating the earliest formulations was insufficient for the task. Eventually mere recitation of what had been said earlier in different contexts actually was less faithful to the apostolic witness than new formulations. McGrath says:

> In the attempt to demarcate the significance of Jesus in such formulae lies the origins of Christian doctrine. . . . The primitive instinct to preserve tradition by reiteration was obliged to give way to the perceived need to continue its history by restatement and interpretation. The dynamism of the New Testament traditions concerning Jesus was compromised through such a process of preservation, in that this process involved petrification, trapping something that was once living in a static form, as a fossil might be preserved in a rock or a fly captured in amber. These are symbols of the past, and of pastness itself—a past which once was living and vibrant but which is now dead, rigid and static. They appear as strange and unfamiliar exhibits in a museum of intellectual history, as anachronisms. The symbol which was intended to express today what was meant in the past degenerates into a symbol of pastness itself. The need for a "rebirth of images" underlies the genesis of doctrine.[7]

In a similar sense, doctrine is an integral part of the Christian community's life. Lindbeck's definition refers to "beliefs and practices that are considered essential to the identity or welfare of the group." Doctrine answers questions like *How should we worship God?* and *How do we bear witness to Christ in the world?* It is Christian practice that gives rise to the problems that doctrine addresses, and doctrine's goal is to shape the practices of the community and its individual members.

Doctrine aims at truth. In the secular sense of true as "worthy of belief," Christian doctrine offers something to the world which it claims as true. In this way, Christians have the obligation to give an account of their faith and hope in ways that engage the best thinking in the world. We need to be apologists who engage the world and explain to outsiders what we believe and why. Yet our understanding of truth differs from that of those outside the faith. In John 14:6 Jesus says of himself, "I am the way, and the truth, and the life." In John 8:31-32 he says, "If you continue in my word, you are truly my disciples; and you will know the truth, and the truth will make you free."[8] This understanding of truth is self-involving, because to know God truly is also to know ourselves. The Christian understanding of truth about God is something like Ellen Charry's view of sapience. In *By the Renewing of Your Minds: The Pastoral Function of Christian Doctrine,* she says, "The patristic age emphasized sapience as the foundation of human excellence. Sapience includes correct information about God but emphasizes attachment to that knowledge. Sapience is engaged knowledge that emotionally connects the knower to the known."[9] Christian doctrine seeks to tell the world the truth about God in such a way that those who accept it, find themselves transformed by it, and then are guided by it in all that they do.

Second, doctrine is practical because it can be transformative. Christian doctrine's goal is to lead human beings toward fulfilling God's purpose in creation. Charry says, "Christian doctrines function pastorally when a theologian unearths the divine pedagogy in order to engage the reader or listener in considering that life with the triune God facilitates dignity and excellence."[10] After reviewing the work of a number of theologians from Paul to Calvin, she concludes:

> Rather, the point is simply that as these major shapers of the Christian tradition formulated, reformulated, and revised Christian doctrine, its moral, psychological, and social implications were uppermost in their minds. Even when refuting their colleagues or opponents who, in the writers' judgment, were distorting the tradition and falling into heresy, they never forgot that God was seeking to draw people to himself for their own good.[11]

Doctrine seeks to create human excellence by teaching human beings the truth about God and themselves.

John Wesley conceived of Christian teaching as being transformative. In the opening sections of "Scripture Way of Salvation," he says:

> Nothing can be more intricate, complex, and hard to be understood, than religion as it has been often described. . . . Yet how easy to be understood, how plain and simple a thing, is the genuine religion of Jesus Christ! Provided only that we take it in its native form, just as it is described in the oracles of God. It is exactly suited by the wise Creator and Governor of the world to the weak understanding and narrow capacity of man in his present state. How observable is this both with regard to the end it

proposes and the means to attain that end! The end is, in one word, salvation: the means to attain it, faith.

It is easily discerned that these two little words—I mean faith and salvation—include the substance of all the Bible, the marrow, as it were, of the whole Scripture. So much the more should we take all possible care to avoid all mistake concerning them, and to form a true and accurate judgment concerning both the one and the other.[12]

Wesley claims that Christian doctrine centers on salvation and that the goal of Christianity is the restoration of the world in general and humanity in particular to the way God intended them to be. His understanding of real religion is set out in the "Preface" to the *Sermons:*

I want to know one thing, the way to heaven—how to land safe on that happy shore. . . .

I have accordingly set down in the following sermons what I find in the Bible concerning the way to heaven, with a view to distinguish this way of God from all those which are the inventions of men. I have endeavoured to describe the true, the scriptural, experimental religion, so as to omit nothing which is a real part thereof, and to add nothing thereto which is not. And herein it is more especially my desire, first, to guard those who are just setting their faces toward heaven (and who, having little acquaintance with the things of God, are the more liable to be turned out of the way) from formality, from mere outside religion, which has almost driven heart-religion out of the world; and secondly, to warn those who know the religion of the heart, the faith which worketh by love, lest at any time they make void the law through faith, and so fall back into the snare of the devil.[13]

Charles Wesley, using the word "experimental" (roughly equivalent to our "experiential"), referred to knowing God and Christ, saying, "This experimental knowledge, and this alone, is true Christianity."[14]

Third, doctrine is practical because its goal is holistic, understood as both orthodoxy and orthopraxis. Randy Maddox has argued that this is one of the characteristics of a theology that sees itself as a practical discipline. He says it must "seek to norm not only ideas and confessions but Christian action in the world.

Thanks to the influence of political and liberation theologies, such a desideratum is now widely accepted."[15] The character of the desired relationship between orthodoxy and orthopraxy merits further elucidation. Jaroslav Pelikan says, "When the Old Testament speaks about 'instruction' or the New Testament about 'the doctrine,' this includes teaching about both confession and conduct, both theology and ethics. A separation between them is fatal, a distinction unavoidable, just as in the New Testament itself 'faith' and 'works' are distinguished without being separated."[16] Pelikan notes that the two branches of theology were not permanently separated until the seventeenth century, but that the distinction between them goes back at least to Athanasius and has its roots in the New Testament itself. Maddox claims that the recovery of theology as a practical discipline should strengthen the relationship between these two. In an analogous way, practical doctrine will pay attention to the ways in which Christian beliefs about God and Christian beliefs about right conduct in the world are intimately related to each other.

United Methodist doctrine is centered on soteriology and thus upon the practice of the Christian faith. While it aims at the correct proclamation of truth, it always seeks truth in the service of Christian discipleship. Thomas Langford, in his *Practical Divinity*, characterizes Wesley's theology by saying:

> Theology is important as it serves the interest of Christian formation. Theology is never an end, but is always a means for understanding and developing transformed living. There was little speculative interest involved in Wesley's theological investigations. He consistently turned theological reflection to practical service. Theology, in his understanding, was to be preached, sung and lived.[17]

Since part of Wesley's body of writings became a substantial part of United Methodist doctrine, his concerns for both correct doctrine and discipleship are embodied in the Church's teaching. In "The Way to the Kingdom," Wesley quotes Romans 14:17 as saying that the kingdom of God is "righteousness and peace and joy in the Holy Ghost," which he construes as a matter of the heart. This means that correct doctrine is not an end in itself. It is a means to having a right relationship with God. He is clear that it is possible to be completely orthodox and yet estranged from God. He says:

> For neither does religion consist in *orthodoxy* or *right opinions;* which, although they are not properly outward things, are not in the heart, but the understanding. A man may be orthodox in every point; he may not only espouse right opinions, but zealously defend them against all opposers; he may think justly concerning the incarnation of our Lord, concerning the ever blessed Trinity, and every other doctrine contained in the oracles of God. He may assent to all the three creeds—that called the Apostles', the Nicene, and the Athanasian—and yet 'tis possible he may have no religion at all, no more than a Jew, Turk, or pagan. He may be almost as orthodox as the devil (though indeed not altogether; for every man errs in something, whereas we can't well conceive him to hold any erroneous opinion) and may all the while be as great a stranger as he to the religion of the heart.[18]

SAVING GRACE AS THE CENTRAL THEME

The third thesis of this chapter is that the central theme of United Methodist doctrine is saving grace. There is a framework of Christian teaching, which addresses basic doctrinal issues but gives greatest emphasis to the grace of God and its saving activity in the world. The Discipline makes this clear in Part II, "Doctrinal Standards and Our Theological Task." The first section, "Our Doctrinal Heritage," begins by discussing the teachings that Christians hold in common. Many key topics are mentioned briefly here: Trinity, creation, incarnation, resurrection, the work of the Holy Spirit, the nature and mission of the church and sacraments, the reign of God, the authority of Scripture, and the unity of the Church. But then it states how United Methodist doctrine gives a particular emphasis within this basic Christian framework:

> The underlying energy of the Wesleyan theological heritage stems from an emphasis upon practical divinity, the implementation of genuine Christianity in the lives of believers. . . .
> Wesley's orientation toward the practical is evident in his focus upon "the scripture way of salvation." He considered doctrinal

matters primarily in terms of their significance for Christian discipleship.

The Wesleyan emphasis upon the Christian life—faith and love put into practice—has been the hallmark of those traditions now incorporated into The United Methodist Church. The distinctive shape of the Wesleyan theological heritage can be seen in a constellation of doctrinal emphases that display the creating, redeeming, and sanctifying activity of God.[19]

Two corollaries of this claim are important to understand. First, United Methodist doctrine gives greatest attention to those matters related to the doctrine of salvation. Conversely, following Wesley, it gives much less attention to speculative matters that, in the eyes of ordinary Christians, are less important to their daily practice. Notice, for example, that Wesley's sermon "On the Trinity" is not included in the fifty-three *Sermons*. There is not a highly developed ecclesiology or doctrine of Scripture. Instead, one-fourth of Wesley's *Sermons* focus on the Sermon on the Mount, construed as a guide to how to live the Christian life. Topics of soteriology— grace, sin, repentance, justification, new birth, assurance, sanctification, and perfection—receive extensive treatment.

Second, some parts of United Methodist doctrine aim at being "plain truth for plain people," seeking to put the truth of the gospel into words that ordinary Christians can understand. In his preface to the *Sermons*, Wesley says, "I design plain truth for plain people. Therefore of set purpose I abstain from all nice and philosophical speculations, from all perplexed and intricate reasonings, and as far as possible from even the show of learning, unless in sometimes citing the original Scripture."[20] Similarly, Wesley wrote the *Notes* "chiefly for plain, unlettered men, who understand only their mother-tongue, and yet reverence and love the word of God, and have a desire to save their souls."[21]

His concerns for truth, for experimental religion, and for a plain style all coalesce into a distinctive whole. At the same time, some important teachings of Christian doctrine are referred to only obliquely or not at all. While others are clearly affirmed, they must be gleaned from a careful reading of all of the doctrinal statements to bring them together into a coherent whole.[22]

IDENTITY

Along with episcopacy, itinerancy, and the roles played by its various conferences, the doctrine of United Methodism is a constitutive part of the identity of United Methodism: "While the Church considers its doctrinal affirmations a central feature of its identity and restricts official changes to a constitutional process, the Church encourages serious reflection across the theological spectrum."[23] The introductory clause of that statement assumes that the Church's doctrinal affirmations are central to its identity, a point not always understood. In the discussion of the denomination's doctrinal history, the Discipline says, "Methodist interest in formal doctrinal standards remained secondary to evangelism, nurture, and mission."[24] Whereas this sentence describes the Methodist Episcopal Church in the early nineteenth century, it accurately characterizes the denomination's practical approach to its doctrine today. Doctrine is intended to serve the mission and ministry of the Church. Yet, the requirements that candidates for ordination study the Church's doctrine and then promise to "preach and maintain" indicate that doctrine is considered by the Church's own statements to be an important part of its identity. Its doctrine shapes its identity in at least four areas: evangelism, nurture, discipline, and discernment.

EVANGELISM

In evangelism, United Methodist doctrine tells the prospective believer what the denomination believes and teaches. When persons are baptized or confirmed, they are asked to repeat the words of the Apostles' Creed along with the congregation.[25] William J. Abraham's account of evangelism as initiation into the reign of God argues that an intellectual commitment to certain truth claims is a part of becoming a Christian.[26] In a practical matter, when a new believer asks about God, United Methodism can talk about the doctrine of the Trinity with reference to Article I of the Articles of Religion, Article 1 of the Confession of Faith, "Upon Our Lord's Sermon on the Mount, VII" and the *Notes*. When asked if the Church of Jesus Christ of Latter Day Saints is a Christian church whose baptism is valid Christian baptism, the denomination can cite its relevant doctrines and say that it is not. Thus, doctrine shapes denominational identity by specifying what it believes and does not believe.[27]

NURTURE

United Methodist doctrine also functions to nurture its members. In an important essay Charles Wood notes the commonly used comparison of doctrine to grammatical principles: "Mastery of the language and conscious knowledge of the 'rules' describing such mastery are two different things, and they do not always coincide. Likewise, understanding Christian doctrinal formulations and understanding things Christianly are two different things."[28] Wood cites a passage from Wesley's sermon "The Way to the Kingdom":

> . . . neither does religion consist in *orthodoxy* or *right opinions*; which, although they are not properly outward things, are not in the heart, but the understanding. A man may be orthodox at every point; he may not only espouse right opinions, but zealously defend them against all opposers; he may think justly concerning the incarnation of our Lord, concerning the ever blessed Trinity, and every other doctrine contained in the oracles of God. He may assent to all the three Creeds. . . . He may be almost as orthodox as the devil . . . and may all the while be as great a stranger as he to the religion of the heart.[29]

Wood then suggests that John Wesley has something quite close to what Wood calls a "grammatical" understanding of doctrine:

> Knowing the content of Christian doctrinal propositions is one thing; knowing God, or having "a heart right toward God and man," is another. A person may have a fine grasp of the first, and be nowhere near the second. But the propositions are not pointless: rightly used, they can be instrumental to the knowledge of God. They represent, and guide, proper Christian usage. It is not the propositions as such but the lived understanding or competence they represent that is of main importance.[30]

Wood goes on to analyze Wesley's view of the Trinity and draws the conclusion that on Wesley's understanding, Christian doctrine is instrumental to the end of Christian understanding and action. Doctrines "have their role, then, in those activities of teaching and reflection in which the conceptual capacities sustaining the knowledge and love of God are developed and strengthened. A key test of their own adequacy is their effectiveness in those activities."[31] Toward this end Wood offers a distinction:

> What we might call "objective doctrine," that is, doctrinal statements and formulations (similar to grammatical principles and paradigms), can be distinguished from what we might call "subjective doctrine," that is, the conceptual substance of the lived understanding of the faith (similar to the actual grammatical structure of a language as it is used by competent speakers); and both can be distinguished from what we might call "active doctrine," that is, the teaching activity in which, usually by means of doctrinal statements of one sort or another, doctrinal competence is fostered.[32]

Wood's proposal has a number of strengths, not the least of which are its ties to contemporary philosophical and theological discussions about the relationships between language and truth. Further, his discussion of how trinitarian language shapes Wesley's thinking about the Christian life lends support to both the grammatical metaphor for doctrine and the centrality of the doctrine of the Trinity in Wesley's theology.

Thus, to adopt Wood's point about how doctrine functions in general and especially for Methodists, one might say that living the Christian life is shaped, in part, by Christian doctrine. Even when individual Christians may not be able to quote doctrinal formulations, those formulations may have so informed their thinking, speaking, and action that they are living out the doctrine implicitly. Studying the various doctrinal statements is important primarily as it tends to shape one's life to be a better Christian.

Just as there is a grammar of language that competent speakers absorb and use but may not be able to articulate, so there is a set of Christian teachings that those who competently live the Christian faith know intuitively but may not be able to articulate. An illustration from my own life may help. I was raised in a Methodist family, the son, grandson, and great grandson of Methodist preachers. I do not recall ever hearing Wesley quoted as I was growing up. A Presbyterian college professor once remarked that I was someone who was concerned with having a "heart strangely warmed" and I did not know what he was referring to. I vaguely knew who John Wesley was, but could have told you very little about him. I enrolled in Albert Outler's course "Wesley and the Wesleyan Tradition" during my first year of seminary, thinking it would be good for me. Little did I anticipate the impact the course would have. The experience of hearing Outler lecture was comparable to my coming home to a place I had never been, or being given a self-description I had not yet heard. Outler's lectures and Wesley's writings told me who I was in ways much deeper than I had imagined possible, yet totally congruent with all that I had known before. To use the grammatical metaphor, Outler and Wesley taught me the deep structure of the language I had been speaking and the worldview I had been living, thereby enabling me to speak and live more authentically.

In a similar way, doctrine functions in Christian communities to shape the hearts of believers so they are right with God. This may not happen through explicit study of doctrine, what Wood calls "active" doctrine. Rather, it happens as the community lives together, worships together, prays together, makes decisions together, and serves God in ministries of evangelism and justice together. George Hunter's *Church for the Unchurched* lists ten characteristics of "apostolic congregations," one of which is that they "have a motivationally sufficient vision for what people, as disciples, can become."[33] Hunter is one of many scholars who examine the theological foundations undergirding the spiritual formation of a congregation collectively and individually. In such activities those who are experienced in the faith lead, both by example and correction, those who are just beginning their Christian journeys. This is Christian nurture.

Occasionally, active doctrine also takes place in the life of the congregation as persons attend confirmation classes, Bible studies, or other learning opportunities where Christian doctrines are the subject matter.[34] Many times people ask "What do we believe?" and seek to learn the teachings of their own denomination or of Christianity generally.

DISCIPLINE

Christian doctrine also functions to set the boundaries of the community, in what Methodists have called their discipline. This discipline can function both positively and negatively. In a positive sense leaders are selected in accordance with their ability to embody the denomination's beliefs in both word and deed. Courses that are taken in preparation for ordination include the study of United Methodist doctrine, polity, and history. The conversations that go on among candidates, their mentor pastors, committees on ordained ministry, and boards of ordained ministry could explore both doctrines as they are expressed in the official texts and doctrines as they are lived out in the practice of both the Christian life and the ordained ministry. Part of the process of examination by the Board of Ordained Ministry includes questions of doctrine and the candidates' understanding of them. This positive approach to the doctrinal discipline of the church culminates in the question asked of each candidate in front of the clergy members of the conference before the full members of the conference vote to admit them into conference membership. The bishop asks each candidate for ordination to give a spoken commitment to "preach and maintain" our doctrines.

Based on this doctrinal formation, there are also negative ways in which doctrinal discipline functions. When a clergy or lay member of the Church teaches in ways that contradict the Church's official teaching, informal pressures are sometimes brought to bear upon that person. Various forms of dialogue and persuasion can also be combined with other steps. A person can be blocked from election to a particular office or appointment to a particular pastorate because her or his theology is in conflict with what the Church teaches. Occasionally, pastors whose teaching has departed too far from that of the congregation can be moved to a different appointment because of this doctrinal conflict. At a farther extreme, the Discipline says that "dissemination of doctrines contrary to the established standards of doctrine of The United Methodist Church" is a chargeable offense that can result in either the expulsion of a clergyperson from the conference or the expulsion of a lay member from membership in the denomination.[35] While trials on this offense are very rare, complaints alleging that someone has violated this provision of their ordination have occurred in the recent past.

DISCERNMENT

Christian doctrine also functions to guide the process of discernment by the church corporately and by Christians individually. The understandings that God was revealed in Christ, that the apostolic witness to Christ was inspired, and that the church down through the centuries has been led by the Holy Spirit in its discernment, lead the church today to ask how it can faithfully proclaim and teach the Christian message. At the same time, the understandings that God chose to speak in Scripture through many different and contrasting voices and that the church has sometimes failed to discern correctly the guidance of the Holy Spirit lead the church to ask whether its teaching needs correction. Changing circumstances lead the church to ask how the message can be better formulated to accomplish the task of appropriate and effective communication with the world. In this complex process of doctrinal reformulation, the official teaching of the church thus guides the discernment of new understanding of the truth. For example, the church's witness against slavery was guided by historic doctrinal teaching that led to the affirmation of the dignity and importance of all human creatures regardless of race. While Scripture appears to condone slavery in certain passages and various parts of the Church have explicitly supported its practice, contemporary opposition to slavery is based precisely on its incompatibility with the most basic tenets of revelation and its doctrinal interpretation.

In The United Methodist Church, contemporary arguments about doctrine often take the form of messy political arguments between different factions in the Church. At their best, however, these discussions are discernment about how best to interpret Scripture in the light of the Church's historic teaching. There is always the awareness that Christian teaching in particular matters can be wrong, and that in all cases it is subject to better formulation and clarification. However, God's word revealed in Scripture and then interpreted and taught by the Church serves as an important guide to the Church's future discernment of the truth of the gospel.

REFORMULATION AND REINVIGORATION

The Church believes that its doctrine is in need of reformulation and reinvigoration. In the section headed "Doctrinal Standards in The United Methodist Church," the Discipline says, "The United Methodist Church stands continually in need of doctrinal reinvigoration for the sake of authentic renewal, fruitful evangelism, and ecumenical dialogue. In this light, the recovery and updating of our distinctive doctrinal heritage—catholic, evangelical, and reformed—is essential."[36] This statement illustrates a deeper principle embedded in the structure of United Methodist doctrine: all Christian doctrine stands under the word of God as revealed in the Bible. In the words of Article IV of the Confession, "Whatever is not revealed in or established by the Holy Scriptures is not to be made an article of faith nor is it to be taught as essential to salvation."[37]

Because of this, United Methodist doctrine is open to any reformulation that is a more faithful interpretation of Scripture. Faithfulness to the word of God in Scripture is the bedrock upon which the doctrinal structure is built. But there is also an awareness that scriptural interpretation is open to human errors[38] and that the increase in knowledge and the changing of social and cultural contexts often make it necessary to find new interpretations of the text, precisely in order to be faithful to the text.

United Methodist doctrine takes into account the changing contexts in which Christians live and seeks to articulate how the gospel should be preached, taught, sung, and lived in different places and times, seeking to engage the world so that the gospel might spread and the reign of God might be proclaimed and lived. One indicator of this becomes clear when one considers the amount of space given the publication of the Social Principles and Resolutions of the Church in comparison with other contemporary doctrinal statements. In the 2000 editions, the former took up 808 pages in the *Book of Resolutions*, while the latter occupied 38 pages of the Discipline. Some of the doctrinal standards were printed in the Discipline and took up 16 pages. The Wesley sermons that are part of United Methodist doctrine are not available in a reasonably priced printed edition in the United States, and the *Notes* are not readily available in the United States at all. While the amount of space allotted does not indicate importance, it does show the practical nature of United Methodist doctrine, which urges Christians to get on with the business of proclaiming and living the gospel in the world.[39]

United Methodism's practical approach to Christian doctrine should not obscure the framework that shapes its understanding of Christian truth. There is a deep and abiding tension within United Methodist doctrine between, on one hand, the variations due to different interpretations, different contexts, and different practical applications required to accomplish the mission, and on the other hand the strong framework that both defines the mission and makes such variations possible without losing integrity. There are constitutional standards, contemporary statements, and liturgy, which delimit and define authentically United Methodist preaching, teaching, and action. A major purpose of this book is to clarify these doctrinal foundations, thereby helping United Methodist theological inquiry be even more fruitful than it has been.

In this task, theology has an important role to play. The Discipline says that while doctrine and theology are interrelated, the distinction between them is an important one to maintain:

> The theological task, though related to the Church's doctrinal expressions, serves a different function. Our doctrinal affirmations assist us in the discernment of Christian truth in ever-changing contexts. Our theological task includes the testing, renewal, elaboration, and application of our doctrinal perspective in carrying out our calling "to spread scriptural holiness over these lands."[40]

Seven words describe the nature of the theological task as the United Methodist Church understands it: critical, constructive, individual, communal, contextual, incarnational, and practical. In all of these ways, the denomination defines an important role for theological research and discussion. The words "testing, renewal, elaboration, and application" indicate that doctrine is not a static entity. As Alister McGrath argues in his *Genesis of Doctrine*, doctrine originated because new questions arose as the Christian church proclaimed the gospel.[41] In order to remain faithful to the gospel, new formulations of it had to be devised.

Over time, some theological formulations then find acceptance in the Church and become doctrinal statements. While Wesley was an ordained priest of the Church of England, his sermons were initially only an individual's proclamations. Some now form part of the doctrine of a church. Reinhard Hütter in *Suffering Divine Things: Theology as Church Practice* understands church doctrine as "what must *unconditionally* be stated, taught, and confessed in continuing adherence to the *doctrina evangelii*, in continuity with how the church in other ages and at other places justifiably (that is, from the perspective of the *doctrina definita* of biblical canon) has adhered to the *doctrina evangelii*, and in delimitation over against concrete errors." Theological doctrine, or dogmatics, is consensus within theological discourse. He continues,

> By contrast, within the framework of theological discourse as a church practice, individual theologians *never* speak for the church as a whole, particularly not when critically examining church doctrine itself. Their churchly disposition, however, often manifests itself in the extent to which their presentations, in the form of interpretation and appropriation of church doctrine, under certain circumstances themselves become *theological doctrine* and thus a point of orientation or a part of church doctrine.[42]

There is every reason to presume that further refinements to United Methodist doctrine will occur in the future, and that theological debates and research will contribute to those developments.

CATHOLIC SPIRIT AND ESSENTIAL DOCTRINES

United Methodist doctrine is committed to what Wesley called a "catholic spirit," referring to the way in which its doctrine is to be taught and its theological task is to be carried out. There are clues about what the term "catholic spirit" means and how it is used in the texts that compose United Methodist doctrine. While the phrase is not used in the *Notes*,[43] there is a whole sermon on the subject and a significant use of the term in another sermon. Catholic spirit, Wesley says, is "catholic love."[44] In his funeral sermon for George Whitefield, with whom he differed bitterly over predestination, he called his friend a man of catholic spirit. He describes the person who has that spirit as

> one who loves as friends, as brethren in the Lord, as joint partakers of the present kingdom of heaven, and fellow-heirs of his eter-

nal kingdom, all, of whatever opinion, mode of worship, or congregation, who believe in the Lord Jesus; who love God and man; who, rejoicing to please and fearing to offend God, are careful to abstain from evil, and zealous of good works. He is a man of a truly catholic spirit who bears all these continually upon his heart; who having an unspeakable tenderness for their persons, and an earnest desire of their welfare, does not cease to commend them to God in prayer, as well as to plead their cause before men; who speaks comfortably to them, and labours by all his words to strengthen their hands in God. He assists them to the uttermost of his power in all things, spiritual and temporal. He is ready "to spend and to be spent" for them; yea, "to lay down his life for his brethren."[45]

This is not to be confused with "latitudinarianism," understood as an indifference to opinions, modes of worship, or congregations.[46] The Discipline captures the essential balance between commitment to truth and commitment to love saying,

This perspective is apparent in the Wesleyan understanding of "catholic spirit." While it is true that United Methodists are fixed upon certain religious affirmations, grounded in the gospel and confirmed in their experience, they also recognize the right of Christians to disagree on matters such as forms of worship, structures of church government, modes of Baptism, or theological explorations. They believe such differences do not break the bond of fellowship that ties Christians together in Jesus Christ. Wesley's familiar dictum was, "As to all opinions which do not strike at the root of Christianity, we think and let think."[47]

At a later point it addresses the same topic saying,

In the name of Jesus Christ we are called to work within our diversity while exercising patience and forbearance with one another. Such patience stems neither from indifference toward truth nor from an indulgent tolerance of error but from an awareness that we know only in part and that none of us is able to search the mysteries of God except by the Spirit of God. We proceed with our theological task, trusting that the Spirit will grant us wisdom to continue our journey with the whole people of God.[48]

In "Catholic Spirit" Wesley argues that errors are an inevitable part of being human. Here he uses the conversation between Jehu and

Jehonadab in 2 Kings 10:15 to discuss how Christians should relate to one another in Wesley's own day. He is clear that this is not an inquiry into the historical situation described in the text. Rather, Wesley uses that encounter to ask what should Christians do now? Wesley answers that we should be aware that people will of necessity think differently and thus disagree. Wise persons know they are wrong somewhere, without knowing specifically where they are wrong. Hence, the example from 2 Kings shows how people who think differently can still be unified and cooperate:

> Every wise man therefore will allow others the same liberty of thinking which he desires they should allow him; and will no more insist on their embracing his opinions than he would have them to insist on his embracing theirs. He bears with those who differ from him, and only asks him with whom he desires to unite in love that single question, "Is thine heart right, as my heart is with thy heart?"[49]

To understand Wesley's point about catholic spirit in this sermon, it is crucial to see that he is discussing tolerance in matters of opinion, and not in regard to essential points of Christianity. He later discusses at some length all of the questions implied in the single question "Is thine heart right?" Taken as a whole, these questions have intellectual, spiritual, and moral implications. Some of them ask about belief in God and Christ. Others ask if Christ is being formed in the believer's heart. Still others ask if the believer's life is being shaped by love so that the person is genuinely displaying her love by her works.[50]

Wesley held strongly to a commitment to truth and an understanding that on the essentials of Christianity, human beings know the truth. In "Christian Perfection" he discusses several ways in which Christians are not perfect, saying first that no one is free from ignorance. He continues,

> Nor, secondly, from mistake, which indeed is almost an unavoidable consequence of it; seeing those who "know but in part" are ever liable to err touching the things which they know not. 'Tis true the children of God do not mistake as to the things essential to salvation. They do not "put darkness for light, or light for darkness," neither "seek death in the error of their life." For they are "taught of God," and the way which he teaches them, the way of

holiness, is so plain that "the wayfaring man, though a fool, need not err therein." But in things unessential to salvation they do err, and that frequently.[51]

Such mistakes are limited not only to facts and the circumstances surrounding them, but also to the interpretation of Scripture, especially "with respect to those parts thereof which less immediately relate to practice. Hence even the children of God are not agreed as to the interpretation of many places in Holy Writ; nor is their difference of opinion any proof that they are not the children of God on either side."[52] Thus, Christians are protected from error in essential doctrines while they know that in matters of opinion they hold some views that are wrong. This is precisely the balance between commitment to truth and tolerance for diversity that lies at the heart of a Wesleyan understanding of catholic spirit. When certainty about the essential doctrines is protected, then Christians can hold fellowship with all those who agree on those essentials. What matters in such relationships is, first of all, mutual love. Each one should admit that on these matters of opinion, each might be wrong and the other side might be right. Commitment to truth requires spending significant time ascertaining what the truth is. Christians should not be indifferent to it. But at the end of the search they should admit that they know of such matters only in part, and perhaps those who differ have a better understanding than they have.

It is thus important to distinguish between what are essential doctrines and what are matters of opinion. That Wesley employs such a distinction is clear in his writings. At several points in the *Sermons* he uses "opinions" as the opposite of the core doctrines of the faith. In "Scriptural Christianity" he says, "I entreat you to observe that here are no *peculiar notions* now under consideration; that the question moved is not concerning *doubtful opinions* of one kind or another; but concerning the undoubted, fundamental branches (if there be any such) of our *common Christianity*."[53]

However, the lists of essential doctrines he gives vary from each other in substantive ways, and he occasionally refers to a doctrine as essential which never shows up in any of his summaries of the essentials.[54] The doctrines that appear most frequently in such summaries are three: original sin, justification by faith, and holiness of heart and life. But in other places he asserts that denying a particular doctrine means you are not a Christian. In the sermon "Original Sin" he discusses belief in original sin as "one grand, fundamental difference" between "Christianity considered as a system of doctrines," and heathenism. He says,

> Hence we may, secondly, learn that all who deny this—call it "original sin" or by any other title—are but heathens still in the fundamental point which differences heathenism from Christianity. . . . But here is the shibboleth: Is man by nature filled with all manner of evil? Is he void of all good? Is he wholly fallen? Is his soul totally corrupted? Or, to come back to the text, is "every imagination of the thoughts of his heart evil continually"? Allow this, and you are so far a Christian. Deny it, and you are but an heathen still.[55]

In the next section, he describes "the proper nature of religion" as *therapeia psuchēs*, the healing of the soul by the grace of God. But there is an intellectual component to the understanding of this process that requires a commitment to at least the doctrine of original sin.

For Wesley all of the doctrines he mentions as essential or "fundamental" relate to the way of salvation or the doctrines of the Trinity and Incarnation. He says in the sermon "The New Birth," "If any doctrines within the whole compass of Christianity may be properly termed fundamental they are doubtless these two—the doctrine of justification, and that of the new birth: the former relating to that great work which God does *for us*, in forgiving our sins; the latter to the great work which God does *in us*, in renewing our fallen nature."[56] In an important passage in the *Notes*, he argues that Scripture has a general tenor that ought to guide its interpretation.[57] For Wesley, the analogy of faith constitutes the heart of the Bible, and it is "that grand scheme of doctrine which is delivered therein, touching original sin, justification by faith, and present, inward salvation. There is a wonderful analogy between all these; and a close and intimate connexion between the chief heads of that faith 'which was once delivered to the saints.'"[58] As one example, he says,

> One very considerable article of this truth is contained in the words above recited, "This is his name whereby he shall be called,

The Lord our righteousness": a truth this which enters deep into the nature of Christianity, and in a manner supports the whole frame of it. Of this undoubtedly may be affirmed what Luther affirms of a truth closely connected with it: it is *articulus stantis vel cadentis ecclesiae*—the Christian church stands or falls with it. It is certainly the pillar and ground of that faith of which alone cometh salvation—of that *catholic* or universal faith which is found in all the children of God, and which "unless a man keep whole and undefiled, without doubt he shall perish everlastingly."[59]

But then Wesley goes on to discuss that while this doctrine is fundamental to the faith,

there is scarce any wherein they are so little agreed, wherein those who all profess to follow Christ seem so widely and irreconcilably to differ. I say "seem," because I am throughly convinced that many of them only seem to differ. The disagreement is more in words than in sentiments: they are much nearer in judgment than in language. And a wide difference in language there certainly is, not only between Protestants and Papists, but between Protestant and Protestant; yea, even between those who all believe justification by faith, who agree as well in this as in every other fundamental doctrine of the gospel.

But if the difference be more in *opinion* than real *experience*, and more in *expression* than in *opinion*, how can it be that even the children of God should so vehemently contend with each other on the point? Several reasons may be assigned for this: the chief is their not understanding one another, joined with too keen an attachment to their *opinions* and particular modes of *expression*.[60]

Wesley used "opinion" in at least two different ways. The passages quoted above from "Scriptural Christianity" and "Christian Perfection" clearly distinguish essential doctrines from matters of opinion. The doctrine of justification by faith is the former while predestination is the latter. At the same time Wesley understands that an essential doctrine like justification by faith can be formulated in a variety of different ways. Such formulations, being individual appropriations of the essential truth, Wesley calls opinions as well.

In "Opinion, Religion and 'Catholic Spirit': John Wesley on Theological Integrity," Randy Maddox suggests, "Wesley typically restricted the use of 'opinions' to contexts concerning an *individual's personal* understanding, appropriation or rejection of authoritative Christian teachings."[61] Maddox is partially right: Wesley does refer to opinions as something that individuals hold. But individuals also hold doctrines that are so scripturally based as not to be held in error. He said of George Whitefield:

> But how shall we improve this awful providence [Whitefield's death]? This is the third thing which we have to consider. And the answer to this important question is easy (may God write it in all our hearts!): by keeping close to the *grand doctrines* which he delivered, and by drinking into his *spirit.*
>
> And, first, let us keep close to the grand scriptural doctrines which he everywhere delivered. There are many doctrines of a less essential nature, with regard to which even the sincere children of God (such is the present weakness of human understanding!) are and have been divided for many ages. In these we may think and let think; we may "agree to disagree." But meantime let us hold fast the essentials of "the faith which was once delivered to the saints," and which this champion of God so strongly insisted on at all times and in all places.[62]

The crucial distinction is between those teachings that are essential to being a Christian, and those on which good Christian persons can disagree. The latter are opinions, and a catholic spirit requires that while one is fixed in her or his own judgment about the truth of them, one must be aware that one might be wrong and thus should honor and respect those of his or her brothers and sisters who disagree on that point.

For United Methodist doctrine the loving spirit that is the goal of Christian doctrine ought to inform all of the practices related to it. It ought to be the rule that guides the thinking, speaking, discerning, listening, and discussing doctrine. Catholic spirit does not mean indifference even in matters of opinion. It does mean teaching and learning the faith in love.

Notes

1. Discipline, 41.
2. Constitution, ¶¶4-5, Discipline 22-3.
3. The United Methodist Church has participated either on its own or through the World Methodist Council in a number of ecumenical groups, dialogues, and

missional ventures during the last century. Examples tending toward doctrinal convergence could include the World Council of Churches, the National Council of Churches, the Consultation on Church Union, observers sent to Vatican II, and bilateral dialogues with the Anglican Communion and the Roman Catholic Church.

4. Discipline, 55.

5. Wood 1985, 67.

6. Wood 1985, 72-73.

7. McGrath, 2-3.

8. All citations from the Bible use the NRSV unless otherwise noted.

9. Charry, 4.

10. Charry, 18.

11. Charry, 233.

12. §§1-2, *Works* 2:155-56.

13. "Preface" to *Sermons on Several Occasions*, §§5-6, *Works* 1:105-6.

14. "Awake, Thou That Sleepest," §III.6, *Works* 1:154. Charles Wesley refers to John 17:3.

15. Maddox 1990, 666.

16. Pelikan 1971, 2.

17. Langford 1983, 20-21.

18. "The Way to the Kingdom," §6, *Works* 1:220-21.

19. Discipline, 45.

20. "Preface" *Sermons*,§3, *Works* 1:104.

21. "Preface" to *Notes*, §3.

22. See, for example, Deschner for one such study.

23. Discipline, 75.

24. Discipline, 54.

25. UMH, 35.

26. Abraham 1989.

27. For a philosophical argument on these matters see Christian.

28. Wood 1998, 169.

29. "The Way to the Kingdom," §1.6, *Works* 1:220-21. Wainwright 2001 suggests "When Wesley appears in his writings to demean orthodoxy, it is *dead* orthodoxy he is aiming at; he is well aware that *living* faith has classic Christian doctrine as the intellectual formulation of its content."

30. Wood 1998, 171. Wood is quoting from Sermon 7, "The Way to the Kingdom," §I.10, *Works* 1:223.

31. Wood 1998, 179.

32. Wood 1998, 179.

33. Hunter, 32.

34. See for example, *Christian Believer* by Abingdon Press and the Alpha program from Holy Trinity Church, Brompton Road, London, England.

35. Discipline, 696-97, ¶2702. The wording is identical for both clergy and laity.

36. Discipline, 59.

37. Discipline, 67. For similar wording, see Article V of the Articles, Discipline 60.

38. See Wesley, "Christian Perfection," §I.5, *Works* 2:102.

39. Runyon 1998 makes this point well by bringing to bear Wesley's theology on contemporary issues. Cobb 1995 makes similar points about the nature of Wesleyan theology.

40. Discipline, 74-75.

41. McGrath 1990, 1-13.

42. Hütter, 140-41. He specifically cites Luther, Melanchthon, and Wesley as examples of this last possibility.

43. In the *Notes* 1 Cor. 1:2, he does say, "Nothing could better suit that catholic love which St. Paul labours to promote in this epistle, than such a declaration of his good wishes for every true Christian upon earth."

44. "Catholic Spirit," §II.4, *Works* 2:94.

45. "On the Death of George Whitefield," §III.7, *Works* 2:344.

46. "Catholic Spirit," §III.1-3, *Works* 2:92-4.

47. Discipline, 50. The quote from Wesley in the last sentence is from "The Character of a Methodist," §1, *Works* 9:34.

48. Discipline, 84.

49. "Catholic Spirit," §I.6, *Works* 2:84-85.

50. Ibid., §§I.12-18.

51. "Christian Perfection," §1.4, *Works* 2:101-2.

52. Ibid., §I.5, 102.

53. "Scriptural Christianity," §IV.4, *Works* 1:175. The phrase in parentheses means that if this is not fundamental to the faith, then nothing is.

54. For example, the doctrine of the Trinity fits this description, as discussed below. Cf. Williams, 16-17 for a helpful summary of Wesley's essential doctrines. Williams isolates several key texts, but he includes "the work of the Holy Spirit" instead of mentioning the new birth and sanctification specifically.

55. "Original Sin," §III.2, *Works* 2:183-4. The text for this sermon is Genesis 6:5.

56. "The New Birth," §1, *Works* 2:187.

57. For a longer analysis of this, see Jones, 43-53.

58. *Notes* Rom. 12:6. Reference is to Jude 3.

59. Sermon 20, "The Lord Our Righteousness," §4, *Works* 1:450-1. Outler's footnote translates the Latin phrase "the doctrine on which the church stands or falls" and then notes the interesting life history of this aphorism that cannot be traced exactly to Luther. The last phrase is taken from the Athanasian Creed.

60. Sermon 20, "The Lord Our Righteousness," §§5-6, *Works* 1:451-52.

61. Maddox 1992, 65. Maddox's argument is helpful in isolating many important distinctions surrounding the concepts of opinion and doctrines in Wesley's thinking. However, his argument is self-contradictory at several key points, notably his claim on p. 64 that Wesley uses 'opinion' to refer to central Christian doctrines." He refers the reader to Wesley's sermon 38, "A Caution Against Bigotry," §II.3, *Works* 2:70. But the text referred to does not mention any of the topics which Maddox later in the article denotes as "essential."

62. Sermon 53, "On the Death of George Whitefield," §III.1, *Works* 2:341.

PART II

THE TEACHING OF
THE UNITED METHODIST CHURCH

CHAPTER THREE

THE TRIUNE GOD

United Methodists confess the historic Christian faith in the triune God. The Articles and Confession both begin with the doctrine of God, perhaps following the opening sentences of the Nicene and Apostles' Creeds. It is also significant that the *Sermons* begin with a section on God's gracious, saving activity.[1] The Bible starts with God's creating activity and teaches that our universe is God's creation. God is the Creator, the Alpha and the Omega, the one in whom we live and move and have our being. Taken as a whole, the Bible describes God's creation of the world, God's interactions with it, and God's recreation of a new heavens and a new earth. Thus, in one sense, the entirety of the Church's doctrine is about God—who God is, what God has done, and what God is going to do. It is also about humanity and how we have understood God, responded to God's initiatives, and the choices we have to make in the light of God's future.

THE TRIUNE GOD

United Methodist doctrinal standards begin with the triune God. The first Article of Religion says, "There is but one living and true God, everlasting, without body or parts, of infinite power, wisdom, and goodness; the maker and preserver of all things, both visible and invisible. And in unity of this Godhead there are three persons, of one substance, power, and eternity—the Father, the Son, and the Holy Ghost."[2] A similar article is placed first in the Confession:

> We believe in the one true, holy and living God, Eternal Spirit, who is Creator, Sovereign and Preserver of all things visible and invisible. He is infinite in power, wisdom, justice, goodness and love, and rules with gracious regard for the well-being and salvation of men, to the glory of his name. We believe the one God reveals himself as the Trinity: Father, Son and Holy Spirit, distinct but inseparable, eternally one in essence and power.[3]

Within the second level of doctrine, Part II of the Discipline also opens with United Methodist confession of faith in God: "United Methodists profess the historic Christian faith in God, incarnate in Jesus Christ for our salvation and ever at work in human history in the Holy Spirit. Living in a covenant of grace under the Lordship of Jesus Christ, we participate in the first fruits of God's coming reign and pray in hope for its full realization on earth as in heaven."[4] Under basic Christian affirmations it says, "With Christians of other communions we confess belief in the triune God—Father, Son, and Holy Spirit. This confession embraces the biblical witness to God's activity in creation, encompasses God's gracious self-involvement in the dramas of history, and anticipates the consummation of God's reign."[5] The UMH offers ten different Affirmations of Faith, three of which are taken directly from biblical texts.[6] While the Nicene Creed is listed first, the three baptismal liturgies all invite the candidates and/or congregation to confess their faith in the words of the Apostles' Creed.[7]

Already we are confronted with the practical nature of United Methodist doctrine, because there is no explicit, extended treatment of the doctrine of God in United Methodist doctrine. None of Wesley's standard sermons focuses on articulating a detailed understanding of matters like God's existence, nature, attributes, Christology, or pneumatology. Wesley says that human beings are ignorant of how "these three are one" and about the attributes of the divine nature.[8]

However, it might be more accurate to say that in focusing United Methodist teaching on the doctrines most directly related to salvation, United Methodist doctrine is in fact an extended treatment of the doctrine of God in the ways that most directly affect humanity. In the opening paragraphs of "The Scripture Way of Salvation" Wesley says:

> Nothing can be more intricate, complex, and hard to be understood, than religion as it has been often described. . . . Yet how easy to be understood, how plain and simple a thing, is the genuine religion of Jesus Christ! Provided only that we take it in its native form, just as it is described in the oracles of God. It is exactly suited by the wise Creator and Governor of the world to the weak understanding and narrow capacity of man in his present state. How observable is this both with regard to the end it proposes and the means to attain that end! The end is, in one word, salvation: the means to attain it, faith.
>
> It is easily discerned that these two little words—I mean faith and salvation—include the substance of all the Bible, the marrow, as it were, of the whole Scripture. So much the more should we take all possible care to avoid all mistake concerning them, and to form a true and accurate judgment concerning both the one and the other.[9]

In this way the doctrine of God underlies all of the rest of United Methodist doctrine.[10] It is part of what John Deschner called Wesley's "presupposed theology."[11] United Methodist doctrine is an unfolding of its understanding of God as Trinity. God's nature as love, God's attributes, and God's activities as creator and governor undergird everything else. Further, the activities of Christ and the Holy Spirit are also significant topics. We will consider each of these in turn.

In addition to the clear affirmations of the doctrine of the Trinity in the Articles and Confession and Discipline cited above, the *Sermons* and *Notes* clearly affirm the doctrine as well. Two such references come in Wesley's series of sermons about the Sermon on the Mount. In the sixth discourse he writes about God's attributes, one of which is "his Trinity in Unity and Unity in Trinity, discovered to us in the very first line of his Written Word, ברא אלהים literally 'the Gods created,' a plural noun joined with a verb of the singular number; as well as in every part of his subsequent revelations, given by the mouth of all his holy prophets and apostles."[12] Typical of Wesley's references to the trinitarian nature of God is his closing of the ninth discourse in the same sermon series. He is explicitly writing a benediction, but uses it to convey his understanding of the three persons: "Now unto God the Father, who hath made me and all the world; unto God the Son, who hath redeemed me and all mankind; unto God the Holy Ghost, who sanctifieth me and all the elect people of God: be honour, and praise, majesty, and dominion, for ever and ever! Amen."[13] In a similar way, when discussing the difference between justification and sanctification, Wesley attributes salvation to God the Father. But he appropriates justification to Christ and sanctification to the Holy Spirit. Wesley explains, "The one implies what God *does for us* through his Son; the other what he *works in us* by his Spirit."[14]

Wesley's *Notes* also contain many trinitarian references. In Matthew 6:13 he comments on the phrase "For thine is the kingdom, and the power, and the glory, for ever" saying, "It is observable, that though the doxology, as well as the petitions, of this prayer, is threefold, and is directed to the Father, Son, and Holy Ghost distinctly; yet is the whole fully applicable both to every Person, and to the ever-blessed and undivided Trinity."[15] The phrase has been dropped from the most authoritative modern Greek text, so the force of Wesley's comment is questionable. Textual criticism has also determined that the crucial clause in 1 John 5:7 in the KJV—"For there are three that bear record in heaven, the Father, the Word, and the Holy Ghost: and these three are one"—is a later addition. The RSV, NRSV, and NIV all agree it does not belong in the text. Wesley was aware of textual arguments against it, but argued that it belonged there. For United Methodist doctrine today the question is what to do with Wesley's comments on a text we no longer recognize as biblical? In almost all such cases, Wesley makes the same points in other contexts.[16]

The basic principle of appropriating the work of the whole Trinity to one of the persons is also made at Hebrews 9:14. There his Note says, "The work of redemption being the work of the whole Trinity. Neither is the Second Person alone concerned even in the amazing condescension that was needful to complete it. The Father delivers up the kingdom to the Son; and the Holy Ghost becomes the gift of the Messiah, being, as it were, sent according to his good pleasure."[17] In other places, comments on the Trinity are "even in those scriptures where one would least expect it," such as at Luke 4:18 and 1 Corinthians 15:28.[18]

United Methodism's commitment to the procession of the Spirit from the Father and the Son is made in four places.[19] Article IV of the Articles affirms it, as does Article III of the Confession. While alternative versions of the Apostles' Creed are printed in the UMH, only the Western version of the Nicene Creed is there, and it includes the filioque clause. Wesley's Note on John 15:26 says:

> The Spirit's coming, and being sent by our Lord from the Father, to testify of him, are personal characters, and plainly distinguish him from the Father and the Son; and his title as *the Spirit of truth*, together with his proceeding from the Father, can agree to none but a divine person. And that he proceeds from the Son, as well as from the Father, may be fairly argued from his being called "the Spirit of Christ," 1 Peter 1:11; and from his being here said to be sent by Christ from the Father, as well as sent by the Father in his name.[20]

Randy Maddox argues in *Responsible Grace* that Wesley's understanding of the Trinity "served implicitly as another 'grammar' of his theological convictions."[21] Geoffrey Wainwright and Charles Wood have argued that this triune approach pervades much of Wesley's theology. Wood says:

> This way of understanding the triune pattern of God's action and the triune character of our human destiny came to both John and Charles Wesley, I suppose, as they took in (or were taken into) the "depth grammar" of the biblical canon. Of course, they were taught that grammar not by "scripture alone" but by a community (or set of communities) of speakers of this Christian language, including their parents, their contemporaries, the authors of the Book of Common Prayer and other shapers of the discourse of their church, and the framers and interpreters of early catholic Christian doctrine.[22]

Geoffrey Wainwright's point is substantially the same without relying on the metaphor of grammar. He says, "Wesley was thoroughly Trinitarian in his understanding of the composition of the Scriptures, in his ways of proceeding with the Scriptures, and in his reading of the content of the Scriptures."[23] This is true despite Wesley's reluctance to use the term "Trinity" and his focus on other doctrines.

Two examples of how this trinitarian grammar affects Wesley's sermons show the deeper structure of his thought. In the sermon "Catholic Spirit" Wesley asks what is implied for Christians in the question from 2 Kings 10:15, "Is thine heart right, as my heart is with thy heart?" Wainwright suggests that the three sections which follow are trinitarian in structure.[24] The first asks, "Is thy heart right with God? Dost thou believe his being, and his perfections? His eternity, immensity, wisdom, power; his justice, mercy, and truth?" Other questions relate to God's governance and the nature of one's faith. Clearly, this is a discussion of the person's relationship with God understood as the Creator, the person of the first article of the Nicene and Apostles' creeds.

The next section asks "Dost thou believe in the Lord Jesus Christ, 'God over all, blessed for ever'?" Here the question focuses on experiencing Christ and being "found in him." Less cognitive assent is being asked for here, and there is stronger focus on relationship and experience.

The next section does not name the Holy Spirit explicitly, but Wainwright says, one must "remember that the source of love in the Christian is the Holy Spirit who, according to Romans 5:5, has been poured into our hearts."[25] Wesley is proposing that belief in the triune God, with the various meanings that the word "belief" has in these sections, is a prerequisite for one's heart being right, and thus also a prerequisite for Christian fellowship.[26]

In yet another instance of how Wesley's trinitarian grammar shapes his understanding of salvation, Wesley summarizes prevenient grace saying,

> If we take this [salvation] in its utmost extent it will include all that is wrought in the soul by what is frequently termed "natural conscience," but more properly, "preventing grace"; all the "drawings" of "the Father," the desires after God, which, if we yield to them, increase more and more; all that "light" wherewith the Son of God "enlighteneth everyone that cometh into the world," *showing* every man "to do justly, to love mercy, and to walk humbly with his God"; all the *convictions* which his Spirit from time to time works in every child of man.[27]

There are the "drawings" of the Father, the "light" given by the Son, and the "convictions" of the Spirit. While all of these are actions of the one God, they are appropriated to the persons. Both Wood and Wainwright take note of what the former calls "a striking trinitarian shape."[28]

The other key texts of United Methodist doctrine are also deeply shaped by the doctrine of the Trinity. The "Hymns, Canticles and Acts of Worship" in the UMH are organized in five sections. "The Glory of the Triune God" is followed by "The Grace of Jesus Christ" and "The Power of the Holy Spirit."[29] This trinitarian pattern is then completed by a section of hymns on the church as "The Community of Faith," and on eschatology with the title of "A New Heaven and a New Earth."

The liturgies approved for the Church's use show an equally trinitarian focus. Because of its placement as the first complete liturgical text in the widely available UMH, "A Service of Word and Table I" is an excellent example of the general tenor of United Methodist liturgy. The opening prayer addresses God, seeks the "inspiration of your Holy Spirit," and prays in the name of Christ. While the rubric for response to the word allows another creed to be used, it is the Apostles' Creed that is printed in the text. The Great Thanksgiving is divided into three main sections, the first of which thanks God the Father for creation and steadfast love. The second is thankful for Christ's life, death, and resurrection. The third invokes the presence and power of the Holy Spirit on the elements and upon the community. The concluding lines of the prayer summarize the trinitarian focus: "Through your Son Jesus Christ, with the Holy Spirit in your holy church, all honor and glory is yours, almighty Father, now and for ever, Amen."[30]

GOD THE FATHER

The first person of the Triune God is called "Father" in all of the constitutional standards of United Methodist doctrine. Contemporary statements have both reaffirmed the traditional language and urged that other names for God be used as well. The other names will be addressed in another section of this chapter.

God's nature is beyond human comprehension, and yet God has graciously chosen to reveal Godself to humanity, preeminently in Jesus Christ and secondarily through Scripture. Because of reflection on that revelation, the church has usually discussed God's nature by examining God's attributes. While recognizing that human knowledge is partial and incomplete, the authority of Scripture suggests that such knowledge, though incomplete, is trustworthy.

When discussing God's attributes, a passage from a sermon that summarizes the whole matter in one reasonably short place is helpful. In "Upon Our Lord's Sermon on the Mount, VI" Wesley refers to the phrase in the Lord's Prayer "hallowed be thy name" and says,

> the name of God is God himself—the nature of God so far as it can be discovered to man. It means, therefore, together with his existence, all his attributes or perfections—his eternity, particularly signified by his great and incommunicable name Jehovah, as the Apostle John translates it, to τὸ Ἀ καὶ τὸ Ὠ, ἀρχὴ καὶ τέλος, ὁ ὢν καὶ ὁ ἦν καὶ ὁ ἐρχόμενος, "the Alpha and Omega, the Beginning and the End; he which is, and which was, and which is to come." His fullness of being," denoted by his other great name, "I am that I am"; his omnipresence;—his omnipotence;—who is indeed the only agent in the material world, all matter being essentially dull and inactive, and moving only as it is moved by the finger of God. And he is the spring of action in every creature, visible and invisible, which could neither act nor exist without the continued influx and agency of his almighty power;—his wisdom, clearly deduced from the things that are seen, from the goodly order of the universe;—his Trinity in Unity and Unity in Trinity, discovered to us in the very first line of his Written Word אלהים בא—literally "the Gods created," a plural noun joined with a verb of the singular number; as well as in every part of his subsequent revelations, given by the mouth of all his holy prophets and apostles; his essential purity and holiness;—and above all his love, which is the very brightness of his glory.[31]

Seven attributes are mentioned here. God's eternity as represented by both the name Jehovah and the citation of Revelation 1:8 and Exodus 3:14. God's omnipresence means that there is no place where God is not. Wesley's comment on John 8:16 makes it clear that even while Christ was on earth he had not left the Father, just as when God comes to earth God has not left heaven.[32] Wesley viewed God's omnipotence as implying that God is in fact the sole agent, all other agents deriving their power from him. God's wisdom is tied to the order in the universe.[33] Wesley's use of "purity" and "holiness" are best understood as words describing the same attribute.[34] Randy Maddox has called our attention to Wesley's understanding that all of these are analogies by which limited human understanding approaches God. It is possible only because God has condescended to communicate with us according to our abilities.[35]

But the most significant attribute for Wesley is love. In the above passage it is termed "the very brightness of his glory." He comments on 1 John 4:8: "God is often styled holy, righteous, wise; but not holiness, righteousness, or wisdom in the abstract, as he is said to be love; intimating that this is his darling, his reigning attribute, the attribute that sheds an amiable glory on all his other perfections."[36] His sermonic comment on the opening words of the Lord's Prayer also stress the love of God.[37] God's name is Father because of God's nature being love. Wesley analyzes the fatherhood of God as creator and preserver.[38] God is loving to all and sustains his creation. Being the Father particularly of our Lord Jesus Christ, he is also the one who saves us. The Lord's Prayer also calls God *our* Father meaning the parent of all humankind. Everyone is loved by God, and anyone who trusts God through the Son will be saved.

Wesley's focus on the love of God was essential to his understanding of God's grace and the saving action of God in the world. In the sermon "The Way to the Kingdom" he refers to 1 Timothy 1:15, John 3:16, and Isaiah 53:5 as containing the substance of the gospel.[39] They talk about Christ's death for our sins, God's love, and God's desire to save sinners. When Wesley talks about salvation, he usually does so by referring to the grace of God. One of his opening paragraphs in "The Scripture Way of Salvation" focuses on prevenient grace. The sermon that he placed first in his *Sermons on Several Occasions* is "Salvation by Faith," which enforces the point that grace is the source of salvation while faith is its condition. Free grace was the source of human creation, sustenance, and salvation. For Wesley, this grace is a manifestation of God's love. In "Satan's Devices" he directly connects grace and love: "Value and esteem more and more that precious truth, 'By grace we are saved through faith.'" Admire more and more the free grace of God in so loving the world as to give "his only Son, that whosoever believeth on him might not perish but have everlasting life. . . . "[40]

Ted Campbell correctly stresses that the attributes should not be seen as simply a collection of terms applied to God. Instead, "they express worship in giving voice to the mystery of God; they express spirituality, because in the quest for sanctification some of the aspects or attributes of divinity are to be acquired, through grace, by the believer."[41] Wesley expresses this directly in his doctrine that humanity is created in the image of God. He suggests humanity was not made merely in God's natural and political images,

> but chiefly in his *moral image,* which, according to the Apostle, is "righteousness and true holiness." In this image of God was man made. "God is love": accordingly man at his creation was full of love, which was the sole principle of all his tempers, thoughts, words, and actions. God is full of justice, mercy, and truth: so was man as he came from the hands of his Creator. God is spotless purity: and so man was in the beginning pure from every sinful blot.[42]

In his *Methodist Doctrine: The Essentials* Campbell argues that while Methodist teaching about God (including United Methodist doctrine) is largely consonant with the teaching of the larger Christian community, Methodists have emphasized the "*personal* nature of God" and "the *love* and compassion that God has for all humankind."[43] Charles Wesley's hymn "Love Divine, All Loves Excelling" brings all of these concerns into one clear text. The first stanza addresses Jesus as Love:

> Love divine, all loves excelling,
> joy of heaven, to earth come down;
> fix in us thy humble dwelling;
> all thy faithful mercies crown!
> Jesus, thou art all compassion,
> pure, unbounded love thou art;
> visit us with thy salvation;
> enter every trembling heart.

The second stanza addresses the Holy Spirit asking that it might "breathe . . . into every troubled breast." The third stanza refers to God the Father as "Almighty" and says "Thee we would be always blessing, serve thee as thy hosts above." The last stanza then talks about human transformation so that we might be restored to God's intended state:

> Finish, then, thy new creation;
> pure and spotless let us be.
> Let us see thy great salvation
> perfectly restored in thee;
> changed from glory into glory,
> till in heaven we take our place,
> till we cast our crowns before thee,
> lost in wonder, love, and praise.[44]

In the same way Charles attributes God's saving activity to love, saying "Amazing love! How can it be that thou, my God, shouldst die for me?"[45] Hundreds of hymns written in the Methodist tradition, such as those of Fannie Crosby, or those non-Methodist hymns embraced by United Methodists today, such as "Here I Am, Lord," by Dan Schutte, could be cited as directly linking the love of God and God's saving activity.

With regard to God's work in the world, the Articles and Confession call God "the maker and preserver of all things"[46] and "Creator, Sovereign and Preserver of all things visible and invisible."[47] Wesley's note on Romans 9:21 distinguishes God's activity into two categories: "Creator, Proprietor, and Lord of all" and "moral Governor and Judge." Most of what he says in the *Notes* and *Sermons* about the former comes in relation to anthropology and humanity's being in God's image.[48]

Wesley gives more attention to the second category, God as moral governor and judge. In a sense, the whole way of salvation is an indication of God's activity in this area. God created the world and continues to love it even as God governs and judges it. In this context God has provided a way of reconciliation. Wesley says:

> I mean here, it is that method of reconciliation with God which hath been chosen and established by God himself, not only as he

is the God of wisdom, but as he is the sovereign Lord of heaven and earth, and of every creature which he hath made. . . .

It may be farther considered that it was of mere grace, of free love, of undeserved mercy, that God hath vouchsafed to sinful man any way of reconciliation with himself; that we were not cut away from his hand, and utterly blotted out of his remembrance. Therefore whatever method he is pleased to appoint, of his tender mercy, of his unmerited goodness, whereby his enemies, who have so deeply revolted from him, so long and obstinately rebelled against him, may still find favour in his sight, it is doubt-less our wisdom to accept it with all thankfulness.[49]

This vision of God's saving activity as the redeemer and judge of all humanity led Wesley to reject any doctrine of predestination that did not include human participation. Wesley allows for election, but it is conditional election—conditional upon humanity's acceptance of the grace that is offered.[50] Wesley's note on 1 Peter 1:2 covers most aspects of his views. Wesley believes in predestination. But his version of it is universal and conditional. All persons have been predestined to be saved if they believe. He gives five reasons that Scripture does not know a doctrine of unconditional predestination. Predestination to hell or heaven is:

1. Cruel respect of persons; an unjust regard of one, and an unjust disregard of another. It is mere creature partiality, and not infinite justice. 2. It is not plain scripture doctrine, if true; but rather, inconsistent with the express written word, that speaks of God's universal offers of grace; his invitations, promises, threatenings, being all general. 3. We are bid to choose life, and reprehended for not doing it. 4. It is inconsistent with a state of probation in those that must be saved or must be lost. 5. It is of fatal consequence; all men being ready, on very slight grounds, to fancy themselves of the elect number.[51]

The last reason leads to a change in the basic conceptions of salvation and faith at the expense of holiness.

In Wesley's understanding, salvation can be lost if one ceases to believe. He interpreted Romans 9:27 to mean that Paul was teaching the possibility of losing one's salvation.[52] It is truly open to everyone on the condition of faith. But if faith is something that can be lost, then one can fall from a state of salvation back into unbelief.

Randy Maddox suggests that Wesley's opposition to predestination was deeply rooted in his doctrine of God. "For the Calvinists, the defining model was a sovereign monarch (in the heat of controversy John put it much less graciously: an omnipresent almighty tyrant!). By contrast, Wesley more commonly employed the model of a loving parent."[53]

Another aspect of God's work in the world is his providence. At several points Wesley disdains talk about "general providence":

> I know not what things they are which are not owing to the providence of God; in ordering, or at least in governing, of which this is not either directly or remotely concerned. I expect nothing but sin; and even in the sins of others I see the providence of God to *me*. I do not say, his *general providence*, for this I take to be a sounding word which means just nothing. And if there be a *particular providence* it must extend to all persons and all things. So our Lord understood it, or he could never have said, "Even the hairs of your head are all numbered." And, "Not a sparrow falleth to the ground" without "the will of your Father which is in heaven." But if it be so, if God presides *universis tanquam singulis, et singulis tanquam universis*—over the whole universe as over every single person, over every single person as over the whole universe— what is it (except only our own sins) which we are not to ascribe to the providence of God?[54]

This coheres with the teaching on God's omnipotence. In "Wandering Thoughts" Wesley describes our resistance to God's particular providence, that is our "murmuring, discontented thoughts, which say, in effect, 'We will not have thee to rule over us'" as sinful.[55]

The coherence of Wesley's teaching on the omnipotence of God is questionable. How God is the sole agent whose providence is responsible for everything except human sin is not clear. Wesley protects human freedom, but even that is to be ascribed to God's grace. One reason his thought is not very coherent here is that it is peripheral to his primary concern—God's saving grace. It is God as loving parent he most wishes to describe, not God the agent whose existence explains causality in the physical world.

JESUS CHRIST

The Articles and Confession are again the starting point for United Methodist Christology. Article II says:

> The Son, who is the Word of the Father, the very and eternal God, of one substance with the Father, took man's nature in the womb of the blessed Virgin; so that two whole and perfect natures, that is to say, the Godhead and Manhood, were joined together in one person, never to be divided; whereof is one Christ, very God and very Man, who truly suffered, was crucified, dead, and buried, to reconcile his Father to us, and to be a sacrifice, not only for original guilt, but also for actual sins of men.[56]

Article III affirms Christ's resurrection and return as judge of all humanity. Confession II says:

> We believe in Jesus Christ, truly God and truly man, in whom the divine and human natures are perfectly and inseparably united. He is the eternal Word made flesh, the only begotten Son of the Father, born of the Virgin Mary by the power of the Holy Spirit. As ministering Servant he lived, suffered and died on the cross. He was buried, rose from the dead and ascended into heaven to be with the Father, from whence he shall return. He is eternal Savior and Mediator, who intercedes for us, and by him all men will be judged.[57]

These statements are in broad agreement with other traditional expressions of Christian teaching, and hence are again repeated in the section headed "Basic Christian Affirmations."[58] Christ's identity as one person of the Trinity who at the same time has both human and divine natures is clear. The creedal outline of his birth, death, burial, and resurrection is made clear as in both the Nicene Creed and the Apostles' Creed. Confession III notes that he lived "as ministering servant" and serves as eternal "Savior and Mediator, who intercedes for us." Article II says that Christ's death was intended to reconcile the Father to us, and that it covers both original guilt and actual sins.

In these ways United Methodist doctrine is tied in to the broad Christian tradition of Christology. Nothing in these articles differentiates United Methodists from the Orthodox, the Roman Catholics, or other Protestants who follow in the Lutheran, Reformed, and Anglican traditions. Indeed, Article II has a history going back through the Thirty-nine Articles of the Church of England to the Augsburg Confession of 1530 and the Württemberg Confession of 1552. The similarities of language with the Nicene Creed, especially the key phrase "one substance with the Father," are clear. In many cases there are key images from Scripture that are mentioned, such as Christ as the Word of God and mediator.

Wesley's *Sermons* and *Notes* add more substance to this framework. It is clear that Wesley believes Christ to be God incarnate. In the first of his thirteen sermons on Matthew 5–7, Wesley describes Jesus in divine terms:

> At the same time with what authority does he teach! Well might they say, "not as the scribes." Observe the manner (but it cannot be expressed in words), the air with which he speaks! Not as Moses, the servant of God; not as Abraham, his friend; not as any of the prophets; nor as any of the sons of men. It is something more than human; more than can agree to any created being. It speaks the Creator of all—a God, a God appears! ὁ ὤν, the being of beings, Jehovah, the self-existent, the supreme, the God who is over all, blessed for ever![59]

At the same time, Wesley affirms that Christ was truly human. He comments on Luke 2:43, "So our Lord passed through and sanctified every stage of human life. Old age only did not become him."[60] At Philippians 2:7-8 he notes, "A real man, like other men. . . . A common man, without any peculiar excellence or comeliness."[61] However, Deschner says that, at places like weeping over Lazarus in John 11, Wesley limits Christ's human nature.[62] There Wesley asserts that "the affections of Jesus were not properly passions, but voluntary emotions, which were wholly in his own power."[63]

Wesley embraced the traditional theological categories of prophet, priest, and king to describe Christ's work. Typically, they were correlated to the doctrine of salvation. At the very beginning of the New Testament *Notes* he says:

> And if we look into ourselves, we shall find a want of Christ in all these respects. We are by nature at a distance from God, alienated

from him, and incapable of a free access to him. Hence we want a mediator, an intercessor, in a word, a Christ, in his priestly office. This regards our state with respect to God. And with respect to ourselves, we find a total darkness, blindness, ignorance of God, and the things of God. Now here we want Christ in his prophetic office, to enlighten our minds, and teach us the whole will of God. We find also within us a strange misrule of appetites and passions. For these we want Christ in his royal character, to reign in our hearts, and subdue all things to himself.[64]

To preach Christ means to preach him in all his offices.[65]

Christ's righteousness is the foundation of human justification. Article IX makes reference to humanity being accounted righteous "only for the merit of our Lord and Saviour Jesus Christ," and Confessions VIII and IX make the same point.[66] Wesley explains this in some detail in "The Lord Our Righteousness," called by Outler one of Wesley's "landmark sermons." There Wesley distinguishes several categories of righteousness. Human justification does not derive from Christ's *divine* righteousness. Christ's *human* righteousness can be divided into *internal* and *external* categories. His *external* righteousness is either *negative*, referring to his avoidance of sin, or *positive*, referring to Mark 7:37, "He did all things well." While some theologians further divide this positive, external righteousness of Christ into Christ's *active* and *passive* righteousness, Wesley argues against such a move. Instead, it is both the active and passive righteousness of Christ that is imputed to all believers, and not imputed to unbelievers.[67] This then is the reason why God can justify sinful humanity without abrogating God's own justice. Later in the same sermon he says,

> And yet again: "All such expressions as these—that we are justified by the grace of God, that Christ is our righteousness, that righteousness was procured for us by the death and resurrection of Christ—import the same thing": namely, that the righteousness of Christ, both his active and passive righteousness, is the meritorious cause of our justification, and has procured for us at God's hand that upon our believing we should be accounted righteous by him.[68]

Elsewhere Wesley calls "the blood and righteousness of Christ" the meritorious cause of our justification.[69] Deschner finds this emphasis on both the active and passive righteousness of Christ to be the foundation for the two-sidedness of Wesley's soteriology, the dual emphasis on both justification and sanctification.[70]

While Wesley affirms the two natures of Christ, John Deschner finds that "Wesley places a heavy emphasis upon the divine nature and shows a certain reserve about the humanity, while at the same time tending to idealize it."[71] Randy Maddox finds a particular reason for this imbalance. He says:

> Wesley's consuming emphasis on the deity of Christ was an expression of his conviction that *God is the one who takes initiative in our salvation*: it is God who died in Christ to make possible our pardon; it is God who awakens us to our need of grace in Christ the Prophet and drives us to Christ the Priest; it is God who initiates our restored relationship in Christ the Priest; and, it is God who guides us as Christ the King, leading us into all holiness and happiness.[72]

HOLY SPIRIT

Lyle Dabney has suggested that pneumatology is the "'unfinished business' of the Protestant theological tradition."[73] His argument that Protestants have typically focused on the doctrine of Christ would account for the relative brevity of Article IV. Confession III restates the content of Article IV and then adds a description of the Spirit's ministry: "We believe in the Holy Spirit who proceeds from and is one in being with the Father and the Son. He convinces the world of sin, of righteousness and of judgment. He leads men through faithful response to the gospel into the fellowship of the Church. He comforts, sustains and empowers the faithful and guides them into all truth."[74] The "Basic Christian Affirmations" in the Discipline expand further on the Confession of Faith statement, tying in the Spirit's activity in both individuals and the church. It says:

> We share the Christian belief that God's redemptive love is realized in human life by the activity of the Holy Spirit, both in personal experience and in the community of believers. This

community is the church, which the Spirit has brought into existence for the healing of the nations. . . .

"Life in the Spirit" involves diligent use of the means of grace such as praying, fasting, attending upon the sacraments, and inward searching in solitude. It also encompasses the communal life of the church in worship, mission, evangelism, service, and social witness.[75]

The relationship between the Holy Spirit and the means of grace is not well developed in United Methodist doctrine. United Methodist ecclesiology would benefit from the further expansion of this brief reference.

The aspect of the Spirit's work that is most fully developed in United Methodist doctrine is its role in sanctification, including assurance, new birth, and perfection. These will be dealt with more fully below. However, three aspects of the Spirit's work should be considered here: as conveyor of grace, as inspirer of Scripture, and as bestower of gifts.

CONVEYOR OF GRACE

When Wesley talks about genuine religion or real Christianity, he frequently refers to what the Holy Spirit is doing in the lives of individuals. His sermon "Scriptural Christianity" distinguishes the extraordinary gifts of the Spirit, which may or may not be present in the church (and even in the early church were bestowed sparingly), from the ordinary fruit of the Spirit, which "none can deny to be essential to all Christians in all ages."[76] In a later sermon he explains it as action and re-action. The life of God in the soul of the believer

> immediately and necessarily implies the continual inspiration of God's Holy Spirit: God's breathing into the soul, and the soul's breathing back what it first receives from God; a continual action of God upon the soul, and re-action of the soul upon God; an unceasing presence of God, the loving, pardoning God, manifested to the heart, and perceived by faith; and an unceasing return of love, praise, and prayer, offering up all the thoughts of our hearts, all the words of our tongues, all the works of our

hands, all our body, soul, and spirit, to be an holy sacrifice, acceptable unto God in Christ Jesus.[77]

At another place Wesley explains that "as soon as ever the grace of God (in the former sense, his pardoning love) is manifested to our soul, the grace of God (in the latter sense, the power of his Spirit) takes place therein."[78] Frequently in Wesley's thought the work of justification is appropriated to the Son, and the work of sanctification to the Spirit. There is some indication in the sermon "The Means of Grace" that in communion, prayer, and the Scriptures it is the Spirit as the power of God who is active in these means. While it is the merit of the Son, it is the power of the Spirit that effects changes in the believer.[79] One of the differences between "the Jewish and the Christian dispensation," according to Wesley, is that at Pentecost the Holy Spirit had been given "in his sanctifying graces," and "then first it was that they who 'waited for the promise of the Father' were made more than conquerors over sin by the Holy Ghost given unto them."[80] Charles Wesley's only direct contribution to United Methodist doctrinal standards, the sermon "Awake, Thou That Sleepest," states that this gift is the fulfillment of Old Testament promises.[81] Thus, the Holy Spirit is understood to be God's powerful agent graciously working in the world.

INSPIRER OF SCRIPTURE

The Holy Spirit is understood to be the primary agent in the writing of Scripture.[82] While human agents are also involved, Wesley emphasizes God's authorship of the text. His clearest statements about revelation are found in the *Notes*. In its "Preface" he says, "Concerning the Scriptures in general, it may be observed, the word of the living God, which directed the first Patriarchs also, was, in the time of Moses, committed to writing. To this were added, in several succeeding generations, the inspired writings of the other Prophets. Afterwards, what the Son of God preached, and the Holy Ghost spake by the Apostles, the Apostles and Evangelists wrote."[83] The apostolic writers of Scripture sometimes had particular revelations, but at other times it was a result of "the divine light which abode with them, the standing treasure of the Spirit of God."[84]

BESTOWER OF GIFTS

Wesley believed that the Holy Spirit's ordinary gifts to the believer related to sanctification. He was aware, of course, of the "extraordinary gifts," such as speaking in tongues. Whether any such were being given in his own day, or would be given in the future, he said, "are questions which it is not needful to decide."[85] Regarding Acts 2:38 he is careful to note that the gift of tongues is not promised to persons in distant ages and nations.[86] However, Maddox suggests that Wesley came to regard his revival as an extraordinary event, which would then account for his leniency in letting women preach.[87] The comment on 1 Corinthians 14:34 says that they may do so if "they are under an extraordinary impulse of the Spirit."[88]

Since that time the modern Pentecostal movement has increased the level of interest in spiritual gifts. The *Book of Resolutions* includes "Guidelines: The United Methodist Church and the Charismatic Movement."[89] This document does not have an explicit theology of the Holy Spirit. Rather, it refers to the gifts of the Holy Spirit in relation to the ecumenical charismatic renewal occurring in mainline Protestant and Catholic churches. It says, "We believe the church needs to pray for a sensitivity to be aware of and respond to manifestations of the Holy Spirit in our world today."[90] In "Guidelines for All" it says, "Be open to new ways in which God by his Spirit may be speaking to the church" and "Seek the gifts of the Spirit which enrich your life and you for ministry."[91]

NAMES AND IMAGES FOR GOD

The constitutional standards of doctrine refer to God and humanity in exclusively masculine terms. In the years since the doctrinal standards of the UMC were formulated, several issues related to inclusive language have arisen and been considered by the Church. "Our Theological Task" acknowledges that new issues continually arise that summon us to fresh theological inquiry. Daily we are presented with an array of concerns that challenge our proclamation of God's reign over all of human existence.

Of crucial importance are concerns generated by great human struggles for dignity, liberation, and fulfillment—aspirations that are inherent elements in God's design for creation. These concerns are borne by theologies that express the heart cries of the downtrodden and the aroused indignation of the compassionate.

. . . Injustices linked to race, gender, class, and age are widespread in our times.

. . . We seek an authentic Christian response to these realities that the healing and redeeming work of God might be present in our words and deeds. Too often, theology is used to support practices that are unjust. We look for answers that are in harmony with the gospel and do not claim exemption from critical assessment. [92]

In light of feminist theological critique, the Church has wrestled with ways to address and refer to God, and ways to describe humanity. Resolution 321 addresses this issue in general. It says:

Whereas, The United Methodist Church affirms the use of biblical language and images in worship and in our common life together, and affirms the use of language that reflects the longstanding commitment to the inclusiveness and diversity of United Methodist members and constituencies,

Therefore, be it resolved, that United Methodist clergy and laity be encouraged to use diverse metaphorical images from the Bible, including masculine/feminine metaphors; use language for humans that reflects both male and female; use metaphors of color, darkness, ability, and age in positive rather than exclusively negative ways; and

Be it further resolved, that publications, audiovisual media, and other materials of The United Methodist Church shall reflect the diverse biblical metaphors, as well as language that reflects the diversity and inclusiveness of humanity.[93]

Taken on its own, the above resolution would suggest that United Methodist doctrine supports language about God that emphasizes diversity. At the same time, the most important services in the UMH and BOW, contained in a section titled "General Services," all use the traditional name of the Trinity—Father, Son, and Holy

Spirit—when addressing God. These services, which include the basic pattern of Sunday worship, four eucharistic services, and four baptismal services, use no feminine imagery for God. While language about human beings is more inclusive, language about God uses traditional formulations or is gender neutral. Guidelines for the BOW were passed and said, "The traditional form of the Trinity (i.e., 'Father, Son, and Holy Spirit') shall be used wherever it is found in the services contained in *The United Methodist Hymnal* and in the ordination services."[94] The Guidelines for language in the UMH are less clear than those of the BOW, but do call for respecting traditional language and retaining the "poet's original forms of address, descriptions and metaphors for God."[95]

In the rest of the UMH and BOW, there are a few places where feminine imagery is used. Brian Wren's "God of Many Names" has as its first stanza:

> God of many names, gathered into One,
> in your glory come and meet us,
> moving, endlessly becoming;
> God of hovering wings, womb and birth of time,
> joyfully we sing your praises, breath of life in every people.[96]

Thomas Troeger's "Source and Sovereign, Rock and Cloud" and Deane Postlethwaite's "The Care the Eagle Gives Her Young"[97] are other examples. In the BOW the optional liturgical resources include a wide variety of names. God is addressed as "loving Parent," "Mother," "Father and Mother," and "Creator, Redeemer, Sustainer."[98] In other prayers, God is compared to a woman giving "life and nourishment to her children," "a woman who searches for a lost coin," "a bakerwoman," the one who has "given birth to our world," and "a mother comforting her children."[99] In the prayer of consecration of a baptismal font, an alternative reading of "in the name of the holy and triune God" is offered for "in the name of the Father, and of the Son, and of the Holy Spirit."[100] Among the many other identifications of God used in the Book of Worship are the following: Creator and Redeemer, Searcher of all our hearts, Covenant Friend, Living God, Guide and Guardian, Señor, Grandfather, Great Spirit, O Great Spirit (Gitchi Manitou,

Awesome of the Awesome), Author of Love, God of all nations, God of Shalom, Creator God, Prince of Peace, Wisdom on High, and Lord God of liberation.[101]

What significance should be attributed to this wide diversity of identifications? United Methodist doctrine gives permission for addressing and describing God in many different ways, acknowledging the finitude of our knowledge of God. Yet, the name of Father, Son, and Holy Spirit is specifically privileged for those services in most general use in the Church and especially for those referring to sacramental and ordination purposes.

Notes

1. Sermon 1, "Salvation by Faith," *Works* 1:117-18. A low point in the recent history of United Methodist doctrinal statements is the opening paragraphs of Part II of the Discipline from 1972 through 1984, which all began with historical background and emphasized the balance between basic but unspecified beliefs and pluralism.

2. Discipline, 59.

3. Discipline, 66-67.

4. Discipline, 41.

5. Discipline, 43.

6. UMH, 880-89. Two of the ten are the "traditional version" of the Apostles' Creed, which omits the words "He descended into hell" and the "ecumenical version" which includes the omitted words and modernizes the language. BOW, 24 suggests nine different possible responses to the reading and preaching of the Word, of which one is "The Apostles' Creed or another creed (see UMH 880-89).

7. UMH, 35, 41, and 46.

8. Sermon 40, "Christian Perfection," §I.2. Quotations are cited in *Works* as being from Job 37:23, Job 26:14, 1 John 5:7 (KJV), and Phil. 2:7. The passage from 1 John is not included in the NRSV or the NIV.

9. Sermon 43, "Scripture Way of Salvation", §§1-2, *Works* 2:155-56.

10. See Wesley's Sermon 55, "On the Trinity," §17 "Especially when we consider that what God has been pleased to reveal upon this head is far from being a point of indifference, is a truth of the last importance. It enters into the very heart of Christianity; it lies at the root of all vital religion."

11. Deschner, xii.

12. Sermon 26, "Upon Our Lord's Sermon on the Mount, VI," §III.7, *Works* 1:581.

13. Sermon 29, "Upon Our Lord's Sermon on the Mount, IX," §29, *Works* 1:649.

14. Sermon 5, "Justification by Faith," §II.1, *Works* 1:187.

15. *Notes* Matt. 6:13.

16. The following is a list of places where the words "Trinity" or "three-one" occur in *Notes*: Matt. 3:17, Matt. 6:13, Luke 4:18, John 8:16, 1 Cor. 15:28, Eph. 2:18, Eph. 4:4, Heb. 9:5, Heb. 9:14, Rev. 4:7-8. Other comments have bearing on the

issues without using these words, such as John 10:30, John 15:26, Acts 10:48, Phil. 2:1, and 1 John 5:7-8.

17. *Notes* Heb. 9:14.

18. *Notes* Luke 4:18, 1 Cor. 15:28.

19. For a brief discussion of this, see Starkey, 31-33.

20. *Notes* John 15:26.

21. Maddox 1994, 140.

22. Wood 1998, 179.

23. Wainwright 2001. See also Wainwright 1990, 26-43.

24. Wainwright 2001.

25. Wainwright 2001.

26. Note that in Sermon 55, "On the Trinity," Wesley says, "But the thing which I here particularly mean is this: the knowledge of the Three-One God is interwoven with all true Christian faith, with all vital religion. . . . But I know not how anyone can be a Christian believer till 'he hath' (as St. John speaks) 'the witness in himself'; till 'the Spirit of God witnesses with his spirit that he is a child of God'— that is, in effect, till God the Holy Ghost witnesses that God the Father has accepted him through the merits of God the Son—and having this witness he honours the Son and the blessed Spirit 'even as he honours the Father.'" §17, *Works* 2:385.

27. Sermon 43, "The Scripture Way of Salvation," §I.2, *Works* 2:156-57.

28. Wood 1998, 177.

29. UMH, viii.

30. UMH, 6-10.

31. Sermon 26, "Upon Our Lord's Sermon on the Mount, VI," §III.7, *Works* 1:580-81.

32. *Notes* John 8:16.

33. See Wesley's *The Wisdom of God in Creation.*

34. For another discussion of these attributes in Wesley's sermons, see Sermon 120, "The Unity of the Divine Being," §2-8, *Works* 4:61-63. For a discussion of the nature of God in all of Wesley's writings, see Maddox 1994, 48-64.

35. Maddox 1994, 50, calling attention to *Notes* Rom. 5:9.

36. *Notes* 1 John 4:8.

37. Sermon 26, "Upon Our Lord's Sermon on the Mount, VI," §III.4-5, *Works* 1:578-79.

38. Sermon 26, "Upon Our Lord's Sermon Upon the Mount, VI," §III.4, *Works* 1:578.

39. Sermon 7, "The Way to the Kingdom," §II.8, *Works* 1:229.

40. Sermon 42, "Satan's Devices," §II.2, *Works* 2:148.

41. Campbell 2000, 97.

42. Sermon 45, "The New Birth," §I.1, *Works* 2:188.

43. Campbell 1999, 46.

44. UMH, 384. Cf. the text and notes, *Works* 7:545-47.

45. UMH, 363. Cf. *Works* 7:322.

46. Article I, Discipline 59.

47. Confession I, Discipline 66.

48. Many of Wesley's most interesting writings on creation and physical science are in his later sermons and other writings. See his *Survey of the Wisdom of God in Creation, or a Compendium of Natural Philosophy,* "Serious Thoughts Occasioned By the Late Earthquake at Lisbon" *Works* 11:1-13, Sermon 54, "On Eternity," Sermon 56, "God's Approbation of His Works," Sermon 67 "On Divine Providence," Sermon 69, "The Imperfection of Human Knowledge," Sermon 77, "Spiritual Worship," and Sermon 103, "What Is Man?"

49. Sermon 6, "The Righteousness of Faith," §II.7-8, *Works* 1:213.

50. See Wesley's quotation of Augustine, "So true is that well-known saying of St. Austin (one of the noblest he ever uttered), *Qui fecit nos sine nobis, non salvabit nos sine nobis*—he that made us *without ourselves* will not save us *without ourselves.*" Sermon 63, "The General Spread of the Gospel" §12, *Works* 2:490. He also uses the phrase in Sermon 85, "On Working Out Our Own Salvation," §III.7, *Works* 3:208.

51. *Notes* 1 Pet. 1:2. See also *Notes* Eph. 1:12, Acts 13:48, Rom. 8:28-29, Rom. 9:18, Rom. 11:5, Rom. 11:28. For Wesleyan sources on predestination outside the doctrinal standards see Sermon 58, "On Predestination," *Works* 2:413-21, Sermon 110, "Free Grace," *Works* 3:542-63, "Predestination Calmly Considered," *Works* (J) 10:204-59, "A Dialogue Between a Predestinarian and His Friend," *Works* (J) 10:259-66 and "Serious Thoughts on the Perseverance of the Saints," *Works* (J) 10:284-98.

52. *Notes* Rom. 9:27.

53. Maddox 1994, 56. References to Wesley are to Sermon 110, "Free Grace" §28 *Works* 3:557 and Sermon 33, "Upon Our Lord's Sermon on the Mount, XIII," §II.2, *Works* 1:692.

54. Sermon 37, "The Nature of Enthusiasm," §28, *Works* 2:56-57.

55. Sermon 41, "Wandering Thoughts," §III.1, *Works* 2:132.

56. Discipline, 60.

57. Discipline, 67.

58. Discipline, 43.

59. Sermon 21, "Upon Our Lord's Sermon on the Mount, I," §9, *Works* 1:474.

60. *Notes* Luke 2:43.

61. *Notes* Phil. 2:7-8.

62. Deschner, 24-25.

63. *Notes* John 11:33.

64. *Notes* Matt. 1:16

65. Sermon 36, "The Law Established Through Faith, II," §1.6, *Works* 2:37-38.

66. Discipline, 61, 69.

67. Sermon 20, "The Lord Our Righteousness," §I.1, *Works* 1:454.

68. Sermon 20, "The Lord Our Righteousness," §I.9, *Works* 1:457. Wesley has abridged and altered John Goodwin's *Imputatio Fidei* and used this passage as his own here. See Outler's note 46 at *Works* 1:457-58.

69. Sermon 43, "The Scripture Way of Salvation," §I.3, *Works* 2:157.

70. Deschner, 192-96.

71. Deschner, 191. Deschner argues that these and other christological presuppositions strongly shape Wesley's theology.

72. Maddox 1994, 117-18.

73. Dabney 2001.

74. Confession III, Discipline, 67.

75. Discipline, 43.

76. Sermon 4, "Scriptural Christianity," §4, 1:161.

77. Sermon 19, "The Great Privilege of Those that are Born of God," §III.2, *Works* 1:442. See also §II.1.

78. Sermon 12, "The Witness of Our Own Spirit," §15, *Works* 1:309. See also Sermon 51, "The Good Steward," §I.8, *Works* 2:286 for a similar reference.

79. Sermon 16, "The Means of Grace," §§II.3, V.1-4, *Works* 1:382, 393-97.

80. Sermon 40, "Christian Perfection," §II.11, *Works* 2:110.

81. Sermon 3, "Awake Thou That Sleepest," §III.4, *Works* 1:153. He quotes Ezek. 36:27 and Isa. 44:3.

82. For a discussion of revelation and the inspiration of Scripture in Wesley's theology as a whole, see Jones, 18-23.

83. *Notes*, Preface, §10. Two sections later he quotes Luther, "Divinity is nothing but a grammar of the language of the Holy Ghost."

84. *Notes* 1 Cor. 7:25.

85. Sermon 4, "Scriptural Christianity," §3, *Works* 1:160.

86. *Notes* Acts 2:38.

87. Maddox 1994, 135.

88. *Notes* 1 Cor. 14:34.

89. BOR, 818-25. Note that the document itself identifies pages 825-33 under the heading "The Charismtic Movement, Its Historical Base, and Wesleyan Framework" as background material.

90. BOR, 820.

91. BOR, 821.

92. Discipline, 83.

93. BOR, 817.

94. The principles underlying the BOW were set in resolutions passed by the 1988 General Conference. The United Methodist Book of Worship Committee and the General Board of Discipleship then sought to implement these resolutions with a set of guidelines. They can be found in the 1992 Advance edition of the *Daily Christian Advocate*, pages R-38 to R-43. For the purpose of this study, the following "specific directives" on R-39-40 are relevant:

"a. The traditional form of the Trinity (i.e., 'Father, Son, and Holy Spirit') shall be used wherever it is found in the services contained in *The United Methodist Hymnal* and in the ordination services.

"b. The word *Lord*, usually referring to Jesus Christ, may be retained where it is considered appropriate.

"c. Masculine pronouns for God may be retained where found in the services contained in *The United Methodist Hymnal* or in other places where their omission would seriously disturb the memory bank of worshipers, but they should be kept to a minimum.

"d. Masculine pronouns for Jesus may be retained where appropriate, but an effort should be made to reduce their frequency.

"e. The ecumenical term 'Christ the King' and the United Methodist alternative term 'Kingdomtide' may be retained in the Calendar, but in general the use of the term 'King' should be minimized.

"f. Feminine images of God taken from, or compatible with, Scripture should be increased in an effort to balance the remaining masculine images. The feminine images already in the services in *The United Methodist Hymnal* should be retained and added to.

"g. There should be greatly increased use of images of God that are neither masculine or feminine, insofar as these are found in, or compatible with, Scripture. Warmly personal images such as 'Friend' and 'Shepherd' are particularly encouraged."

95. *Report of the Hymnal Revision Committee to the 1988 General Conference of the United Methodist Church, Advance Daily Christian Advocate* 1.

96. Brian Wren, "God of Many Names," UMH, 105. © Hope Publishing Co. Used by permission.

97. UMH, 113, 118.

98. See respectively BOW, 170, 398, 466, and 563.

99. See respectively BOW, 438, 454, 469, 484, and 586.

100. BOW, 641.

101. See respectively BOW, 167, 289, 301, 460, 465, 468, 487, 491, 492, 493, 494, 520, 525, and 547.

CHAPTER FOUR

SCRIPTURE ALONE . . . YET NEVER ALONE

SCRIPTURE ALONE . . .

Scripture's authority is foundational for the rest of United Methodist doctrine. Article V makes the claim that any doctrines that cannot be found in Scripture are not to be required. It says, "The Holy Scripture containeth all things necessary to salvation; so that whatsoever is not read therein, nor may be proved thereby, is not to be required of any man that it should be believed as an article of faith, or be thought requisite or necessary to salvation."[1] In similar words Confession IV says that it "reveals the Word of God so far as it is necessary for our salvation. It is to be received through the Holy Spirit as the true rule and guide for faith and practice."[2] Wesley's *Sermons*, *Notes*, and the contemporary statements of the Church all claim to rest on scriptural authority.

One way of talking about this is to say that United Methodists believe in Scripture alone and that Scripture properly interpreted is never alone. In the "Preface" to *Sermons*, Wesley says,

> I want to know one thing, the way to heaven—how to land safe on that happy shore. God himself has condescended to teach the way: for this very end he came from heaven. He hath written it

down in a book. O give me that book! At any price give me the
Book of God! I have it. Here is knowledge enough for me. Let me
be *homo unius libri*.[3]

"Homo unius libri" or "man of one book" sounds exclusively bib-
licist. Yet, only five sections later (two pages in the Bicentennial edition of the *Works*) Wesley quotes Homer's *Iliad* in Greek.[4] Thus,
Wesley never intended the Bible to be the only book that people
read, and he frequently appeals to Scripture along with other
authorities. Recent scholarship has outlined the relationships that
exist among Scripture, Christian antiquity, reason, experience, and
the Church of England in Wesley's theology as a whole.[5] I will
argue below that the current statement in "Our Theological Task"
restates the heart of Wesley's position with a few important
changes.

The evidence for United Methodist doctrine claiming to believe
in "Scripture alone" starts with the Articles and Confession. Both
documents make explicit appeal only to Scripture. It should be
noted, however, that neither affirms Scripture's inerrancy. The
Articles say it "containeth all things necessary to salvation" but do
not affirm that everything that it says is true. The Confession
makes a similar point in saying that the Bible "reveals the Word of
God so far as it is necessary for our salvation."[6] When the Articles
criticize the doctrines of purgatory and transubstantiation and the
practice of "having public prayer" in a language not understood by
the people, they explicitly appeal to the Bible.[7] In other places,
appeal is made to "Christ's ordinance and commandment" or to
"the Gospel," which also appear to be scriptural appeals.[8] The
argument in Article XXII "Of the Rites and Ceremonies of
Churches" is of interest in this regard because it specifically claims
the freedom of "particular churches" to develop different rites and
ceremonies according to differing circumstances. The only limit is
that "nothing be ordained against God's Word." Individual members of those churches are required not to "openly break the rites
and ceremonies of the church to which he belongs" so long as they
are not "repugnant to the Word of God, and are ordained and
approved by common authority."[9] The related article in the
Confession requires that worship should be "consistent with the
Holy Scriptures."[10]

The relationship of Article V and Confession IV to the rest of these documents is significant. It can reasonably be said that they provide the basis on which the rest of these documents claim to rest, and the warrants for any possible revision thereto. Each of these articles has a sentence that requires scriptural warrant for Christian doctrine. The second sentence in Confession IV says, "Whatever is not revealed in or established by the Holy Scriptures is not to be made an article of faith nor is it to be taught as essential to salvation."[11]

Imagine that one part of United Methodist doctrine is judged by the competent authorities to contradict the Bible or that those authorities found that the Scripture's teaching should be seen differently, so that it came to be understood that earlier generations had been mistaken in their interpretation of the text. In such a case Article V and Confession IV would require doctrinal changes, even in the Articles and Confession themselves. In a more likely scenario, however, the continued discernment of the Church as to the best interpretation of Scripture and its best application to a new cultural or ecclesiastical situation would suggest a revision of doctrine, again with the goal being to teach those things "revealed in" and "established by" the Bible.

The other crucial point taught in the Articles and Confession is that whatever is not contrary to Scripture is permissible. Thus, varieties of worship styles and allegiances to different forms of government are all permitted. Wesley makes the same point in his sermon "The Witness of Our Own Spirit" saying, "Whatever the Scripture neither forbids nor enjoins (either directly or by plain consequence) [a Christian] believes to be of an indifferent nature, to be in itself neither good nor evil: this being the whole and sole outward rule whereby his conscience is to be directed in all things."[12] The basis of this strong approach to the authority of Scripture is an understanding that it is the inspired, trustworthy revelation of God's Word. Regarding the doctrine of revelation, there is a tension between Wesley's *Sermons* and *Notes* and the rest of the doctrinal standards. Wesley comes close to a dictation theory of inspiration. In the Preface to the *Notes* he says:

> Concerning the Scriptures in general, it may be observed, the word of the living God, which directed the first Patriarchs also, was, in the time of Moses, committed to writing. To this were

added, in several succeeding generations, the inspired writings of the other Prophets. Afterwards, what the Son of God preached, and the Holy Ghost spake by the Apostles, the Apostles and Evangelists wrote. . . . The Scripture, therefore, of the Old and New Testament is a most solid and precious system of divine truth. Every part thereof is worthy of God; and all together are one entire body, wherein is no defect, no excess. It is the fountain of heavenly wisdom, which they who are able to taste, prefer to all writings of men, however wise, or learned, or holy.[13]

Similarly, his note on 2 Timothy 3:16 reflects the traditional Reformation emphasis on the Holy Spirit's double inspiration, of both the writers and the readers. But it should be noted that Wesley says that both the writers of the text and the text itself are inspired:

But what is the *rule* whereby men are to judge of right and wrong; whereby their conscience is to be directed? . . . But the Christian rule of right and wrong is the Word of God, the writings of the Old and New Testament: all which the prophets and "holy men of old" wrote "as they were moved by the Holy Ghost"; "all" that "Scripture" which was "given by inspiration of God," and which is indeed "profitable for doctrine," or teaching the whole will of God; "for reproof" of what is contrary thereto; "for correction" of error; and "for instruction (or training us up) in righteousness."

This "is a lantern unto a" Christian's "feet, and a light in all his paths." This alone he receives as his rule of right or wrong, of whatever is really good or evil.[14]

For Wesley, the two are clearly intertwined: inspired persons do not write uninspired texts. While he is aware that there is a human element in the composition of the Scriptures, his emphasis is on the divine authorship of the text. Thus, what it commands is trustworthy and not to be ignored.[15]

The Articles and Confession are more circumspect in their claims. Nowhere do they call the text of Scripture "inspired." The Articles never call the Bible "the Word of God." They do say that the Scriptures contain what is necessary and sufficient for salvation and in them everlasting life is offered by Christ. Similarly, the Confession says that the Bible "reveals the Word of God."[16] The statement on Scripture in "Our Theological Task" also refers to the human beings who have been inspired by the Holy Spirit.[17] These texts all guard against identifying the Word of God with the words of the text. They thus allow much more room for error in nonessential matters as well as for the variety of human expressions that are obvious to the critically trained reader of Scripture.[18]

Scripture as a Means of Grace

Nevertheless, all of these texts see that God's word is revealed in Scripture and thus serves as "the true rule and guide for faith and practice."[19] In the General Rules and *Sermons*, Scripture is a means of grace. The third of the General Rules says that Methodists should evidence their desire for salvation "by attending upon all the ordinances of God," including "Searching the Scriptures."[20] In his sermon "The Means of Grace," Wesley's exegesis of that phrase from John 5:39 is questionable.[21] While his Greek translation may be permissible, no modern English translation follows his example. However, the essential point is that "reading, hearing, and meditating" on the Scriptures is one of the ordinary channels by which God conveys "preventing, justifying, or sanctifying grace" to human beings.[22] Toward the end of the sermon, Wesley offers a typical case of how these various channels are used by God to save the individual's soul. Lots of things might awaken the person to his or her need for God. Wesley then suggests that person might hear a sermon. Scripture then plays an important role in what follows: "If he finds a preacher who speaks to the heart, he is amazed, and begins 'searching the Scriptures,' whether these things are so. The more he *hears* and *reads*, the more convinced he is; and the more he *meditates* thereon day and night. Perhaps he finds some other book which explains and enforces what he has heard and read in Scripture."[23] More will be said in chapter 8 about the means of grace in general. Looking at the *Sermons* as an example of Christian piety and spiritual formation shows that John Wesley was deeply formed by Scripture. A simple glance at the Bicentennial Edition of *The Works of John Wesley* will show the great frequency of scriptural quotations employed there.[24]

Understanding that searching the Scriptures is a means of grace is directly related to the first of two types of authority that United

Methodists attribute to Scripture. "Our Theological Task" says that faithful Christian witness must consider both "the sources from which we derive our theological affirmations and the criteria by which we assess the adequacy of our understanding and witness."[25] Scripture is both the chief source and the primary criterion of Christian witness. Some philosophers have called its authority "causative," in that it shapes our thinking and speech.[26] We have seen that Scripture is used in the individual's journey toward full salvation. In addition, when something is taught in Scripture it should not be ignored. Regarding expressions in the Bible that teach Christian perfection, Wesley says:

> But are they not found in the oracles of God? If so, by what authority can any messenger of God lay them aside, even though all men should be offended? We have not so learned Christ; neither may we thus give place to the devil. Whatsoever God hath spoken, that will we speak, whether men will hear or whether they will forbear: knowing that then alone can any minister of Christ be "pure from the blood of all men," when he hath "not shunned to declare unto them all the counsel of God."[27]

In "The Law Established by Faith, II," he makes a similar point in saying that "to 'preach Christ' is to preach all things that Christ hath spoken: all his promises; all his threatenings and commands; all that is written in his Book."[28] His note on 1 Peter 4:11 says that Christians should "speak as the oracles of God . . . both as to matter and manner." This means treating all of the Scripture, that people should "repent, believe, obey," and if any of that is left out, one is not preaching Christ.[29] Thus, the portions of Scripture's message that we dislike or feel uncomfortable with are nevertheless authoritative.

The other type of authority that Scripture exercises is normative authority. In the *Book of Discipline* this is referred to as being a criterion of our witness. Another way of expressing it is to say that when we are deciding what is true and what is truly Christian, we should use the Bible as the ultimate authority for our decisions. We have seen that the Articles and Confession restrict this function of being a criterion of truth to "matters of faith and practice." Nowhere in United Methodist doctrine is there a claim for authority in matters of geology, astronomy, or other physical sciences.

Because of this limitation, United Methodist teaching is not worried about the inerrancy of Scripture with regard to these matters. Thus, it can engage in a dialogue with modern science about how science and religion are compatible. The Discipline says:

> Since all truth is from God, efforts to discern the connections between revelation and reason, faith and science, grace and nature, are useful endeavors in developing credible and communicable doctrine. We seek nothing less than a total view of reality that is decisively informed by the promises and imperatives of the Christian gospel, though we know well that such an attempt will always be marred by the limits and distortions characteristic of human knowledge.[30]

NEW TESTAMENT AND OLD TESTAMENT TOGETHER

The Confession of Faith says that both the Old and New Testaments reveal the Word of God:

> The Old Testament is not contrary to the New; for both in the Old and New Testament everlasting life is offered to mankind by Christ, who is the only Mediator between God and man, being both God and Man. Wherefore they are not to be heard who feign that the old fathers did look only for transitory promises. Although the law given from God by Moses as touching ceremonies and rites doth not bind Christians, nor ought the civil precepts thereof of necessity be received in any commonwealth; yet notwithstanding, no Christian whatsoever is free from the obedience of the commandments which are called moral.[31]

In Wesley's writings, this same approach is repeated many times.[32] His note on Romans 8:33 makes reference to the "the gospel having the most strict connexion with the Books of the Old Testament." In "The Means of Grace," Wesley refers to 2 Timothy 3:15 and notes that Paul is praising the Old Testament:

> Behold this, lest ye one day "wonder and perish," ye who make so small account of one half of the oracles of God! Yea, and that half of which the Holy Ghost expressly declares that it is "profitable," as a means ordained of God for this very thing, "for

doctrine, for reproof, for correction, for instruction in righteousness": to the end [that] "the man of God may be perfect,
throughly furnished unto all good works."[33]

For both Article VI and Wesley, it is Christ who is speaking in the
Old Testament. John Deschner's study of Wesley's Christology
suggests that for Wesley, Christ is present and speaking in the Old
Testament, that Christ sent the prophets and gave them their message, and that there are types of Christ in the text. Deschner says,
"The continuity of Old and New Testaments is a presupposition of
considerable importance for Wesley, for it is the formal ground of
the continuity of law and gospel, of Israel and the church."[34]

Nevertheless, this continuity does not imply identity. Wesley
believed that Christians were living under a different dispensation,
where privileges and possibilities were available that had not been
available under the previous dispensation.[35] On 1 John 2:8 he writes,
"For there is no comparison between the state of the Old Testament
believers, and that which ye now enjoy: the *darkness* of that dispensation *is passed away; and* Christ *the true light now shineth* in your
hearts."[36] The Old Testament is light, but it is like that of a lamp
whereas the light of the New Testament is the light of the day.[37]

Another aspect of the relation between the Old Testament and the
New is the claim in both Article VI and Wesley's writings that the
law of the Old Testament is best understood as having three parts:
moral, ceremonial, and political. This distinction bears on the question of how the laws of the Old Testament are binding on Christians.
The article says clearly that political and ceremonial laws are not
applicable to Christians, but moral laws are. Wesley's *Notes* makes
frequent references to the distinction, but nowhere does he give
any systematic way of distinguishing which commandments from
the Old Testament fall into which category.[38] Presumably he
regarded texts like Exodus 20:7 and Micah 6:8 as obviously moral,[39]
while circumcision and the dietary laws were ceremonial.[40]

WHOLENESS OF SCRIPTURE

Article VI and Wesley consider the Bible to be whole. While there
are two dispensations or covenants, there is also an underlying

unity. Hence, Wesley frequently appeals to the whole Scripture or its general tenor constituted by the analogy of faith.[41] This key concept is appealed to once in one of the *Sermons* and again in the *Notes* on Romans 12:6.[42] Wesley translates that verse "Having then gifts differing according to the grace that is given us, whether *it be* prophecy, *let us prophesy* according to the analogy of faith" and comments,

> St. Peter expresses it, "as the oracles of God"; according to the general tenor of them; according to that grand scheme of doctrine which is delivered therein, touching original sin, justification by faith, and present, inward salvation. There is a wonderful analogy between all these; and a close and intimate connexion between the chief heads of that faith "which was once delivered to the saints." Every article therefore concerning which there is any question should be determined by this rule; every doubtful scripture interpreted according to the grand truths which run through the whole.[43]

This crucial text makes two important points. First, the wholeness of Scripture is constituted by its "grand scheme of doctrine." David Kelsey, in *The Uses of Scripture in Recent Theology*, suggests that to call something "scripture" is to see it as whole.[44] For United Methodist doctrine, the wholeness of Scripture is constituted by this basic pattern of doctrine. The most likely interpretation of the phrase "present, inward salvation" is what Wesley elsewhere calls inward and outward holiness or sanctification.[45]

The second crucial point is that the interpretation of every text should be seen in the light of this general tenor. While Wesley says as much in this note, why should it be taken as a key for interpreting Scripture? The answer lies in the thesis of this book: the heart of United Methodist doctrine is a particular understanding of salvation. Upon this interpretation rests the conclusion that a body of doctrine claiming to be founded on Scripture would in fact find the unity of Scripture in that doctrinal scheme. Wesley finds that the "general tenor" of Scripture is constituted by the connection or analogy between sin, justification, and sanctification; he then writes a body of sermons that elucidate this "grand scheme of doctrine"; the General Conference adds to this a section entitled "Distinctive Wesleyan Emphases" that also focuses on these doctrines; and all of them work together to show this is how United Methodist doctrine interprets Scripture.

Related to this understanding of the general tenor of Scripture as a process of the persons' development from sin to perfection is one of Wesley's rules of interpreting Scripture.[46] It is clearly stated and explained in one of his sermons where he argues that the law and the gospel "agree perfectly well together." He continues,

> Yea, the very same words, considered in different respects, are parts both of the law and of the gospel. If they are considered as commandments, they are parts of the law: if as promises, of the gospel. Thus, "Thou shalt love the Lord thy God with all thy heart," when considered as a commandment, is a branch of the law; when regarded as a promise, is an essential part of the gospel—the gospel being no other than the commands of the law proposed by way of promises. Accordingly poverty of spirit, purity of heart, and whatever else is enjoined in the holy law of God, are no other, when viewed in a gospel light, than so many great and precious promises. . . .
> We may yet farther observe that every command in Holy Writ is only a covered promise.[47]

Following this rule, Wesley's exegesis of Matthew 5:48 interprets it as a promise that "sums up" and "seals" the preceding commandments. He even translates the Greek *esesthe oun hymeis* not in the words of the KJV as "be ye therefore perfect" but with "you shall be perfect." Note that the Greek is susceptible of being rendered by both the present imperative and future indicative forms of the verb.

. . . YET NEVER ALONE

There is one sense in which United Methodist doctrine teaches that Scripture alone is the authority for the theological task, and thus for the reformulation of doctrine. Yet, there is another sense in which United Methodist doctrine teaches that Scripture is never alone; it is always interpreted with tradition, reason, and experience.

Again we start with the Articles and Confession. We noted above that both documents appeal only to Scripture as the warrant of their teachings. However, both implicitly draw upon tradition.

They were influenced by previous creeds and statements of Christian faith, and in some cases use key words that have a long history in Christian teaching. In Article 1, for example, the use of the word "person" for each member of the Trinity and the claim that they are all of "one substance" is a nonscriptural teaching developed during the creedal formulation of the fourth century councils at Nicaea and Constantinople.

Elsewhere I have argued that Wesley appealed to five sources of authority, even though he never makes reference in the *Sermons* or *Notes* to these five authorities as a group.[48] In "The Nature of Enthusiasm" he recommends discerning the will of God "by applying the plain Scripture rule, with the help of experience and reason, and the ordinary assistance of the Spirit of God."[49] He does say in the "Preface" to the *Sermons* that if he is in doubt about the meaning of Scripture, he "consult[s] those who are experienced in the things of God, and then the writings whereby, being dead, they yet speak."[50] He also appeals to past theologians, creeds, and other traditional sources. Wesley's use of all these sources is made clear in the notes to the Bicentennial Edition of *Works*.

Within United Methodist doctrine all of this is stated clearly in "Our Theological Task." As noted above, the task of theology is related to doctrine in that it "includes the testing, renewal, elaboration, and application of our doctrinal perspective."[51] In two places United Methodist doctrine says, "The living core of the Christian faith was revealed in Scripture, illumined by tradition, vivified in personal experience, and confirmed by reason."[52] Such a formulation does not discuss possible conflicts between the four sources. It later says:

> While we acknowledge the primacy of Scripture in theological reflection, our attempts to grasp its meaning always involve tradition, experience, and reason. Like Scripture, these may become creative vehicles of the Holy Spirit as they function within the Church. They quicken our faith, open our eyes to the wonder of God's love, and clarify our understanding.[53]

Note that here, all four sources have been acknowledged as "creative vehicles of the Holy Spirit." Indeed, at one point the Discipline says "what matters most is that all four guidelines be brought to bear in faithful, serious, theological consideration."[54]

The phrase "what matters most" is hard to understand when Scripture is labled "primary" three times in the same section. One would expect that "what mattered most" would be faithfulness to Scripture as properly understood. It goes on to claim that the unity of these four is biblical:

> Scripture witnesses to a variety of diverse traditions, some of which reflect tensions in interpretation within the early Judeo-Christian heritage. However, these traditions are woven together in the Bible in a manner that expresses the fundamental unity of God's revelation as received and experienced by people in the diversity of their own lives.[55]

This unity is founded on the fact that Scripture norms the other three, but the other three are indispensable in the proper interpretation of Scripture.

TRADITION

The Articles and Confession are highly traditional texts, in many instances preserving language carefully worked out over the centuries of Christian teaching and reflection on the gospel. Yet they do not explicitly affirm or deny the authority of tradition.

While Wesley understood Christian antiquity and the Church of England as the authoritative portions of Christian tradition, he made use of many other parts of it.[56] In recent years the concept of tradition has been broadened through ecumenical dialogues, so that the statement in "Our Theological Task" makes three important but brief comments.[57]

First, it says, "Tradition is the history of that continuing environment of grace in and by which all Christians live, God's self-giving love in Jesus Christ. As such, tradition transcends the story of particular traditions." Here United Methodist doctrine seeks to acknowledge that tradition is the history of God's interaction with God's people, which both includes and transcends the particular parts of the story. Thus, United Methodism's commitment to the unity and catholicity of Christianity means that any appeals to tradition must ultimately take into account this most broad understanding of the term.

Second, "Christian tradition precedes Scripture, and yet Scripture comes to be the focal expression of the tradition." A great deal of scholarly reflection and ecumenical dialogue during the twentieth century emphasized that there is a closer relationship between Scripture and tradition than is sometimes thought.

Third, "We are now challenged by traditions from around the world that accent dimensions of Christian understanding that grow out of the sufferings and victories of the downtrodden." Too often tradition is seen as the history of European and American Christians, rather than the diverse flowering of many different expressions of Christianity. The larger understanding of tradition suggests that particular traditions representing African, Latin American, and Asian traditions must be included as well.

EXPERIENCE

In Wesley's view, experience is to be considered in two ways.[58] As a goal of the Christian life, it has importance because it shows what God is doing in the life of the believer. Thus, the experience of assurance is something all Christians should not rest without.

In the second sense, as a source of doctrine, experience is the weakest of the sources and criteria for theology. Wesley lists objections to his doctrine of assurance in "The Witness of the Spirit, II." He says: "It is objected, first, 'Experience is not sufficient to prove a doctrine which is not founded on Scripture.' This is undoubtedly true, and it is an important truth. But it does not affect the present question, for it has been shown that this doctrine is founded on Scripture. Therefore experience is properly alleged to confirm it."[59]

"Our Theological Task" defines experience as "the personal appropriation of God's forgiving and empowering grace."[60] It is not only individual, but also corporate, and it draws attention to many facets of human experience that pose problems for us.

REASON

The crisis of biblical authority in Western culture during the last three hundred years resulted in part from developments in biblical interpretation and significant conflicts within theology, philosophy, history, and the natural and social sciences.[61] As these disciplines developed, the importance of reason over various forms of traditional evidence was argued to the point that the very possibility of revelation as a source of knowledge has been widely questioned and debated.

United Methodist doctrine counts reason as an important source and criterion of theology. Analyses of Wesley's understanding of reason have shown that he thought highly of it.[62] However, he gives very little attention to the subject in his standard *Sermons* and *Notes*, and the importance of reason to his thought is implicit in those texts.

"Our Theological Task" affirms that reason is important. It claims that "all truth is from God" and offers a goal: "a total view of reality that is decisively informed by the promises and imperatives of the Christian gospel." These "reasoned understandings of Christian faith" will enable Christians "to grasp, express, and live out the gospel in a way that will commend itself to thoughtful persons who are seeking to know and follow God's ways."[63]

Reason does six things:

> By reason we read and interpret Scripture.
> By reason we determine whether our Christian witness is clear.
> By reason we ask questions of faith and seek to understand God's action and will.
> By reason we organize the understandings that compose our witness and render them internally coherent.
> By reason we test the congruence of our witness to the biblical testimony and to the traditions that mediate that testimony to us.
> By reason we relate our witness to the full range of human knowledge, experience, and service.[64]

In other places, reason is said to "confirm" revelation. But what happens when Christian teaching is seen as unreasonable or unbelievable to thinking, rational persons? United Methodist doctrine says that Scripture is primary, but seeks to make Scripture's teaching understandable and clear to such persons.

OPENNESS TO DOCTRINAL REFORMULATION

The closing paragraph of "Our Doctrinal History" says, "The United Methodist Church stands continually in need of doctrinal reinvigoration for the sake of authentic renewal, fruitful evangelism, and ecumenical dialogue. In this light, the recovery and updating of our distinctive doctrinal heritage—catholic, evangelical, and reformed—is essential."[65] It goes on to include in this task both the "repossession of our traditions as well as the promotion of theological inquiry."

Thus it can be seen that the United Methodist Church is open to the reformulation of its doctrine. While effecting change may be difficult, the standards of doctrine are in principle changeable. Specifically, Article V, Confession IV, and the claims for the primacy of Scripture in *Sermons*, *Notes*, and the Discipline all say that whenever Scripture teaches something contrary to United Methodist doctrine, it is the doctrine that must change.

Notes

1. Discipline, 60.

2. Discipline, 67.

3. Preface to Sermons, §5, *Works* 1:105. Wesley also uses the phrase "homo unius libri" in Sermon 107, "On God's Vineyard," §I.1, *Works* 3:504.

4. "Preface," §10, *Works* 1:107.

5. See Jones, Ted Campbell 1991, Matthews, and Maddox 1994, 26-47. For a popular version of these views, see Gunter, et al.

6. Discipline, 60, 67.

7. Articles XIV, XV, XVIII, XXI, and XXII, Discipline, 62-64.

8. Articles XI, XIX, XVI, and XXV, Discipline, 63-64.

9. Article XXII, Discipline 65.

10. Confession XIII, Discipline, 70.

11. Discipline, 67.

12. Sermon 12, "The Witness of Our Own Spirit," §6, *Works* 1:303.

13. *Notes*, Preface, §10.

14. Sermon 12, "The Witness of Our Own Spirit," §6, *Works* 1:302-3.

15. For a more complete discussion, see Jones 1995, 17-36, and Maddox 1994, 26-40.

16. Discipline, 60-61, 67.

17. Discipline, 78.

18. It is interesting here that the sixteenth-century Articles of Religion is more guarded and cautious in its claims about Scripture than is Wesley. See Green, 46-58, for the suggestion that the original article was formulated to guard against Catholic assertions about the role of tradition.

19. Discipline, 67.

20. Discipline, 74.

21. The NRSV has "You search the scriptures"; the NIV has "You diligently study the Scriptures" but offers a footnote with the alternative reading, "Study

diligently." The confusion comes because *ereunate* can be either the imperative or indicative form.

22. Sermon 16, "The Means of Grace," §II.1, *Works* 1:381.

23. Sermon 16, "The Means of Grace," §V.1, *Works* 1:394.

24. See Jones, 129-59, for a discussion of Wesley's use of Scripture.

25. Discipline, 77.

26. Wood 1996, 190.

27. "Christian Perfection," §2, *Works* 2:99-100.

28. Sermon 35, "The Law Established by Faith, I," §I.11, *Works* 2:25. See also Sermon 36, "The Law Established by Faith, II," §I.5, *Works* 2:37 for a similar statement.

29. *Notes* 1 Pet. 4:11. Note the reference to the doctrinal core of Scripture, what he elsewhere calls "the analogy of faith" as the teaching of the oracles of God.

30. Discipline, 82.

31. Articles VI, Discipline, 61.

32. See Jones, 53-58 for a more complete discussion.

33. "The Means of Grace," §III.9, *Works* 1:388.

34. Deschner, 86-87.

35. Sermon 40, "Christian Perfection," §II.11, *Works* 2:110.

36. *Notes* 1 John 2:8. See similar comments at 2 Cor. 3:6-9.

37. *Notes* 2 Pet. 1:19.

38. See for example, *Notes* Eph. 2:14, Gal. 2:4, and Gal. 3:19.

39. See Sermon 2, "The Almost Christian," §I.4, *Works* 1:132 and Sermon 15, "The Great Assize," §IV.3, 1:372.

40. This is so obvious to Wesley that his sermon "The Circumcision of the Heart" simply states that "the distinguishing mark of a true follower of Christ, of one who is in a state of acceptance with God, is not either outward circumcision or baptism, or any other outward form, but a right state of soul—a mind and spirit renewed after the image of him that created it—is one of those important truths that can only be 'spiritually discerned.'" See Sermon 17, "The Circumcision of the Heart," §3, *Works* 1:402.

41. For a more complete discussion, see Jones, 43-53.

42. Sermon 5, "Justification by Faith," §2, *Works* 1:183.

43. *Notes* Rom. 12:6. The scriptural references are to 1 Pet. 4:11 and Jude 3.

44. Kelsey, 106 distinguishes "wholeness" from being unitary. Wholeness means that it functions to a certain end, whereas unity implies consistency and coherence. He argues that different theologians will discern different patterns of wholeness.

45. See "Preface" to *Explanatory Notes Upon the Old Testament*, *Works* (J) 14:253; and Sermon 122, "Causes of the Inefficacy of Christianity," §6, *Works* 4:89.

46. For a discussion of this, see Jones, 104-27.

47. "Upon Our Lord's Sermon on the Mount, V," §II.2-3, *Works* 1:554-55.

48. See Jones, 62-103. The five are Scripture, Christian antiquity, the Church of England, experience, and reason. See also Ted Campbell 1991b, 154-61.

49. Sermon 37, "The Nature of Enthusiasm," §38, *Works* 2:59.

50. "Preface," §5, *Works* 1:106.

51. Discipline, 75.

52. On 77 the Discipline attributes this view to Wesley. Later, in ¶315.9(g), 196 it states it as the Church's teaching.

53. Discipline, 78-79.

54. Discipline, 77.

55. Discipline, 79.

56. For a brief introduction to Wesley's views, see Gunter, et al., 63-75. The best treatment of Wesley's views on Christian antiquity is Campbell, 1991a. Jones, 81-94 has a discussion of antiquity's relation to Scripture in Wesley's theology.

57. Discipline, 80.

58. See Jones, 94-101, Maddox 1995, 44-46, and Gunter, et al., 107-27.

59. Sermon 11, "The Witness of the Spirit, II," §IV.1, *Works* 1:293.

60. Discipline, 81.

61. See Reventlow, Baird, and Frei for important discussions of the history of biblical interpretation from 1600 to the present.

62. The best study of Wesley's thought on this subject remains Matthews. But see Maddox 1994, 34-35 for a good discussion on the possibility of natural theology in Wesley. Also see Gunter, et al., 77-106.

63. Discipline, 82.

64. Discipline, 82.

65. Discipline, 59.

CHAPTER FIVE

CREATION, SIN, LAW, GRACE, AND REPENTANCE

United Methodist teaching about humanity requires holding in tension four key concepts all deeply rooted in Scripture: creation, sin, grace, and law. Human beings are created in God's image, yet original sin has so corrupted that image that no person can be saved on his or her own. Original sin leads inexorably to actual sins. Yet no person is ever left alone, because God's grace is freely given to all, enabling them to fulfill the law that was intended for their salvation. First we will discuss each of the four, and then the turning of one's life toward God in repentance.

CREATION BY GRACE

The heart of United Methodist doctrine is saving grace, so, not surprisingly, grace is also the starting point of its anthropology. The opening sentence of the first of the *Sermons* makes it clear that God's creation of humankind was an act of grace:

All the blessings which God hath bestowed upon man are of his mere grace, bounty, or favour: his free, undeserved favour, favour altogether undeserved, man having no claim to the least of his mercies. It was free grace that "formed man of the dust of the ground, and breathed into him a living soul," and stamped on that soul the image of God, and "put all things under his feet."[1]

God's grace is an expression of God's essential nature, which is love. Article I and Confession I both affirm God's loving nature and creative activity. "Our Social Creed" says,

> We believe in God, Creator of the world; and in Jesus Christ, the Redeemer of creation. We believe in the Holy Spirit, through whom we acknowledge God's gifts, and we repent of our sin in misusing these gifts to idolatrous ends.
>
> We affirm the natural world as God's handiwork and dedicate ourselves to its preservation, enhancement, and faithful use by humankind.[2]

This builds on the affirmation given earlier that "All creation is the Lord's, and we are responsible for the ways in which we use and abuse it. Water, air, soil, minerals, energy resources, plants, animal life, and space are to be valued and conserved because they are God's creation and not solely because they are useful to human beings. God has granted us stewardship of creation."[3]

The BOR speaks about God's creation and our misuse of it.[4] The *Sermons* articulate a clear understanding of stewardship of our bodies, souls, worldly goods, and talents.[5] God's creation of the whole world is clearly affirmed in the *Notes*.[6] The restoration of all things will involve the whole of creation.[7]

HUMANITY CREATED IN THE IMAGE OF GOD

Within God's creation, humanity occupies a special place. Among the "Basic Christian Affirmations" is the statement, "The created order is designed for the well-being of all creatures and as the place of human dwelling in covenant with God."[8] When the *Sermons* and *Notes* talk about God's activity as creator, they most frequently focus on God making humankind in God's own image.

Specifically, the *Sermons* note that humanity was created in God's image in three different senses of the term.[9] Wesley says:

> And, first, why must we be born again? What is the foundation of this doctrine? The foundation of it lies near as deep as the cre-

ation of the world, in the scriptural account whereof we read, "And God," the three-one God, "said, Let us make man in our image, after our likeness. So God created man in his own image, in the image of God created he him." Not barely in his *natural image*, a picture of his own immortality, a spiritual being endued with understanding, freedom of will, and various affections; nor merely in his *political image*, the governor of this lower world, having "dominion over the fishes of the sea, and over the fowl of the air, and over the cattle, and over all the earth"; but chiefly in his *moral image*, which, according to the Apostle, is "righteousness and true holiness." In this image of God was man made. "God is love": accordingly man at his creation was full of love, which was the sole principle of all his tempers, thoughts, words, and actions. God is full of justice, mercy, and truth: so was man as he came from the hands of his Creator. God is spotless purity: and so man was in the beginning pure from every sinful blot. Otherwise God could not have pronounced *him* as well as all the other works of his hands, "very good." This he could not have been had he not been pure from sin, and filled with righteousness and true holiness. For there is no medium. If we suppose an intelligent creature not to love God, not to be righteous and holy, we necessarily suppose him not to be good at all; much less to be "very good."[10]

Several important points should be brought out with regard to this passage.

The first sense in which we were created in the image of God is the natural image. Thus, we share God's nature in that we are immortal spirits who have various divine capacities: understanding, freedom of the will, and affections. The *Sermons* and *Notes* throughout presuppose that human beings are immortal souls temporarily joined to bodies. He says explicitly,

> God has entrusted us with our *soul*, an immortal spirit made in the image of God, together with all the powers and faculties thereof— understanding, imagination, memory; will, and a train of affections either included in it or closely dependent upon it; love and hatred, joy and sorrow, respecting present good and evil; desire and aversion, hope and fear, respecting that which is to come.[11]

Creation in God's natural image implies that each person is essentially a spirit and that death is separation from the body leading eventually to eternal judgment.[12]

Humanity was also created in God's political image. Wesley devotes very little space to the development of this idea. His note on Romans 8:19 makes a passing reference to the whole visible creation, which will benefit from the glory of the children of God. Sermon 51, "The Good Steward," talks about our care for the "worldly goods" with which God has entrusted us.[13] But it is only as human technology has advanced sufficiently and the environmental problems associated with increasing population, pollution, and the endangerment of species have increased that United Methodists have become concerned for how well we exercise our role as "governor over this lower world." The Social Principles, with its concerns for the natural world, nurturing community, social community, economic community, political community, and world community, should be read, in part, as a witness about how this political aspect of the image of God should be exercised today.

For Wesley the most important way in which creation in the image of God should be understood concerns the moral image. For him, it is clear from 1 John 4:8 that "God is love." On that verse the *Notes* say that love is God's "reigning attribute, the attribute that sheds an amiable glory on all his other perfections." Thus, to be created in the moral image of God is to be created "full of love, which was the sole principle of all his tempers, thoughts, words, and actions."[14] Justice, mercy, and truth characterize this image as well.

This understanding of creation in the moral image of God is foundational to the rest of United Methodist doctrine. It underlies the soteriology of the *Sermons* and *Notes*. The note on Romans 14:17 concisely makes a point that is echoed throughout the rest of the authoritative texts: "*For the kingdom of God*—That is, true religion, does not consist in external observances. *But* in *righteousness*—The image of God stamped on the heart; the love of God and man, accompanied with the *peace* that passeth all understanding, *and joy in the Holy Ghost*."[15] In short, the doctrines of sanctification, Christian perfection, personal holiness, and social justice all have to do with the renewal of this moral image of God. This is the first piece in United Methodist understanding of God's saving grace. Creation is by God, and human beings are created in God's image, especially like God's reigning attribute, love.

ORIGINAL SIN AND ACTUAL SINS

The anthropology of United Methodist doctrine appropriately begins with creation in the image of God, but it never rests there. The image that was God's intention has been disfigured by sin. Human nature was created good, but at its very deepest levels it is marred by sin.

The Articles and Confession talk about this as the Fall. In Article VII, it is clearly stated that a corrupt human nature is engendered in all of Adam's offspring.[16] Confession VII puts forward the same point without mentioning Adam: "We believe man is fallen from righteousness and, apart from the grace of our Lord Jesus Christ, is destitute of holiness and inclined to evil. Except a man be born again, he cannot see the Kingdom of God. In his own strength, without divine grace, man cannot do good works pleasing and acceptable to God."[17] Wesley's sermon "The New Birth" locates the source of this corruption of human nature and destitution of holiness in Adam's disobedience. Human beings were made in God's image, but they had the freedom to disobey God's commandments. This they did, and God's promise in Genesis 2:17 was fulfilled: Adam and Eve died on that day.

> Accordingly in that day he did die: he died to God, the most dreadful of all deaths. He lost the life of God: he was separated from him in union with whom his spiritual life consisted. The body dies when it is separated from the soul, the soul when it is separated from God. But this separation from God Adam sustained in the day, the hour, he ate of the forbidden fruit. And of this he gave immediate proof; presently showing by his behaviour that the love of God was extinguished in his soul, which was now "alienated from the life of God." Instead of this he was now under the power of servile fear, so that he fled from the presence of the Lord.[18]

This spiritual death, Wesley argues, is the "loss of the life and image of God."[19] Because all of humanity were "in Adam's loins," Wesley can explain the text from 1 Corinthians 15:22 that "in Adam all died." He continues,

> The natural consequence of this is that everyone descended from him comes into the world spiritually dead, dead to God, wholly

"dead in sin"; entirely void of the life of God, void of the image of God, of all that "righteousness and holiness" wherein Adam was created. Instead of this every man born into the world now bears the image of the devil, in pride and self-will; the image of the beast, in sensual appetites and desires. This then is the foundation of the new birth—the entire corruption of our nature.[20]

Thus, United Methodist doctrine teaches that there is a human problem, and that it is sin. As "Our Doctrinal Heritage" puts it, "As sinful creatures, however, we have broken that covenant, become estranged from God, wounded ourselves and one another, and wreaked havoc throughout the natural order. We stand in need of redemption."[21] Moreover, the nature of the human problem is such that humanity cannot fix its own problem. Article VIII, "Of Free Will," says, "The condition of man after the fall of Adam is such that he cannot turn and prepare himself, by his own natural strength and works, to faith, and calling upon God; wherefore we have no power to do good works, pleasant and acceptable to God, without the grace of God by Christ preventing us, that we may have a good will, and working with us, when we have that good will."[22] This article not only makes it clear that humanity cannot save itself, but also points to the grace of God as the way in which genuine salvation comes. The word "preventing" here has the meaning of "to go before with spiritual guidance and help."[23] Thus, it is a reference to the prevenient grace of God discussed later in this chapter.

Wesley understands that when Adam sinned, all of humanity was changed forever. He says in "Justification by Faith," "By the sin of the first Adam, who was not only the father but likewise the representative of us all, we all 'fell short of the favour of God,' we all became 'children of wrath,' or, as the Apostle expresses it, 'Judgment came upon all men to condemnation.'"[24] Adam as the father of all humankind points to a kind of biological transmission theory of original sin. Adam as the representative of humanity sinned, and thus legally brought his penalty upon all of the rest of us as well.[25]

Thus, the *Sermons* sometimes refer to the "natural" human being. Two of the *Sermons* interpret Ephesians 5:14 "Awake thou that sleepest, and arise from the dead, and Christ shall give thee light"[26] as applying to sinful human beings who don't know that they need God:

> The poor unawakened sinner, how much knowledge soever he may have as to other things, has no knowledge of himself. In this respect "he knoweth nothing yet as he ought to know." He knows not that he is a fallen spirit, whose only business in the present world is to recover from his fall, to regain that image of God wherein he was created. . . .
>
> Full of all diseases as he is, he fancies himself in perfect health.[27]

As Wesley understands it, the natural person is so mired in sin that he or she does not even know how bad the situation is. This is true "whether he be a gross, scandalous transgressor, or a more reputable and decent sinner, having the form though not the power of godliness."[28] Humanity is in a difficult position after Adam's sin. Each person is a sinner, and yet unaware of his or her own need.

Original Sin

The result of the fall is that human beings have a corrupted nature. This is first of all an explanation for the state of humanity as a whole. The sermon "Original Sin" begins with a reference to both pagan and Christian accounts of the dignity and self-sufficiency of humanity. Wesley then asks, "But in the meantime, what must we do with our Bibles? For they will never agree with this. These accounts, however pleasing to flesh and blood, are utterly irreconcilable with the scriptural."[29] He goes on to discuss the sermon's text, Genesis 6:5, "And God saw that the wickedness of man was great in the earth, and that every imagination of the thoughts of his heart was only evil continually." His exegesis leads to the conclusion that human beings are the same now as they were back then.

Yet original sin is also important as a description of each individual's condition and need for God. Wesley says that understanding oneself as a sinner is one of the first steps in the way of salvation:

> Know thyself to be a sinner, and what manner of sinner thou art.
> Know that corruption of thy inmost nature, whereby thou art

very far gone from original righteousness, whereby "the flesh lus-
teth" always "contrary to the Spirit," through that "carnal mind
which is enmity against God," which "is not subject to the law of
God, neither indeed can be." Know that thou art corrupted in
every power, in every faculty of thy soul, that thou art totally corrupted in every one of these, all the foundations being out of
course. The eyes of thine understanding are darkened, so that
they cannot discern God or the things of God.[30]

This view of original sin is total. The *Notes* referring to Romans 6:6
says it is "that entire depravity and corruption which by nature
spreads itself over the whole man, leaving no part uninfected."[31]
The liturgy for the Baptismal Covenant I asks each person being
baptized, or the parents of the infant being baptized, "Do you
renounce the spiritual forces of wickedness, reject the evil powers
of this world, and repent of your sin?"[32] Similar or identical questions are asked in the other liturgies of baptism.

Moreover, three corollaries of this doctrine are brought out in the
sermon "Original Sin." First, the doctrine is the foundation of the
whole way of salvation. If humanity is not fallen, then there is "no
occasion for this work in the heart, this 'renewal in the spirit of our
mind.'"[33] Elsewhere Wesley refers to the doctrine of original sin as
the "general ground of the whole doctrine of justification."[34]

Second, original sin is one of the essential doctrines of
Christianity. It differentiates Christian teaching from all sorts of
heathenism:

> Hence we may, secondly, learn that all who deny this—call it
> "original sin" or by any other title—are but heathens still in the
> fundamental point which differences heathenism from
> Christianity. They may indeed allow that men have many vices;
> that some are born with us; and that consequently we are not
> born altogether so wise or so virtuous as we should be; there
> being few that will roundly affirm we are born with as much
> propensity to good as to evil, and that every man is by nature as
> virtuous and wise as Adam was at his creation. But here is the
> shibboleth: Is man by nature filled with all manner of evil? Is he
> void of all good? Is he wholly fallen? Is his soul totally corrupted?
> Or, to come back to the text, is "every imagination of the thoughts
> of his heart evil continually"? Allow this, and you are so far a
> Christian. Deny it, and you are but an heathen still.[35]

There is something about the doctrine of original sin that is so basic to the way of salvation that denying it means, for Wesley, denying the core of Christian teaching. Presumably, if the existence of the problem is denied, then the solution is unnecessary.

Third, original sin understood as a loss of the image of God is thus understood as a disease. Genuine religion is the healing of this sickness. Wesley says it is *therapeia psychēs*, the therapy of the soul. "Hereby the great Physician of souls applies medicine to heal *this sickness*; to restore human nature, totally corrupted in all its faculties."[36] God does this by giving us knowledge of himself, faith, repentance, and lowliness of heart, and by instilling in us the love of God. Thus, the great end of religion is "to renew our hearts in the image of God, to repair that total loss of righteousness and true holiness which we sustained by the sin of our first parent."[37]

ACTUAL SINS

Wesley understands human action as arising from human tempers, or the habitual disposition of the heart. With human nature so diseased, it is inevitable that human beings will commit actual sins. These sins are of two kinds: sins of omission, where an obligatory action was not taken, and sins of commission, where a wrong act was done. Sins of commission can be inward, relating to thoughts, feelings, tempers, and other actions not observable by others. They can also be outward, the words and deeds that can be observed. The *Sermons* have a clear definition of the word "sin": "By 'sin' I here understand outward sin, according to the plain, common acceptation of the word: an actual, voluntary 'transgression of the law'; of the revealed, written law of God; of any commandment of God acknowledged to be such at the time that it is transgressed."[38] This is the understanding of sin that is normally talked about in 1 John 3:9 when it says that Christians do not commit sin. However, there are a number of further distinctions that help Wesley refine his teaching.

There are involuntary sins that are really not sins "properly so called" as Wesley puts it.[39] Wesley calls these "sins of infirmity" or "sins of surprise" because they arise either out of our ignorance or other failings, or from our being caught unawares. In all such cases, there is no sense of our willingly breaking God's law by either action or inaction.

Inward sins are those which affect our tempers, will, and thoughts. While Christians do not commit outward sins, this inward sin clings to us. Wesley quotes the Article IX of the Thirty-nine Articles which says that sin "remains" in the heart of the believer. He says that it does not reign there, but that the Christian life is one of struggle between the flesh and the spirit.[40] This type of sin affects our inner lives and cleaves to our actions. The sermon "Repentance of Believers" argues that there is a type of repentance and a type of faith necessary to those who have entered upon the Christian life. A number of ways in which the believer's soul is affected by sins of pride, self-will, and inordinate affection are discussed. He quotes again 1 John 2:16's threefold characterization of sin as "the desire of the flesh, or the desire of the eye, or the pride of life." He says that sin remains in their hearts, and "cleaves to their actions" since even the best deeds are sometimes done for mixed motivations.[41]

The problem of sin is universal. All human beings are infected by it, and it infects each and every part of them. The note on Romans 3:23 says: *"For all have sinned*—In Adam, and in their own persons; by a sinful nature, sinful tempers, and sinful actions. *And are fallen short of the glory of God*—The supreme end of man; short of his image on earth, and the enjoyment of him in heaven."[42]

STRUCTURAL SOCIAL SIN

The contemporary statements of United Methodist doctrine make another distinction that is not explicit in the constitutional standards. One of the "Distinctive Wesleyan Emphases" is a commitment to mission and service, which says that "Scriptural holiness entails more than personal piety; love of God is always linked with love of neighbor, a passion for justice and renewal in the life of the world."[43]

More contemporary statements of United Methodist doctrine also affirm that there is a human problem. Frequently they do not make reference to the Fall, to Adam's sin, or to original sin by name:

The perils of nuclear destruction, terrorism, war, poverty, violence, and injustice confront us. Injustices linked to race, gender, class, and age are widespread in our times. Misuse of natural resources and disregard for the fragile balances in our environment contradict our calling to care for God's creation. Secularism pervades high-technology civilizations, hindering human awareness of the spiritual depths of existence.[44]

Even though these problems are not explicitly described as aspects of human sin here, the larger context of United Methodist doctrine says that such problems are directly linked to humanity's violation of God's laws and separation from the relationship God intended.

The word "sin" is used only three times in the Social Principles. It occurs first in the preamble where United Methodists "confess our many sins against God's will for us as we find it in Jesus Christ."[45] The last section, "Our Social Creed" has a similar usage.[46] But the third use is one of the most illuminating for the theology that underlies all of the Social Principles and many of the Resolutions. In the section "Rights of Racial and Ethnic Persons" it says,

> Racism is the combination of the power to dominate by one race over other races and a value system that assumes that the dominant race is innately superior to the others. Racism includes both personal and institutional racism. Personal racism is manifested through the individual expressions, attitudes, and/or behaviors that accept the assumptions of a racist value system and that maintain the benefits of this system. Institutional racism is the established social pattern that supports implicitly or explicitly the racist value system. Racism plagues and cripples our growth in Christ, inasmuch as it is antithetical to the gospel itself. White people are unfairly granted privileges and benefits that are denied to persons of color. Therefore, we recognize racism as sin and affirm the ultimate and temporal worth of all persons.[47]

By calling institutional racism sin, United Methodist doctrine either expands upon or contradicts the definition used in the *Sermons*. On the one hand, racism violates a known law of God, and so its character as sin is clear. However, whether institutional racism has a voluntary character or not is more difficult to determine. In this definition, it is defined as a social pattern that embodies the "racist value system." This whole approach to sin takes advantage of the body of knowledge gathered by social scientists, philosophers, and theologians in the last two centuries. When Wesley argues for the kind of involuntary sin that cleaves to our action despite our best intention, he appears to have left significant room for this broadened understanding of sin.

GRACE

So far the picture of fallen humanity portrayed by United Methodist doctrine looks bleak. It is crucial to understand that the portrait of the natural human being given here is incomplete without also acknowledging the universal, saving grace of God, which has been given to every human being.

Article VIII, discussed above, has a crucial phrase about God's grace. Humanity is incapable of doing good works "without the grace of God by Christ preventing us."[48] Confession VII makes a similar point with the phrase "apart from the grace of our Lord Jesus Christ."[49]

Given this description of the human problem, it is by the grace of God that salvation is possible. The opening paragraphs of the first sermon in the *Sermons* make the point strongly:

> All the blessings which God hath bestowed upon man are of his mere grace, bounty, or favour: his free, undeserved favour, favour altogether undeserved, man having no claim to the least of his mercies. It was free grace that "formed man of the dust of the ground, and breathed into him a living soul," and stamped on that soul the image of God, and "put all things under his feet." . . .
>
> If then sinful man find favour with God, it is "grace upon grace" χάριν ἀντὶ χάριτος. If God vouchsafe still to pour fresh blessings upon us—yea, the greatest of all blessings, salvation—what can we say to these things but "Thanks be unto God for his unspeakable gift!" And thus it is. Herein "God commendeth his love toward us, in that, while we were yet sinners, Christ died" to save us. "By grace," then, "are ye saved through faith."[50]

Wesley defines grace in the sermon "The Witness of Our Own Spirit." He says,

By "the grace of God" is sometimes to be understood that free love, that unmerited mercy, by which I, a sinner, through the merits of Christ am now reconciled to God. But in this place it rather means that power of God the Holy Ghost which "worketh in us both to will and to do of his good pleasure." As soon as ever the grace of God (in the former sense, his pardoning love) is manifested to our soul, the grace of God (in the latter sense, the power of his Spirit) takes place therein.[51]

At several points in the *Notes* he refers to grace as love, as in his comment on 2 Corinthians 8:9: "*The grace*—The most sincere, most free, and most abundant love."[52] Grace is thus described as being rooted in God's nature as love. It is favor given despite sin. It is a gift. It is known by its effects. It restores the knowledge of right and wrong, convinces of sin, pardons, and gives power over sin, thereby healing the disease.

Since grace is God's love, it ought to be understood in relational terms. Just as other relationships have different stages of development, so does the human being's relationship with God. At different stages God's love will take different forms. Grace is all one, but it will do different things depending on what the human being needs at particular points. Hence the distinctions between prevenient, justifying, and sanctifying grace.

PREVENIENT GRACE

Prevenient grace is the love of God at work in our lives from the very beginning. When Article VIII talks about "the grace of God by Christ preventing us" the words "prevent" and "prevenient" are the verb and adjectival forms of the same root word which means "come before."[53] To affirm prevenient grace is to say that God is actively loving all of humanity. Wesley frequently referred to the human conscience and argued that it was not "natural" but a supernatural gift of God's grace. This point along with his reference to the text of John 1:9 are included in his description of salvation as a process that starts with this gracious love of God:

If we take this in its utmost extent it will include all that is wrought in the soul by what is frequently termed "natural conscience," but more properly, "preventing grace"; all the "drawings" of "the Father," the desires after God, which, if we yield to them, increase more and more; all that "light" wherewith the Son of God "enlighteneth everyone that cometh into the world," *showing* every man "to do justly, to love mercy, and to walk humbly with his God."[54]

Outler, suggesting the importance of this idea in Wesley's theology, notes that preventing grace allows for human involvement since Christians have affirmed, following the Second Council of Orange in 529, that the work of the Holy Spirit is resistible and that of the Father is not. Randy Maddox makes the important point that this understanding of prevenient grace balances Wesley's affirmation of total depravity. Specifically, prevenient grace partially restores our human faculties so that we might be able to accept or reject saving grace.[55] "Our Doctrinal Heritage" acknowledges prevenient grace as "the divine love that surrounds all humanity and precedes any and all of our conscious impulses" and "prompts our first wish to please God, our first glimmer of understanding concerning God's will, and our 'first slight transient conviction' of having sinned against God."[56]

This understanding of grace explains how United Methodist doctrine can affirm two important things at the same time. First, every good gift in humanity's process of salvation comes from God. It is "grace upon grace." We are saved by grace alone. At the same time, humanity is given the ability, by grace, to respond or not respond. Because God loves us, God does not coerce us.[57] This pattern of human response being given to God's prevenient grace is crucial to Wesley's idea of salvation. It is God who saves, but humans must cooperate. Yet even their ability to cooperate, the faith that responds, is made possible by God's grace:

> And hence we may, thirdly, infer the absolute necessity of this re-action of the soul (whatsoever it be called) in order to the continuance of the divine life therein. For it plainly appears God does not continue to act upon the soul unless the soul re-acts upon God. He prevents us indeed with the blessings of his goodness. He first loves us, and manifests himself unto us. While we are yet afar off he calls us to himself, and shines upon our hearts. But if we do not then love him who first loved us; if we will not hearken to his voice; if we turn our eye away from him, and will not

attend to the light which he pours upon us: his Spirit will not always strive; he will gradually withdraw, and leave us to the darkness of our own hearts. He will not continue to breathe into our soul unless our soul breathes toward him again; unless our love, and prayer, and thanksgiving return to him, a sacrifice wherewith he is well pleased.[58]

Several Wesleyan hymns stress the universality of God's grace and its invitation into a saving relationship:

> Come, sinners, to the gospel feast;
> let every soul be Jesus' guest.
> Ye need not one be left behind,
> for God hath bid all humankind.[59]

United Methodist doctrine teaches universal redemption, that is, the change in status of every human being because of the death of Christ on the cross. Christ died for everyone and not just a few. This gracious activity of God both restores the faculties that humans need in order to respond to the offer of salvation and continually woos the lost soul to return home. This is not the same as universal salvation. Tragically, some refuse God's gracious offer of salvation.

The other ways in which grace affects humanity relate to other stages in the way of salvation. Grace convicts us of sin and helps us repent. Justifying grace pardons us and restores us to right relationship with God. Sanctifying grace "breaks the power of cancelled sin [and] sets the prisoner free."[60]

LAW

The law has an important role to play in the United Methodist understanding of these early stages of salvation. By "the law" it should be clear that the Articles of Religion and the *Sermons* distinguish between different parts of the body of Old Testament commandments. Article VI says:

The Old Testament is not contrary to the New; for both in the Old and New Testament everlasting life is offered to mankind by Christ. . . . Although the law given from God by Moses as touching ceremonies and rites doth not bind Christians, nor ought the civil precepts thereof of necessity be received in any commonwealth; yet notwithstanding, no Christian whatsoever is free from the obedience of the commandments which are called moral.[61]

Sermons and *Notes* use the distinction at several points as well.[62] It is such a deep assumption he regards it as common among Christians.[63] Thus, in all that follows, any reference to "the law" is to the moral law because that is the only one binding on Christians.

Wesley is deeply concerned with charting a middle course between two extremes. On the one hand he is seeking to avoid the moralism that reduces Christianity to a set of behaviors which characterize good persons. He criticizes such persons as having "the form of godliness without the power."[64] On the other hand, he is strongly opposed to antinomianism. He preaches salvation by faith in such a way that people understand that faith establishes the law. [65]

For Wesley, the law's origin was part of God's gracious creation. It was given to the angels before the creation of humanity, and it was engraved on the hearts of the first humans.[66] Wesley refers to John 1:9 for one proof that the law continues to be given to all humanity. Wesley has a high view of the law's relationship to God. He says,

> Now this law is an incorruptible picture of the high and holy One that inhabiteth eternity. It is he whom in his essence no man hath seen or can see, made visible to men and angels. It is the face of God unveiled; God manifested to his creatures as they are able to bear it; manifested to give and not to destroy life; that they may see God and live. It is the heart of God disclosed to man. Yea, in some sense we may apply to this law what the Apostle says of his Son—it is "the streaming forth" or outbeaming "of his glory, the express image of his person."[67]

Later he says, "The law of God (speaking after the manner of men) is a copy of the eternal mind, a transcript of the divine nature."[68] Thus he explains the meaning of Romans 7:12, "Wherefore the law *is* holy, and the commandment holy, and just, and good."[69] This law is fulfilled by the great commandments. He says:

"This is the law and the prophets." Whatsoever is written in that law which God of old revealed to mankind, and whatsoever precepts God has given by "his holy prophets which have been since the world began," they are all summed up in these few words, they are all contained in this short direction. And this, rightly understood, comprises the whole of that religion which our Lord came to establish upon earth.[70]

Wesley then argues that the law thus understood has three uses. First, it convinces the world of sin. Wesley told his preachers that preaching the law was a way of awakening sinners to see their spiritual condition correctly. He says that sometimes people are awakened by the message of reconciliation, such as 2 Corinthians 5:19, "but it is the ordinary method of the Spirit of God to convict sinners by the law."[71] The second use of the law brings the sinner into life. While the law "drives us by force," it remains that "love is the spring of all."[72] The third use of the law is that it acts as a guide and tutor to believers, thus keeping us alive.[73]

Having made this clear in Sermon 34, his offering two other sermons titled "The Law Established Through Faith" is understandable. Faith thus understood does not "make void the law," but enables the law to fulfill its intended purpose of restoring persons to the perfection that God intended for them in creation. In justification one's relationship to the law changes; one begins to keep the law because one desires it.[74] Being born again means being filled with faith, hope, and love. Love brings, as one of its fruits,

universal obedience to him we love, and conformity to his will; obedience to all the commands of God, internal and external; obedience of the heart and of the life, in every temper and in all manner of conversation. And one of the tempers most obviously implied herein is the being "zealous of good works"; the hungering and thirsting to do good, in every possible kind, unto all men; the rejoicing to "spend and be spent for them," for every child of man, not looking for any recompense in this world, but only in the resurrection of the just.[75]

One's relationship to the law thus changes. After the natural person is awakened by the law's commands, the legal person obeys the law because he or she is very conscious of God's wrath. The General Rules set as the only requirement for joining a Methodist society a desire to flee from God's wrath.[76] At justification one is born again, one's heart is circumcised, and one desires to keep the law for its own sake. Sin still remains and urges us to violate God's commandments, but it does not reign. Thus, the ruling desire in our hearts is to "establish the law."

The two sermons are also clear about the ways in which Christians both establish and make void the law. Christians establish the law by preaching everything Christ has revealed, all his promises and his threatenings.[77] We have to preach Christ in all his offices. We "make void the law" if we focus on a truncated gospel that deals only with Christ's priestly office. We must also preach Christ as prophet and king.

The second way to establish the law is to preach the kind of faith that does not supersede holiness, but produces it:

> In order to this we continually declare (what should be frequently and deeply considered by all who would not "make void the law through faith") that faith itself, even Christian faith, the faith of God's elect, the faith of the operation of God, still is only the handmaid of love. As glorious and honourable as it is, it is not the end of the commandment. God hath given this honour to love alone. Love is the end of all the commandments of God.[78]

Similarly, we make void the law if we teach any other kind of faith.

The third way of establishing the law is to establish it in our hearts and lives. Its opposite, "the *living* as if faith was designed to excuse us from holiness,"[79] is the most common way in which humanity "makes void the law." The General Rules—do no harm, do good, and attend upon all the ordinances of God—can be construed as one formulation of how to follow in the path of holiness. Faith enables us to pursue holiness. Wesley says:

> Faith alone it is which effectually answers this end, as we learn from daily experience. For so long as we walk by faith, not by sight, we go swiftly on in the way of holiness. While we steadily look, not at the things which are seen, but at those which are not seen, we are more and more crucified to the world and the world crucified to us. Let but the eye of the soul be constantly fixed, not on the things which are temporal, but on those which are eternal, and our affections are more and more loosened from earth and fixed on things above. So that faith in general is the most direct

and effectual means of promoting all righteousness and true holiness; of establishing the holy and spiritual law in the hearts of them that believe.[80]

Related to this is a deep understanding of how the gospel and the law are related in Scripture. One of Wesley's rules for interpreting the Bible is that "commandments are covered promises."[81] He says:

> Yea, the very same words, considered in different respects, are parts both of the law and of the gospel. If they are considered as commandments, they are parts of the law: if as promises, of the gospel. Thus, "Thou shalt love the Lord thy God with all thy heart," when considered as a commandment, is a branch of the law; when regarded as a promise, is an essential part of the gospel—the gospel being no other than the commands of the law proposed by way of promises. Accordingly poverty of spirit, purity of heart, and whatever else is enjoined in the holy law of God, are no other, when viewed in a gospel light, than so many great and precious promises.
>
> There is therefore the closest connection that can be conceived between the law and the gospel. On the one hand the law continually makes way for and points us to the gospel; on the other the gospel continually leads us to a more exact fulfilling of the law. The law, for instance, requires us to love God, to love our neighbour, to be meek, humble, or holy. We feel that we are not sufficient for these things, yea, that "with man this is impossible." But we see a promise of God to give us that love, and to make us humble, meek, and holy. We lay hold of this gospel, of these glad tidings: it is done unto us according to our faith, and "the righteousness of the law is fulfilled in us" through faith which is in Christ Jesus.
>
> We may yet farther observe that every command in Holy Writ is only a covered promise.[82]

In one key text, Wesley's translation makes this point well. For Matthew 5:48, the KJV has "Be ye therefore perfect, even as your Father which is in heaven is perfect."[83] Wesley's translation in the *Notes* is "Therefore ye shall be perfect, as your Father who is in heaven is perfect." The Greek text is *Esesthe oun hymeis teleioi hōs ho patēr hymōn ho ouranios teleios estin.* The word *esesthe* can be translated either as the present imperative "you be" or as the future indicative "you shall be." Wesley's translation is grammatically possible. Most translators for reasons of the context construe this verse as a command. Wesley's principle that commands are also promises suggests that the ambiguity of the Greek should be preserved. "You shall be perfect" could be construed as either imperative or future indicative. In his view the larger doctrinal context means that the promise aspect should be emphasized. His comment on the verse makes this clear:

> And how wise and gracious is this, to sum up, and as it were seal, all his commandments with a promise; even the proper promise of the gospel, that he will "put" those "laws in our minds, and write them in our hearts!" He well knew how ready our unbelief would be to cry out, This is impossible! and therefore stakes upon it all the power, truth, and faithfulness of Him to whom all things are possible.[84]

In short, United Methodist doctrine places a strong emphasis on the law. Maddox says, "Wesley's understanding of human nature and the human problem gives primacy of place to therapeutic concerns, like those more characteristic of Eastern Christianity, and integrates the more typically Western juridical concerns into this orientation."[85] This characteristic blending of both juridical and therapeutic concerns is manifest in Wesley's understanding of the uses of the law. The law both condemns us and, after our pardon, heals us. A commandment's double role as both law and gospel, obligation and promise, is possible because the lawgiver and the enabler of its fulfillment are the same Person.

REPENTANCE

In his note on Matthew 3:8, Wesley distinguishes between legal repentance and evangelical repentance: "The former, which is the same that is spoken of here, is a thorough conviction of sin. The latter is a change of heart (and consequently of life) from all sin to all holiness."[86] The first type of repentance comes as the first step in the way of salvation. Creation in the image of God, original sin, and God's prevenient grace describe aspects of the universal human condition. God's grace restores the human faculties that allow for the possibility of faith, and God uses a variety of ways to draw humanity closer to him. In legal repentance, persons become aware of their spiritual condition. God's grace convinces them of their need for him, and of their sinful state. The *Sermons* often refer to this as awaking from sleep.[87] Wesley interprets Romans 7:7-25 as giving voice to the struggle of the person "reasoning, groaning, striving, and escaping from the legal to the evangelical state."[88] There is a deep awareness that repentance is not easy and the struggle against the reign of sin in one's life is difficult. In the sermon "The Spirit of Bondage and Adoption," Wesley describes the process in great detail:

> By some awful providence, or by his Word applied with the demonstration of his Spirit, God touches the heart of him that lay asleep in darkness and in the shadow of death. He is terribly shaken out of his sleep, and awakes into a consciousness of his danger. Perhaps in a moment, perhaps by degrees, the eyes of his understanding are opened, and now first (the veil being in part removed) discern the real state he is in. Horrid light breaks in upon his soul; such light as may be conceived to gleam from the bottomless pit, from the lowest deep, from a lake of fire burning with brimstone. He at last sees the loving, the merciful God is also "a consuming fire"; that he is a just God and a terrible, rendering to every man according to his works, entering into judgment with the ungodly for every idle word, yea, and for the imaginations of the heart. He now clearly perceives that the great and holy God is "of purer eyes than to behold iniquity"; that he is an avenger of everyone who rebelleth against him, and repayeth the wicked to his face; and that "it is a fearful thing to fall into the hands of the living God."[89]

Repentance is preeminently knowledge of one's own spiritual state. In "The Way to the Kingdom" he says directly, "And first, repent, that is, know yourselves."[90] But where this knowledge is really fixed in the soul, the person also experiences the affections that go along with it. He says:

> If to this lively conviction of thy inward and outward sins, of thy utter guiltiness and helplessness, there be added suitable affections—sorrow of heart for having despised thy own mercies; remorse and self-condemnation, having the mouth stopped,

shame to lift up thine eyes to heaven; fear of the wrath of God abiding on thee, of his curse hanging over thy head, and of the fiery indignation ready to devour those who forget God and obey not our Lord Jesus Christ; earnest desire to escape from that indignation, to cease from evil and learn to do well—then I say unto thee, in the name of the Lord, "Thou art not far from the kingdom of God." One step more and thou shalt enter in. Thou dost "repent."[91]

Wesley's theory of human behavior is that whatever is in the mind will manifest itself in the affections and from there determine human behavior. Thus, there also should be "works meet for repentance," which will show forth in the life of the truly repentant person. The General Rules say, "wherever this [desire to flee from the wrath to come] is really fixed in the soul it will be shown by its fruits. It is therefore expected of all who continue therein that they should continue to evidence their desire of salvation" by following the three rules.[92]

Wesley's discussions of humility are rooted in this kind of self-knowledge. If the unawakened person in the natural state believes himself to be basically fine, the process of repentance is where one comes to know the truth about oneself. Convincing grace leads the person to a new self-understanding. He says,

No man has a title to the praise of God unless his heart is circumcised by humility, unless he is little, and base, and vile in his own eyes; unless he is deeply convinced of that inbred "corruption of his nature, whereby he is very far gone from original righteousness," being prone to all evil, averse to all good, corrupt and abominable; having a "carnal mind," which "is enmity against God, and is not subject to the Law of God, nor indeed can be"; unless he continually feels in his inmost soul that without the Spirit of God resting upon him he can neither think, nor desire, nor speak, nor act, anything good or well-pleasing in his sight.[93]

Again, Wesley's translation of a key New Testament text shows the theological approach to his understanding of it. He renders the first two of the beatitudes as "Happy *are* the poor in spirit: for theirs is the kingdom of heaven. Happy *are* they that mourn: for they shall be comforted."[94] Wesley translates *makarioi* as "happy." The Jerusalem Bible and the Today's English Version similarly translate the Greek. His comment emphasizes that the persons being described as happy are those who are penitent, and are thus mourning their sins or the sins of others. These persons receive the kingdom of heaven if they endure to the end.[95]

Evangelical repentance is the kind that transforms the life of the believer through sanctifying grace. Because sin remains in our hearts even after justification, we know that we are guilty sinners, deserving of God's punishment. Yet, this repentance is different from what was experienced previously because persons understand themselves to be, at the same time, sinners and children of God.[96] Wesley reads Romans 7:7-25 as applying to someone in the stage of legal repentance. Nevertheless, he says that those who interpret those verses as a description of Christians struggling to root out the remaining sin in their lives have a measure of truth as well.[97]

The great difference here is that evangelical repentance, whereby sin, guilt, and dependence on the grace of God are acknowledged, is knowingly conjoined to love and acceptance by God. Justification is the restoration of a relationship through pardon. Repentance after justification means a self-awareness of one's sin, guilt, and helplessness that nevertheless do not threaten the relationship. Wesley says that the antidote is faith, and that faith and repentance mirror each other in the life of the believer:

> By repentance we feel the sin remaining in our hearts, and cleaving to our words and actions. By faith we receive the power of God in Christ, purifying our hearts and cleansing our hands. By repentance we are still sensible that we deserve punishment for all our tempers and words and actions. By faith we are conscious that our advocate with the Father is continually pleading for us, and thereby continually turning aside all condemnation and punishment from us. By repentance we have an abiding conviction that there is no help in us. By faith we receive not only mercy, but "grace to help in *every* time of need." Repentance disclaims the very possibility of any other help. Faith accepts all the help we stand in need of from him that hath all power in heaven and earth. Repentance says, "Without him I can do nothing": faith says, "I can do all things through Christ strengthening me."[98]

For the believer there is an underlying confidence that the disease of sin is being healed. Like a sick person receiving treatment from a trusted physician, the sinner is confident of cure, yet still experiences the problems associated with the disease.

Wesley's view of repentance does not stress the idea of turning around one's life; rather, it stresses one's self-understanding. This change in one's mind is closely related to the Greek word for repentance, *metanoia*. However, Wesley believes that a genuine change in mind will lead to changed behavior, "works meet for repentance." If such works are not present, the change in mind was not real.

The hymn "Depth of Mercy" gives poetic voice to the person who has experienced justification and is now aware of backsliding:[99]

> Depth of mercy! Can there be
> mercy still reserved for me?
> Can my God his wrath forbear,
> me, the chief of sinners, spare?
>
> I have long withstood his grace,
> long provoked him to his face,
> would not hearken to his calls,
> grieved him by a thousand falls.
>
> I my Master have denied,
> I afresh have crucified,
> oft profaned his hallowed name,
> put him to an open shame.
>
> There for me the Savior stands,
> shows his wounds and spreads his hands.
> God is love! I know, I feel;
> Jesus weeps and loves me still.
>
> Now incline me to repent,
> let me now my sins lament,
> now my foul revolt deplore,
> weep, believe, and sin no more.[100]

Repentance is the awakening of the sinner to one's need for God, one's own guilt, and one's inability to solve it on one's own. If the religion of Jesus Christ is the answer to the human problem, and God has chosen not to help without the cooperation of those he loves, then repentance is the stage where each person acknowledges one's problem and begins seeking the answer.

Notes

1. Sermon 1, "Salvation by Faith," §1, *Works* 1:117-18.

2. Discipline, 122.

3. Discipline, 96. See also Discipline, 83 where "Our Theological Task" refers to "our calling to care for God's creation."

4. BOR, 77-78.

5. Sermon 51, "The Good Steward," *Works* 2:282-98.

6. *Notes* Heb. 11:3, John 1:1-3.

7. *Notes* Rom. 8:19-21.

8. Discipline, 43.

9. For a discussion of these three senses of the image of God in all of Wesley's thought, see Runyon, 13-19. Maddox 1994, 65-93 discusses Wesley's anthropology in greater depth.

10. Sermon 45, "The New Birth," §I.1, *Works* 2:188-89.

11. Sermon 51, "The Good Steward," §I.2, *Works* 2:284.

12. See *Notes* 1 Thess. 5:23 for an explicit though parenthetical statement of this presupposition. For Wesley's understanding of the last judgment, see Sermon 15, "The Great Assize," §§2-3, *Works* 1:356, where he says that every human being will face it.

13. Sermon 51, "The Good Steward," §I.7, *Works* 2:286.

14. Sermon 45, "The New Birth," §I.1, *Works* 2:188.

15. *Notes* Rom. 14:17. In an analysis of the index to the Bicentennial edition of Wesley's Sermons (which covered all 151, not just the standard 53) this verse was his seventh most frequently quoted text in the whole Bible. See Jones 155-56. For this same point about the nature of "true religion," see sermon 7, "The Way to the Kingdom," §§I.1-13, *Works* 1:218-25.

16. Discipline, 61.

17. Discipline, 68.

18. Sermon 45, "The New Birth," §I.2, *Works* 2:189.

19. Ibid., §I.3, *Works* 2:190.

20. Ibid., §I.4, *Works* 2:190.

21. Discipline, 43.

22. Discipline, 61.

23. *Compact Edition of the Oxford English Dictionary*, "prevent" I.4, 2:2294.

24. Sermon 5, "Justification by Faith," §I.9, *Works* 1:187.

25. Maddox 1994, 73-83 offers a thoughtful and comprehensive study of Wesley's changing anthropology. He argues on p. 74 that a full understanding of Wesley's various statements requires attention to the time period of the comment, the occasion of the comment, and the internal tensions between Wesley's juridical and therapeutic concerns. Such an approach is essential to an adequate understanding of Wesley's theology. However, two changes in approach need to be

noted in considering United Methodist doctrine. First, the development over time is muted in significance, because The United Methodist Church has taken responsibility for all of these statements. Second, the Wesley scholar has the ability to consider all of Wesley's writings while the student of United Methodist doctrine must be limited to the authoritative texts. For the Church, these tensions about how the problem of original sin is transmitted are left unresolved. Wesley's leaving these side-by-side in various places as well as juxtaposed in a paragraph like this one is typical of his concern for practical doctrine rather than speculative theology. See his comment to Dr. John Robertson, "The fact I know, both by Scripture and by experience. I know it is transmitted: but *how* it is transmitted I neither know nor desire to know," 24 September 1753, *Works* 26:519. Maddox suggests that Wesley really was more concerned to know about this than he indicates here. The standards of doctrine suggest that Wesley was actually content to leave this unresolved. This is an excellent example of where theological reflection can and should consider doctrinal ambiguities in the service of the Church's witness.

26. KJV.

27. Sermon 3, "Awake, Thou That Sleepest," §§I.2-3, *Works* 1:143. See also Sermon 9, "The Spirit of Bondage and Adoption," §§I.1-8, *Works* 1:251-55.

28. Sermon 9, "The Spirit of Bondage and Adoption," §I.8, *Works* 1:254-55.

29. Sermon 44, "Original Sin," §4, *Works* 2:173.

30. Sermon 7, "The Way to the Kingdom," §II.1, *Works* 1:225.

31. *Notes* Rom. 6:6.

32. UMH, 34.

33. Sermon 44, "Original Sin," §III.4, *Works* 2:184.

34. Sermon 5, "Justification by Faith," §I.9, *Works* 1:187.

35. Sermon 44, "Original Sin," §III.2, *Works* 2:183-84.

36. Sermon 44, "Original Sin," §III.3, *Works* 2:184.

37. Sermon 44, "Original Sin," §III.5, *Works* 2:185.

38. Sermon 19, "The Great Privilege of Those that are Born of God," §II.2, *Works* 1:436.

39. He says in the *Plain Account of Christian Perfection*, "To explain myself a little farther on this head: (1.) Not only sin, properly so called, (that is, a voluntary transgression of a known law,) but sin, improperly so called, (that is, an involuntary transgression of a divine law, known or unknown,) needs the atoning blood. (2.) I believe there is no such perfection in this life as excludes these involuntary transgressions which I apprehend to be naturally consequent on the ignorance and mistakes inseparable from mortality. (3.) Therefore *sinless perfection* is a phrase I never use, lest I should seem to contradict myself. (4.) I believe, a person filled with the love of God is still liable to these involuntary transgressions. (5.) Such transgressions you may call sins, if you please: I do not, for the reasons above-mentioned," *Works* (J) 11:396. See also Sermon 76, "On Perfection," §II.9 *Works* 3:79 where he defends his definition of "sin" as scriptural.

40. Sermon 13, "On Sin in Believers," §§I.3, 6, III.3, *Works* 1:318-19, 322.

41. Sermon 14, "The Repentance of Believers," §I.13, *Works* 1:342-43.

42. *Notes* Rom. 3:23.

43. Discipline, 47.

44. Discipline, 83.

45. Discipline, 96.

46. Discipline, 122.

47. Discipline, 104.

48. Discipline, 61.

49. Discipline, 68.

50. Sermon 1, "Salvation by Faith," §§1, 3, *Works* 1:117-18.

51. Sermon 12, "The Witness of Our Own Spirit," §15, *Works* 1:309.

52. *Notes* 2 Cor. 8:9. See also Gal. 1:15, Gal. 2:21, and Eph. 1:6.

53. *Compact Edition of the Oxford English Dictionary*, "prevent" I.4, 2:2294.

54. Sermon 43, "The Scripture Way of Salvation," §I.2, *Works* 2:156-57. The *Notes* on John 1:9 refer to Christ enlightening everyone as natural conscience.

55. Maddox 1994, 87-90.

56. Discipline, 46.

57. The most insightful of Wesley's sermons on this topic is not a part of United Methodist doctrine: Sermon 85, "On Working Out Our Own Salvation." In §III.7, *Works* 3:208-9 he says, "Secondly, God worketh in you; therefore you *must* work: you must be 'workers together with him' (they are the very words of the Apostle); otherwise he will cease working. The general rule on which his gracious dispensations invariably proceed is this: 'Unto him that hath shall be given; but from him that hath not,' that does not improve the grace already given, 'shall be taken away what he assuredly hath' (so the words ought to be rendered). Even St. Augustine, who is generally supposed to favour the contrary doctrine, makes that just remark, *Qui fecit nos sine nobis, non salvabit nos sine nobis*: 'he that made us without ourselves, will not save us without ourselves.' He will not save us unless we 'save ourselves from this untoward generation'; unless we ourselves 'fight the good fight of faith, and lay hold on eternal life'; unless we 'agonize to enter in at the strait gate,' 'deny ourselves, and take up our cross daily,' and labour, by every possible means, to 'make our own calling and election sure.'"

58. Sermon 19, "The Great Privilege of Those that are Born of God," §III.3, *Works* 1:442.

59. UMH, 339, 616. See also *Works* 7:81. The editors of the UMH split Charles Wesley's hymn into two parts, one used for invitation and one for communion, each with the same first stanza.

60. "O For a Thousand Tongues to Sing," UMH, 57, stanza 4.

61. Discipline, 61.

62. E.g., Sermon 34, "The Original, Nature, Properties and Use of the Law," §§1, II.1, *Works* 2:4, 8; Sermon 35, "The Law Established Through Faith, I," §§3, II.5, *Works* 2:21, 27; Upon Our Lord's Sermon on the Mount, V," §II.1, *Works* 2:551; *Notes* Mark 12:31, Luke 1:6, John 3:3, Rom. 3:20, Gal. 2:4, Gal. 3:19, Eph. 2:14, and 1 Tim. 1:8. For further discussion of this regarding Wesley's conception of Scripture, see Jones, 56-58.

63. *Notes* Acts 13:39.

64. *Notes* Matt. 13:28. See also Sermon 3, "Awake, Thou That Sleepest," §III.11, *Works* 1:157.

65. Sermon 35, "The Law Established Through Faith, I," §II.5, *Works* 2:27.

66. Most of the following paragraphs is a summary of Wesley's argument in sermon 34, "The Original, Nature, Properties and Use of the Law," *Works* 2:4-19. This is the most detailed exposition of this subject in United Methodist doctrine.

67. Sermon 34, "The Original, Nature, Properties and Use of the Law," *Works* §II.3, 2:9.

68. Sermon 34, "The Original, Nature, Properties and Use of the Law," *Works* §II.6, 2:10.

69. KJV.

70. Sermon 30, "Upon our Lord's Sermon on the Mount, X," §23, *Works* 1:661.

71. Sermon 34, "The Original, Nature, Properties and Use of the Law," §IV.1, *Works* 2:15.

72. Sermon 34, "The Original, Nature, Properties and Use of the Law," §IV.2, 2:16.

73. Sermon 34, "The Original, Nature, Properties and Use of the Law," §IV.3, 2:16. In this claim, Wesley is siding with Calvin and the Reformed tradition against the Lutherans.

74. Note the phrase used in Q26 in the "Large Minutes," number 10: "And in general, do not mend our Rules, but keep them; not for wrath, but for conscience' sake," *Works* (J) 8:310.

75. Sermon 18, "The Marks of the New Birth," §III.5, *Works* 1:427.

76. Discipline, 72.

77. Sermon 36, "The Law Established by Faith, II," §1.5, *Works* 2:37.

78. Sermon 36, "The Law Established by Faith, II," §II.1, *Works* 2:38.

79. Sermon 35, "The Law Established by Faith, I," §III.1, *Works* 2:29.

80. Sermon 36, "The Law Established by Faith, II," §III.2, *Works* 2:41.

81. For discussion of this see Jones, 124.

82. "Upon Our Lord's Sermon on the Mount, V," §§II.2-3, *Works* 1:554-55.

83. Both the NRSV and the NIV follow the KJV at this point. They have "Be perfect, therefore, as your heavenly Father is perfect."

84. *Notes* Matt. 5:48.

85. Maddox 1994, 67.

86. *Notes* Matt. 3:8.

87. Sermon 3, "Awake, Thou That Sleepest," *Works* 1:142-58.

88. *Notes* Rom. 7:14.

89. Sermon 9, "The Spirit of Bondage and Adoption," §II.1, *Works* 1:255. Wesley is referring to the following biblical verses: Ps. 107:10 (Luke 1:79), Eph. 1:18, Rev. 19:20, Deut. 4:24 (Heb. 12:29), Prov. 24:12, Hab. 1:13, Deut. 7:10, and Heb. 10:31.

90. Sermon 7, "The Way to the Kingdom," §II.1, *Works* 1:225. See also Sermon 14, "The Repentance of Believers," §I.1, *Works* 1:336.

91. Sermon 7, "The Way to the Kingdom," §II.7, *Works* 1:229. The biblical references here are to Luke 18:13, Isa. 1:16-17, and Mark 12:34.

92. Discipline, 72.

93. Sermon 17, "The Circumcision of the Heart," §II.1, *Works* 1:409.

94. *Notes* Matt. 5:3-4.

95. *Notes* Matt. 5:3-4.

96. Sermon 14, "The Repentance of Believers," §I.1, *Works* 1:336.

97. Sermon 14, "The Repentance of Believers," §I.10, *Works* 1:341.

98. Sermon 14, "The Repentance of Believers," §II.6, *Works* 1:349-50.

99. In the 1780 *Collection of Hymns for the Use of the People Called Methodist* it was put in the section labeled "Convinced of Backsliding." See *Works* 7:284-85.

100. UMH, 355.

CHAPTER SIX

JUSTIFICATION BY GRACE THROUGH FAITH

One of the theses of this study is that the central theme of United Methodist doctrine is saving grace. The idea of God's saving grace pervades the teaching of the Church, and God's action of saving the world receives the most attention and occupies the most central position in that body of teaching. We have seen how the general tenor of Scripture is the analogy of faith—that "grand scheme of doctrine" describing original sin, justification, and sanctification. In one metaphor Wesley compares religion to a house. Repentance is the porch, justification is the door, and sanctification is the whole house.[1] While the goal is being in the house, one must cross the porch and go through the doorway to get there. Similarly, in most cases, crossing the porch is of moderate duration, passing through the doorway is of short duration, and exploring the house could and should take a lifetime.

We have seen that repentance is the graciously given knowledge of oneself as a guilty sinner helpless in attaining salvation. Given the diagnosis of the human problem as sin, and the characterization of sin as a disease distorting the image of God, it follows that Christianity is best characterized as *therapeia psychēs*. Wesley explains:

> Hereby the great Physician of souls applies medicine to heal *this sickness;* to restore human nature, totally corrupted in all its

faculties. God heals all our atheism by the knowledge of himself, and of Jesus Christ whom he hath sent; by giving us faith, a divine evidence and conviction of God and of the things of God— in particular of this important truth: Christ loved *me,* and gave himself for *me.* By repentance and lowliness of heart the deadly disease of pride is healed; that of self-will by resignation, a meek and thankful submission to the will of God. And for the love of the world in all its branches the love of God is the sovereign remedy. Now this is properly religion, "faith thus working by love," working the genuine, meek humility, entire deadness to the world, with a loving, thankful acquiescence in and conformity to the whole will and Word of God.[2]

Genuine religion is best understood as the therapy of the soul. Christianity is the way in which God is transforming God's creation away from its sin and restoring the original God present in the first creation. This means the changing of individuals and of entire social systems.

A common mistake about salvation is to relate it only to life after death. The *Sermons* emphasize that salvation is a present reality, not merely something achieved after death. In "The Scripture Way of Salvation" Wesley focuses on the tense of the verb *sesōmenoi* in Ephesians 2:8. While he follows the KJV (both in the sermon and in the *Notes*) in translating it as "Ye *are* saved," he argues that with equal propriety it could be translated "Ye *have been* saved."[3] Both the NRSV and the NIV use the latter translation. Thus, salvation is something that relates to human life in the present.

Another way in which salvation is misunderstood, according to United Methodist doctrine, is to limit it to only one moment in time. In the same sermon Wesley describes salvation as a process. If salvation is the therapy of the soul, then healing often requires a lifelong process of removing the disease and restoring the image of God. He says,

> If we take this in its utmost extent it will include all that is wrought in the soul by what is frequently termed "natural conscience," but more properly, "preventing grace"; all the "drawings" of "the Father," the desires after God, which, if we yield to them, increase more and more; all that "light" wherewith the Son of God "enlighteneth everyone that cometh into the world," *showing* every man "to do justly, to love mercy, and to walk humbly

with his God"; all the *convictions* which his Spirit from time to time works in every child of man. Although it is true the generality of men stifle them as soon as possible, and after a while forget, or at least deny, that ever they had them at all.[4]

While it begins with God's prevenient grace given to the individual before he or she is aware of it, salvation continues through the rest of the process. Repentance, justification, sanctification, and perfection are all further stages through which the grace of God leads the person in the process of salvation.

The Mission Statement of the United Methodist Church is contained in the phrase "to make disciples of Jesus Christ." However, it is explained as a process that has five steps:

> We make disciples as we:
> —proclaim the gospel, seek, welcome and gather persons into the body of Christ;
> —lead persons to commit their lives to God through baptism and profession of faith in Jesus Christ;
> —nurture persons in Christian living through worship, the sacraments, spiritual disciplines, and other means of grace, such as Wesley's Christian conferencing;
> —send persons into the world to live lovingly and justly as servants of Christ by healing the sick, feeding the hungry, caring for the stranger, freeing the oppressed, and working to develop social structures that are consistent with the gospel; and
> —continue the mission of seeking, welcoming and gathering persons into the community of the body of Christ.[5]

This statement corresponds to the various stages of salvation as persons are invited to hear the gospel, make commitments through faith, grow as disciples, and then serve the world in Christ's name.

SALVATION

Whereas Wesley understands salvation in the broad sense as stretching back to all of what God has done for us, including prevenient grace, he says that, in the narrow sense, salvation has two parts: justification and sanctification.[6] Understanding the proper relationship between these reveals the balance and general structure of United Methodist doctrine.

A crucial explanation of this relationship comes in the sermon "Justification by Faith." He says,

> But what is it to be "justified"? What is "justification"? This was the second thing which I proposed to show. And it is evident from what has been already observed that it is not the being made actually just and righteous. This is *sanctification*; which is indeed in some degree the immediate *fruit* of justification, but nevertheless is a distinct gift of God, and of a totally different nature. The one implies what God *does for us* through his Son; the other what he *works in us* by his Spirit. So that although some rare instances may be found wherein the term "justified" or "justification" is used in so wide a sense as to include sanctification also, yet in general use they are sufficiently distinguished from each other both by St. Paul and the other inspired writers.[7]

When Wesley says sanctification is a distinct gift, he means it is logically distinct. In order of time, and thus in order of human experience, the two are simultaneous. Yet logically each is "a distinct gift of God, and of a totally different nature." The same point is made in another sermon:

> Justification implies only a relative, the new birth a real, change. God in justifying us does something *for* us: in begetting us again he does the work *in* us. The former changes our outward relation to God, so that of enemies we become children; by the latter our inmost souls are changed, so that of sinners we become saints. The one restores us to the favour, the other to the image of God. The one is the taking away the guilt, the other the taking away the power, of sin. So that although they are joined together in point of time, yet are they of wholly distinct natures.[8]

From this and other sources several aspects of the distinction can be drawn out. The most important is the one made above: justification is something God does for us through Christ, while sanctification is something God does in us through the Holy Spirit. Justification is a change in humanity's relationship to God. Sin has broken the relationship, and by the merits of Christ God offers humanity forgiveness and restores us to being God's children. It is thus a relative change, a change in status. In the words of the hymn, the sinner can say,

> Just as I am, without one plea,
> but that thy blood was shed for me,
> and that thou bidst me come to thee,
> O Lamb of God, I come, I come.[9]

In justification, the sinner receives pardon because Christ's righteousness is imputed to that person. At this stage, it is salvation from the guilt of sin and from fear.

Sanctification differs from this in that while God accepts people just as they are, God never leaves them just as they are. At the same moment that they are justified, they are also sanctified. Sanctification is a real change, where righteousness is imparted to human beings. It is freedom from the power of sin. It is the transformation of the person from sin to holiness and growth toward having the mind of Christ.

The metaphor of the house makes it clear that justification is of short duration if not momentary. Moving through the porch may take a long period of time, but moving through the door is relatively short. Further, the entire rest of the journey is in the house so long as one chooses to stay there. Sanctification is a process of gradually changing the person from the sinful state to becoming increasingly perfect. Indeed, we will see in the next chapter that the goal of sanctification, sometimes called entire sanctification, is that perfection or maturity which was God's intention for humanity in creation.

To summarize the distinction then, let us juxtapose the characteristics of the two aspects of salvation. Justification is a relative change; sanctification is a real change. Justification is imputed righteousness; sanctification is imparted righteousness. Justification is freedom from the guilt of sin and fear; sanctification is freedom from the power of sin. Both are gifts of God's grace received by faith. Charles Wesley said in the hymn, which has normally been placed first in Methodist hymnals,

> He breaks the power of canceled sin,
> he sets the prisoner free;

> his blood can make the foulest clean;
> his blood availed for me.[10]

Justification cancels sin. Sanctification frees and cleanses humanity from sin.

UNIVERSAL REDEMPTION

When Wesley characterized prevenient grace in the terms of John 1:8, he was committing himself to the idea that God's saving grace is freely offered to all human beings. His note on John 3:16 is one place where he argues that God loves everyone, "even those that despise his love," and that all should believe Christ was given for them.[11] This led Wesley to argue against the doctrine of predestination and its corollaries. While some of Wesley's strongest statements on the subject lie outside of the doctrinal standards,[12] the basic elements of his teaching are interwoven throughout his writings and aptly summarized in his note on 1 Peter 1:2. He says there:

> *Elect*—By the free love and almighty power of God taken out of, separated from, the world. Election, in the scripture sense, is God's doing anything that our merit or power have no part in. The true predestination, or fore-appointment of God is, 1. He that believeth shall be saved from the guilt and power of sin. 2. He that endureth to the end shall be saved eternally. 3. They who receive the precious gift of faith, thereby become the sons of God; and, being sons, they shall receive the Spirit of holiness to walk as Christ also walked. Throughout every part of this appointment of God, promise and duty go hand in hand. All is free gift; and yet such is the gift, that the final issue depends on our future obedience to the heavenly call. But other predestination than this, either to life or death eternal, the scripture knows not of.[13]

Wesley argues that God elected the whole world.[14] Every human being was predestined to salvation. This election is conditional upon the person's acceptance of the gift through faith. Whether persons are eternally saved is also conditional upon their continued faith and acceptance of God's sanctifying grace. Wesley's note on Philippians 2:13 offers a type of divine-human cooperation in the process of salvation:

> *For it is God*—God alone, who is with you, though I am not. *That worketh in you according to his good pleasure*—Not for any merit of yours. Yet his influences are not to supersede, but to encourage, our own efforts. *Work out your own salvation*—Here is our duty. *For it is God that worketh in you*—Here is our encouragement. And O, what a glorious encouragement, to have the arm of Omnipotence stretched out for our support and our succour![15]

Maddox refers to this as responsible or co-operant grace, where the grace of God is given in such a way to ensure that it is not effectual unless the person chooses to accept it and use it by faith.[16]

A helpful way to look at these issues is to compare Wesley's views to the "Five Points" of Calvinism formulated in the canons of the Synod of Dort.[17] Outler says, "The 'Five Points' came to be listed in a familiar acronym, TULIP: *T*otal depravity, *U*nconditional election, *L*imited atonement, *I*rresistible grace, and the *P*erseverance of the saints."[18] Wesley agreed with the Calvinists on total depravity, with the exception that he interpreted "total" to mean that every part of the human creature was depraved with some vestige of the image of God remaining. With regard to the other four points, Wesley taught conditional election, unlimited atonement, resistible grace, and the present assurance of salvation through the witness of the Holy Spirit.

Contemporary statements of United Methodist doctrine do not address the issue of predestination in significant ways. However, the UMH carries the message of invitation extended to all. John Stockton wrote "Only Trust Him" in 1874:

> Come, every soul by sin oppressed,
> there's mercy with the Lord;
> and he will surely give you rest, by trusting in his Word.
> Only trust him, only trust him, only trust him now.
> He will save you, he will save you, he will save you now.[19]

A Laotian hymn carries a similar message:

> Come, all of you, come, men and women, come forward,
> drink of the water provided for you;

> all of you who are thirsty, come to me to drink
> from the water of life, provided by Jesus your Lord.[20]

In both of these hymns the words "every" and "all" offer the invitation universally. If every person would accept God's grace, then all would be saved.

JUSTIFICATION

Both Article IX and Confession IX affirm that we are justified not by works but, to use the words of the former, "we are accounted righteous before God only for the merit of our Lord and Saviour Jesus Christ, by faith."[21] Both articles also use the phrase "accounted righteous" as equivalent to "justified." Wesley says:

> The plain scriptural notion of justification is pardon, the forgiveness of sins. It is that act of God the Father whereby, for the sake of the propitiation made by the blood of his Son, he "showeth forth his righteousness (or mercy) by the remission of the sins that are past." . . . To him that is justified or forgiven God "will not impute sin" to his condemnation. He will not condemn him on that account either in this world or in that which is to come. His sins, all his past sins, in thought, word, and deed, "are covered," are blotted out; shall not be remembered or mentioned against him, any more than if they had not been. God will not inflict on that sinner what he deserved to suffer, because the Son of his love hath suffered for him. And from the time we are "accepted through the Beloved," "reconciled to God through his blood," he loves and blesses and watches over us for good, even as if we had never sinned.[22]

On Wesley's understanding, human beings are justified when God forgives their sins and accepts them as God's children. The proper relationship between them is restored. The breach caused by human sin is covered and they are reconciled to God. This is a relative change. Human beings have not done anything to deserve this, nor are they changed in this process. Rather, God "accounts them righteous."

It is in this sense that the term "imputed righteousness" is used. The righteousness of Christ was both passive and active, involving both suffering and action according to God's will. When a sinner believes, God counts that person as righteous, imputing to him the righteousness of Christ. In this God is not deceived. God knows our sins and knows full well that God is forgiving them for the sake of Christ if we accept the gift through faith.[23]

Ground of Justification

The ground or basis on which God can offer this salvation is the sacrifice of Christ upon the cross.

> Justification is another word for pardon. It is the forgiveness of all our sins, and (what is necessarily implied therein) our acceptance with God. The price whereby this hath been procured for us (commonly termed the "meritorious cause" of our justification) is the blood and righteousness of Christ, or (to express it a little more clearly) all that Christ hath done and suffered for us till "he poured out his soul for the transgressors."[24]

Wesley's dispute over meritorious and formal causes of salvation may be obscure to modern readers because the multiple senses of the word "cause" that were familiar in medieval and reformation theology have been abandoned.[25] Wesley is seeking to avoid the doctrine of predestination while affirming that the reason God can grant us salvation, the meritorious cause, is the righteousness of Christ. Article IX makes it clear that "we are accounted righteous before God only for the merit of our Lord and Saviour Jesus Christ, by faith, and not for our own works or deservings."[26]

Faith

Both Article IX and Confession IX make it clear that the condition of justification is faith. Confession IX says "penitent sinners are justified or accounted righteous before God only by faith in our Lord Jesus Christ."[27]

Randy Maddox's important study of Wesley's theology argues persuasively that, for Wesley, grace is responsible. By this he means

God's grace gives human beings the ability to respond, and will not save them unless they do so. The response called for is faith. However, the kind of faith Wesley is relying on is both simple and complex. It is simple in that one step can bring it about. It is complex in that believing in God inherently brings with it a whole way of life. In this way it is analogous to getting married, which also involves a pledge of faith and is a simple action, but similarly brings with it major changes and a whole new way of living.

In the *Sermons* Wesley utilizes three interrelated definitions of faith.[28] All three are contained in one section of "The Circumcision of the Heart," with a footnote from Wesley acknowledging the change in his theology made in 1738. He says:

> "All things are possible to him that" thus "believeth": "the eyes of his understanding being enlightened," he *sees* what is his calling, even to "glorify God, who hath bought him with" so high "a price, in his body and in his spirit, which now are God's" by redemption, as well as by creation. He feels what is "the exceeding greatness of his power" who, as he raised up Christ from the dead, so is able to quicken us—"dead in sin"—"by his Spirit which dwelleth in us." "This is the victory which overcometh the world, even our faith": that faith which is not only an unshaken assent to all that God hath revealed in Scripture, and in particular to those important truths, "Jesus Christ came into the world to save sinners"; he "bare our sins in his own body on the tree"; "he is the propitiation for our sins; and not for ours only, but also for the sins of the whole world";[29] but likewise the revelation of Christ in our hearts: a divine evidence or conviction of his love, his free, unmerited love to me a sinner; a sure confidence in his pardoning mercy, wrought in us by the Holy Ghost—a confidence whereby every true believer is enabled to bear witness, "I know that my Redeemer liveth"; that *I* "have an advocate with the Father," that "Jesus Christ the righteous is" *my* Lord, and "the propitiation for *my* sins." I know he "hath loved *me*, and given himself for *me*." He "hath reconciled *me*, even *me* to God"; and *I* "have redemption through his blood, even the forgiveness of sins."[30]

Before distinguishing the three senses of the word "faith," it is important to affirm that in all cases the faith is directed to Christ, or to God in Christ.[31] Our faith is in Christ, particularly in his righteousness.[32] Thus the truths of Scripture that describe the salvation offered by Christ's death on the cross are an important basis for all three senses of "faith."

First, Wesley says that faith is "an unshaken assent to all that God hath revealed in Scripture," meaning those truths that describe God's offer of salvation in Christ. Wesley refers to faith as assent in other places as well.[33] There is thus a cognitive component to faith which rests on the authority of Scripture. Yet Wesley is very clear that, however necessary assent to these truths may be, saving faith is much more than mere assent. He says that a person "may assent to all the three creeds—that called the Apostles', the Nicene, and the Athanasian—and yet 'tis possible he may have no religion at all."[34]

Wesley's second understanding of faith uses the traditional words of the Reformation that faith is trust or confidence in Christ. This is a disposition of the heart, given by God, that includes abandoning trust in one's own righteousness, acknowledging one's sin and one's need for God, and having confidence that God's forgiveness and salvation includes oneself. If assent believes that Christ died for the whole world intellectually, then this kind of belief involves one's heart making a personal commitment to Christ. Ephesians 5:2 says, "And walk in love, as Christ also hath loved us, and hath given himself for us an offering and a sacrifice to God for a sweetsmelling savour." Romans 5:10 says, "For if, when we were enemies, we were reconciled to God by the death of his Son, much more, being reconciled, we shall be saved by his life." Colossians 1:14 says, "In whom we have redemption through his blood, *even* the forgiveness of sins."[35] Wesley paraphrases these verses by changing the plural pronouns to the singular first-person and italicizing "me" and "I." The universal affirmations about what God is doing have become personal and self-involving because the believer trusts and has confidence in God through Christ.

Wesley's third understanding of faith builds on the second but adds the metaphor of spiritual senses. The crucial text supporting this sense of the word is Hebrews 11:1. Wesley quotes it, saying:

> Faith in general is defined by the Apostle, ἔλεγχος πραγμάτων οὐ βλεπομένων—"an evidence," a divine "evidence and conviction" (the word means both), "of things not seen" not visible, not perceivable either by sight or by any other of the external senses. It implies both a supernatural *evidence* of God and of the things of

God, a kind of spiritual *light* exhibited to the soul, and a super-natural *sight* or perception thereof. . . . By this twofold operation of the Holy Spirit—having the eyes of our soul both *opened* and *enlightened*—we see the things which the natural "eye hath not seen, neither the ear heard." We have a prospect of the invisible things of God. We see the *spiritual world*, which is all round about us, and yet no more discerned by our natural faculties than if it had no being; and we see the *eternal world*, piercing through the veil which hangs between time and eternity.[36]

Faith is like a gift that enables the individual to perceive things that were previously hidden. Where one once could not see spiritual truth, now faith enables one to see it. Wesley's description of the new birth draws the parallel with physical birth.[37] Just as a baby suddenly experiences a world never seen before and sensations not available in the womb, so faith bestows new senses on the justified person. What the justified person perceives is variously described as "the invisible things of God," "the spiritual world," and "the eternal world." The contrast between not having faith and having faith is drawn very starkly in "The New Birth":

While a man is in a mere natural state, before he is born of God, he has, in a spiritual sense, eyes and sees not; a thick impenetrable veil lies upon them. He has ears, but hears not; he is utterly deaf to what he is most of all concerned to hear. His other spiritual senses are all locked up; he is in the same condition as if he had them not. Hence he has no knowledge of God, no intercourse with him; he is not at all acquainted with him. He has no true knowledge of the things of God, either of spiritual or eternal things. Therefore, though he is a living man, he is a dead Christian.[38]

When one is born again, the eyes of understanding are opened; one can see the truth, hear the voice of God, and feel the working of the Spirit in one's heart. Wesley continues,

And all his spiritual senses are then "exercised to discern" spiritual "good and evil." By the use of these he is daily increasing in the knowledge of God, of Jesus Christ whom he hath sent, and of all the things pertaining to his inward kingdom. And now he may properly be said *to live*: God having quickened him by his Spirit, he is alive to God through Jesus Christ. He lives a life which the world knoweth not of, a "life" which "is hid with Christ in God." God is continually breathing, as it were, upon his soul, and his soul is breathing unto God. Grace is descending into his heart, and prayer and praise ascending to heaven. And by this intercourse between God and man, this fellowship with the Father and the Son, as by a kind of spiritual respiration, the life of God in the soul is sustained: and the child of God grows up, till he comes to "the full measure of the stature of Christ."[39]

This kind of faith is a gift that is accepted by the individual. Faith is not something one does. That would turn it into another work. Rather, this awareness of spiritual reality is a gift from God that the individual either accepts or rejects.

The relationship between the elements of the way of salvation at this initial stage often appears to be confusing. This is because a number of things happen simultaneously to the believer. Repentance should be understood as a kind of low-level faith, where one understands oneself as a sinner, understands that one needs God, sees that a change in heart is necessary, and despairs of doing it on one's own. At the moment of justification God gives saving faith to the believer, and the believer trusts in God for salvation. Various means of receiving this gift are possible. It may come through reading Scripture, through hearing the word of God preached, through the sacraments, through Christian conversation, or in any number of ways. It might even be in combination. But there comes a time when one sees the world differently than before; the change is so radical that the different worldview allows one to say that one is living in a different world. Spiritual senses awaken and give new information that one did not have before. The truths of Scripture that had been meaningless before become real. Thus, this saving faith is well described as building on one's assent to the truth of the gospel attained through trust and reliance on the God described therein, and one's new awareness of the spiritual reality in which one has always lived.

FAITH AND WORKS

In a number of respects, United Methodist doctrine has the logical shape of "Yes, but. . . ." Scripture alone is the authority, but when Scripture is properly interpreted it always involves tradition, reason, and experience. Christians may be given the gift of entire sanctification where they do not sin, but sin will always be a part of every Christian's life. In each of these cases, there is an important ambiguity in one of the key terms. "Scripture" means a set of writings canonized by the church, so the word "our" involves the whole of the Christian church and implies that proper interpretation of Scripture involves the whole church, our whole minds, and all the experiential resources we can bring to bear. The word "sin" has a broader meaning and a narrower meaning for Wesley. The narrow meaning is "an intentional violation of a known law of God," and in this sense of the word entire sanctification is deliverance from the power of sin. In its broader meaning of any violation of any law of God, human beings will always be sinners through ignorance, mistake, or infirmities.

In a similar way, faith is the only necessary condition of justification and sanctification, but good works are also necessary for salvation. Wesley is clear about the first part of this apparently contradictory statement. He says faith "is the condition: none is justified but he that believes; without faith no man is justified. And it is the only condition: this alone is sufficient for justification. Everyone that believes is justified, whatever else he has or has not. In other words: no man is justified till he believes; every man when he believes is justified."[40] Yet Wesley is also clear about the necessity of good works. However, the contradiction is only apparent, because the ambiguity here rests on two senses of "necessity." Speaking strictly, it is only faith that is necessary for salvation. It is immediately necessary. But good works are necessary for a lively faith, and so they are remotely necessary.[41] In other words, salvation requires faith, which in turn requires good works for the continuance of faith. This is made clear in the "Wesleyan Distinctives" section of "Our Doctrinal Heritage":

> Faith is the only response essential for salvation. However, the General Rules remind us that salvation evidences itself in good works. For Wesley, even repentance should be accompanied by "fruits meet for repentance," or works of piety and mercy.
>
> Both faith and good works belong within an all-encompassing theology of grace, since they stem from God's gracious love "shed abroad in our hearts by the Holy Spirit."[42]

188

The distinction between two senses of "necessary" is clarified when one considers what Wesley calls the difference in degree.[43] This relates to whether something is necessary conditionally or unconditionally. Faith is necessary to salvation unconditionally. Good works are necessary only conditionally, that is, if there is time and opportunity. The thief on the cross in Luke 23:39-43 is Wesley's example of this. He believed in Christ and was told "Truly I tell you, today you will be with me in Paradise."[44] This would be impossible if the good works that are the fruit of genuine repentance and faith were unconditionally necessary for salvation. The man was dying and lacked time; his movements were confined and he lacked opportunity. In his case, faith alone was necessary. However, for the vast majority of human beings good works are necessary for continuance in faith because those persons have both the time and opportunity for them.

The General Rules exemplify this in their language, which also follows the "Yes, but . . ." structure. The only requirement for joining the Methodist Societies was "a desire to flee from the wrath to come, and to be saved from their sins." The Rules then articulate something that is necessary to a lively and continuing desire for salvation: "But wherever this is really fixed in the soul it will be shown by its fruits. It is therefore expected of all who continue therein that they should continue to evidence their desire of salvation," by doing no harm, doing good, and attending upon all the ordinances of God.[45]

This is the United Methodist way of resolving the apparent contradiction between Paul and James in the New Testament. Using the example of Abraham, Paul says in Romans 3:28: "Therefore we conclude that a man is justified by faith without the deeds of the law."[46] James, also using the example of Abraham, says, "Ye see then how that by works a man is justified, and not by faith only."[47] Wesley makes two arguments to show that the two authors are really trying to say the same thing. First, he says that James, purposely using the same "phrases, testimonies, and examples" as Paul had used, "refutes not the doctrine of St. Paul, but the error of those who had abused it."[48] Wesley says that James 2:14—"What doth it profit, my brethren, though a man say he hath faith, and have not works? can *that* faith save him?"—is a summary of the verses following.[49] He says that James is talking not about saving faith, but about a person who claims to have faith but really does not:

> It is not, *though he have faith*; but, *though he say he have faith*. Here, therefore, true, living faith is meant: but in other parts of the argument the apostle speaks of a dead, imaginary faith. He does not, therefore, teach that true faith *can*, but that it *cannot*, subsist without works: nor does he oppose faith to works; but that empty name of faith, to real faith working by love. *Can that faith* "which is without works" *save him*? No more than it can profit his neighbour.[50]

United Methodist doctrine thus understands true, saving faith to be the kind that, given time and opportunity, will result in good works. Any supposed faith that does not in fact lead to such behaviors is not genuine, saving faith.

The second argument Wesley mounts in this matter points to an unusual use of "justified." He resolves Paul's and James's differing descriptions of Abraham by using two senses of the word. Wesley says that Paul described Abraham as justified or *accounted righteous* by faith before Isaac was born. He then construes James as pointing to Abraham's being justified or *made righteous* by works when he offered Isaac as a sacrifice on the altar. The problem with this note is that everywhere else Wesley distinguishes justification, the relative change that God does for us, from sanctification, the real change that God does in us.

Wesley is aware that the New Testament writers use the word "justified" in other ways as well. In "Justification by Faith" he notes some Pauline usages that diverge from his strict definitions. He says,

> Indeed the Apostle in one place seems to extend the meaning of the word much farther, where he says: "Not the hearers of the law, but the doers of the law shall be justified." Here he appears to refer our justification to the sentence of the great day. And so our Lord himself unquestionably doth when he says, "By thy words thou shalt be justified"; proving thereby that "for every idle word men shall speak they shall give an account in the day of judgment." But perhaps we can hardly produce another instance of St. Paul's using the word in that distant sense. In the general tenor of his writings it is evident he doth not; and least of all in the text before us,[51] which undeniably speaks, not of those who have already "finished their course," but of those who are

now just setting out, just beginning "to run the race which is set before them."[52]

This text also points to another use of "justification" and its cognates. Wesley held to the doctrine that at the last judgment, believers are justified, that is, acquitted. His note on Matthew 12:37 is crucial: *"For by thy words* (as well as thy tempers and works) *thou shalt* then *be* either acquitted or condemned. Your words as well as actions shall be produced in evidence for or against you, to prove whether you was a true believer or not. And according to that evidence you will either be acquitted or condemned in the great day."[53] At the last day, one is justified again. As always, salvation is by faith. But for this justification works play a greater role because they are part of the evidence whether the person was a believer or not.[54] Again, works are remotely necessary, but because of the increased time and opportunity they are important evidence for determining whether one truly believed or not. Confession X makes this clear: "We believe good works are the necessary fruits of faith and follow regeneration but they do not have the virtue to remove our sins or to avert divine judgment. We believe good works, pleasing and acceptable to God in Christ, spring from a true and living faith, for through and by them faith is made evident."[55]

EVANGELISM AND THE MISSION OF THE CHURCH

The mission statement of the United Methodist Church, to make disciples of Jesus Christ, is described as a process with different stages. The first two relate directly to the doctrine of justification. Part of the Church's mission is to "proclaim the gospel, seek, welcome and gather persons into the body of Christ" and to "lead persons to commit their lives to God through baptism and profession of faith in Jesus Christ."[56] These phrases describe the Church's ministry of evangelism in which the Church seeks out persons who are not believers and shares the good news of Christ with them. Seen in the context of United Methodist doctrine, the phrase "proclaim the gospel" includes the demands of the law, the need for repentance, and the offer of salvation by grace through faith. While many definitions of evangelism exist, a number of them focus on

191

the church's ministry in helping persons receive justification and entry into the Christian life.

"Our Doctrinal History" calls for "doctrinal reinvigoration" with the expected outcome of "fruitful evangelism."[57] A careful understanding of the doctrine of justification will accomplish this by focusing on the saving grace of God, the proper place of human response to that grace, the nature of saving faith, and the role of good works in the way of salvation.

Notes

1. "The Principles of a Methodist Farther Explained," *Works* 9:227.

2. Sermon 44, "Original Sin," §III.3, *Works* 2:184.

3. Sermon 43, "The Scripture Way of Salvation," §I.1, *Works* 2:156.

4. Sermon 43, "The Scripture Way of Salvation," §I.2, *Works* 2:156-57.

5. Discipline, 88.

6. Sermon 43, "The Scripture Way of Salvation," §I.3, *Works* 2:157.

7. Sermon 5, "Justification by Faith," §II.1, *Works* 1:187.

8. Sermon 19, "The Great Privilege of Those that are Born of God," §2, *Works* 1:431-32.

9. Charlotte Elliott, UMH, 357.

10. UMH, 57.

11. *Notes* John 3:16.

12. See Sermon 110, "Free Grace," Sermon 58, "On Predestination," and *Predestination Calmly Considered*.

13. *Notes* 1 Pet. 1:2.

14. For a helpful discussion of Wesley's views in general, see Gunter 1989, 227-66.

15. *Notes* Phil. 2:13. See Sermon 85, "On Working Out Our Own Salvation," *Works* 3:199-209.

16. Maddox 1994, 92, 147-48.

17. For the canons of the Synod of Dort, see Schaff 3:550-97. The canons are given under five heads of doctrine, whose titles are: "Of Divine Predestination," "Of the Death of Christ, and the Redemption of Men thereby," "Of the Corruption of Man, his Conversion to God and the Manner thereof," and "Of the Perseverance of the Saints."

18. *Works* 1:81, footnote 50.

19. John H. Stockton, UMH, 337.

20. Laotian hymn, trans. Cher Lue Vang, UMH, 350.

21. Discipline, 61.

22. Sermon 5, "Justification by Faith," §II.5, *Works* 1:189-90.

23. Sermon 20, "The Lord Our Righteousness," §§II.1-9, *Works* 1:453-57.

24. Sermon 43, "The Scripture Way of Salvation," §I.3, *Works* 2:157-58.

25. See Outler's "Introductory Comment" to Sermon 20, "The Lord Our Righteousness," *Works* 1:445-46, Sermon 43, "The Scripture Way of Salvation," footnote 8, *Works* 2:157-58, and *Works* 1:80-81.

26. Discipline, 61.

27. Discipline, 69.

28. Matthews, 184-246.

29. At this point in the text Wesley inserted a mark referring to the following footnote: "The following part of this paragraph is now added to the sermon formerly preached." The sermon was originally preached January 1, 1733, and this footnote was added for its publication in the second volume of *Sermons on Several Occasions* in 1748.

30. Sermon 17, "The Circumcision of the Heart," §7, *Works* 1:405.

31. Sermon 1, "Salvation by Faith," §I.4, *Works* 1:120.

32. "There is no true faith, that is, justifying faith, which hath not the righteousness of Christ for its object." Sermon 20, "The Lord Our Righteousness," §II.1, *Works* 1:454.

33. In the *Sermons* see Sermon 1, "Salvation by Faith," §§I.4-5, *Works* 1:120-21, Sermon 7, "The Way to the Kingdom," §II.10, *Works* 1:230, and Sermon 18, "The Marks of the New Birth," §§I.2-3, *Works* 1:418.

34. Sermon 7, "The Way to the Kingdom," §I.6, *Works* 1:220.

35. These three citations are KJV.

36. Sermon 43, "The Scripture Way of Salvation," §II.1, *Works* 2:160-61.

37. Sermon 45, "The New Birth," §II.4, *Works* 2:192-93.

38. Sermon 45, "The New Birth," §II.4, *Works* 2:192.

39. Sermon 45, "The New Birth," §II.4, *Works* 2:193.

40. Sermon 43, "The Scripture Way of Salvation," §III.1, *Works* 2:162.

41. Sermon 43, "The Scripture Way of Salvation," §III.2, *Works* 2:162-63.

42. Discipline, 47.

43. The use of "degree" here is somewhat obscure. Wesley has in mind the different levels of intensity. See *The Compact Edition of the Oxford English Dictionary*, 1:674-75, definition 6.

44. NRSV.

45. Discipline, 72-74.

46. KJV.

47. James 2:24, KJV.

48. *Notes* James 2:14. Note that Wesley here includes Hebrews in a list of books written by Paul.

49. This is Wesley's translation of the verse in the *Notes*.

50. *Notes* James 2:14.

51. Rom. 4:5.

52. Sermon 5, "Justification by Faith," §II.5, *Works* 1:190.

53. *Notes* Matt. 12:37.

54. For helpful discussions, see Deschner 177-81, Lindström 205-15, and Maddox 1994, 171.

55. Discipline, 69.

56. Discipline, 88.

57. Discipline, 59.

Chapter Seven

Sanctification, Christian Perfection, and the Last Judgment

Careful attention to Confession XI, supplemented by other authoritative texts, will bring out most of the key points in the United Methodist teaching on sanctification. Three additional subjects—assurance, repentance after justification, and the last judgment—will also be treated. This article says:

> We believe sanctification is the work of God's grace through the Word and the Spirit, by which those who have been born again are cleansed from sin in their thoughts, words and acts, and are enabled to live in accordance with God's will, and to strive for holiness without which no one will see the Lord.
>
> Entire sanctification is a state of perfect love, righteousness and true holiness which every regenerate believer may obtain by being delivered from the power of sin, by loving God with all the heart, soul, mind and strength, and by loving one's neighbor as one's self. Through faith in Jesus Christ this gracious gift may be received in this life both gradually and instantaneously, and should be sought earnestly by every child of God.
>
> We believe this experience does not deliver us from the infirmities, ignorance, and mistakes common to man, nor from the

possibilities of further sin. The Christian must continue on guard against spiritual pride and seek to gain victory over every temptation to sin. He must respond wholly to the will of God so that sin will lose its power over him; and the world, the flesh, and the devil are put under his feet. Thus he rules over these enemies with watchfulness through the power of the Holy Spirit.[1]

SANCTIFICATION BY GRACE THROUGH FAITH

The article starts with the affirmation that sanctification is something God does in persons. Like the rest of salvation, it is by God's grace through human faith. It is logically distinguished from justification in that it is a real change God works in persons. Because sanctification is a real change that results in a greater holiness, it is easy for persons to assume that it is earned by the individual's doing good works. Wesley wants to correct that misinterpretation. He says,

> I have continually testified in private and in public that we are sanctified, as well as justified, by faith. And indeed the one of these great truths does exceedingly illustrate the other. Exactly as we are justified by faith, so are we sanctified by faith. Faith is the condition, and the only condition of sanctification, exactly as it is of justification. It is the condition: none is sanctified but he that believes; without faith no man is sanctified. And it is the only condition: this alone is sufficient for sanctification. Everyone that believes is sanctified, whatever else he has or has not. In other words: no man is sanctified till he believes; every man when he believes is sanctified.[2]

This means, however, that both justification and sanctification are simultaneous. When someone is justified, at the same time one is sanctified, but not entirely sanctified. Whereas justification is an instantaneous change in status, sanctification is a process that goes on for the rest of the person's life. Using the metaphor of the house again, sanctification is living in the house forever, unless one chooses to leave.

SANCTIFICATION AS A PROCESS OF CLEANSING AND GROWTH

At the time of the union of the Methodist Episcopal, Methodist Episcopal South, and Methodist Protestant Churches in 1939, a statement about sanctification from the Methodist Protestant tradition was placed at the end of the Articles of Religion:

> Sanctification is that renewal of our fallen nature by the Holy Ghost, received through faith in Jesus Christ, whose blood of atonement cleanseth from all sin; whereby we are not only delivered from the guilt of sin, but are washed from its pollution, saved from its power, and are enabled, through grace, to love God with all our hearts and to walk in his holy commandments blameless.[3]

Thus, sanctification ought to be understood in conjunction with the creation of humanity in the image of God. Two metaphors are used to explain this process. First, if sin is a disease, sanctification is its cure. By cleansing humanity from its disfigurement, humanity is restored to its original nature. The individual is freed from the power of sin in one's life.

Second, images of growth are also used. In sanctification one grows to be more like Christ. As one becomes more like Christ, the power of sin gradually decreases. More and more the Spirit shapes the believer's faith, hope, and love. The Christian life is one of growing in grace toward perfection in love, until one attains the mind which was in Christ Jesus. Wesley comments on Ephesians 4:12-13:

> Verse 12. In this verse is noted the office of ministers; in the next, the aim of the saints; in the 14th, 15th, 16th, the way of growing in grace. And each of these has three parts, standing in the same order. *For the perfecting the saints*—The completing them both in number and their various gifts and graces. *To the work of the ministry*—The serving God and his church in their various ministrations. *To the edifying of the body of Christ*—The building up this his mystical body in faith, love, holiness.
>
> Verse 13. *Till we all*—And every one of us. *Come to the unity of the faith, and knowledge of the Son of God*—To both an exact agreement in the Christian doctrine, and an experimental knowledge of Christ as the Son of God. *To a perfect man*—To a state of spiritual manhood both in understanding and strength. *To the measure*

of the stature of the fulness of Christ—To that maturity of age and spiritual stature wherein we shall be filled with Christ, so that he will be all in all.[4]

Note that in his comment on verse 13, Wesley rephrases "perfect man" as "spiritual manhood," and then refers to "maturity of age and spiritual stature." Wesley is aware that *teleios* and its cognates, which are usually translated as "perfect," also mean "mature." In the KJV, this can be seen at Hebrews 5:14 where *teleiōn* is translated "full age." This linguistic nuance is made clearer in the NRSV when in a number of places it uses "mature" where the KJV uses "perfect."[5]

Wesley makes it clear in Christian Perfection that there is a gradual process of growth in the Christian life. He says, "But it should be premised that there are several stages in Christian life as well as in natural: some of the children of God being but new-born babes, others having attained to more maturity." He then quotes 1 John 2:12-27 and Ephesians 4:13 to show that the use of "little children," "young men," and "fathers" refers to stages of spiritual growth. It is the last group, people who have "grown up to the measure of the stature of the fullness of Christ," that Wesley was speaking of in his doctrine of Christian perfection. In the original edition of the sermon he claimed that only these were "properly Christians." In the 1750 edition and all those following, he said that only those were "perfect Christians."[6]

Part of the reason for this process of growth is the awareness that God's grace is shaping the human heart. Sanctification is divided into two types of holiness, inward and outward. Wesley's understanding of human psychology was that outward behaviors are the result of inward tempers. Maddox says,

> It is equally important to note that Wesley assumed that these motivating affections were not simply transitory, but can (and should) be habituated into enduring dispositions. . . . He was using "temper" in this connection in a characteristic eighteenth-century sense of an enduring or *habitual* disposition of a person. . . . From the motivating disposition of these tempers would then flow holy words and actions.[7]

Into this framework can be put many of the aspects of sanctification. One's heart is circumcised by God, giving it humility, faith, hope, and love. This is the inward holiness that is the foundation of all else. It is fulfilling the Great Commandments to love God with all that we are and to love our neighbors as ourselves. Sin, which is frequently described by Wesley as "the desire of the flesh, and the desire of the eye, and the pride of life,"[8] diminishes as love increases in our hearts. Sanctification is a process of increasing the virtues and decreasing sinful desires. As the power of sin decreases, one's behaviors improve and inward sin diminishes as well.

This process is a struggle. It does not usually come quickly and it is seldom easy:

> Let us therefore hold fast the sound doctrine "once delivered to the saints," and delivered down by them with the written word to all succeeding generations: that although we are renewed, cleansed, purified, sanctified, the moment we truly believe in Christ, yet we are not then renewed, cleansed, purified altogether; but the flesh, the evil nature, still remains (though subdued) and wars against the Spirit. So much the more let us use all diligence in "fighting the good fight of faith." So much the more earnestly let us "watch and pray" against the enemy within. The more carefully let us "take to" ourselves and "put on the whole armour of God"; that although "we wrestle" both with "flesh and blood, and with principalities and powers, and wicked spirits in high places, we may be able to withstand in the evil day, and having done all, to stand."[9]

It is important to remember that salvation is by grace through faith. Since salvation has two main parts, the cause and condition of our salvation applies to both parts. Thus, we are sanctified as well as justified by grace through faith. Too often modern thought is cast either in terms of a biological model where a creature grows "naturally" on its own, or in terms of human accomplishment where individuals struggle and accomplish their goals through hard work and smart thinking. Instead, this process of sanctification is to be received as a gift from God. The person's acceptance of the gift is faith, and this sets up a cooperation between the Holy Spirit's work in her and her use of that grace which transforms her over time. Wesley describes it as action and re-action:

> From what has been said we may learn, secondly, what the life of God in the soul of a believer is, wherein it properly consists,

and what is immediately and necessarily implied therein. It immediately and necessarily implies the continual inspiration of God's Holy Spirit: God's breathing into the soul, and the soul's breathing back what it first receives from God; a continual action of God upon the soul, and re-action of the soul upon God; an unceasing presence of God, the loving, pardoning God, manifested to the heart, and perceived by faith; and an unceasing return of love, praise, and prayer, offering up all the thoughts of our hearts, all the words of our tongues, all the works of our hands, all our body, soul, and spirit, to be an holy sacrifice, acceptable unto God in Christ Jesus.[10]

The priority of God's grace is clear. In the following paragraph Wesley notes that the human response or "re-action" is necessary for grace to continue.[11]

Charles Wesley's hymns make this divine-human synergy clear:

> O Thou who camest from above,
> the pure celestial fire to impart,
> kindle a flame of sacred love
> upon the mean altar of my heart.
>
> There let it for thy glory burn
> with inextinguishable blaze,
> and trembling to its source return,
> in humble prayer and fervent praise.
>
> Jesus, confirm my heart's desire
> to work and speak and think for thee;
> still let me guard the holy fire,
> and still stir up thy gift in me.
>
> Ready for all thy perfect will,
> my acts of faith and love repeat,
> till death thy endless mercies seal,
> and make my sacrifice complete.[12]

One of the corollaries of the belief that human beings are sanctified by grace through faith is that the believer trusts in four things.[13] The first is that God has in fact promised this in the Scriptures. Wesley's key text here is Deuteronomy 30:6, "And the LORD thy God will circumcise thine heart, and the heart of thy seed, to love the LORD thy God with all thine heart, and with all thy soul, that thou mayest live."[14] The second is that God is able to do it. The third is "that God is able and willing to do it *now*." And the fourth is that God does it and that believers experience the fulfillment of the biblical promises. Wesley then offers a paragraph that has led to a great deal of controversy within the Wesleyan movement, whether sanctification is gradual or instantaneous. He clearly favors the latter. He says,

> "But does God work this great work in the soul *gradually* or *instantaneously*?" Perhaps it may be gradually wrought in some. I mean in this sense—they do not advert to the particular moment wherein sin ceases to be. But it is infinitely desirable, were it the will of God, that it should be done instantaneously; that the Lord should destroy sin "by the breath of his mouth" in a moment, in the twinkling of an eye. And so he generally does, a plain fact of which there is evidence enough to satisfy any unprejudiced person.[15]

Thus, Wesley's reliance on God's omnipotence, God's graciousness, and the strong desire for accomplishing the goal lead him to believe and teach that with God anything is possible. Confession XI, referred to at the start of this chapter, simply states, "this gracious gift may be received in this life both gradually and instantaneously."

Several ways of interpreting this point are possible. One is to stress the gradual progress of the individual in the Christian life, acknowledging that at some single point, all voluntary sin disappears. Thus, entire sanctification is instantaneous because it happened in an instant. At various times in the history of Methodism this instant was presumed to be the moment of death, at which point the soul was cleansed to be welcomed into paradise. However, the holiness movement interpreted Wesley's writings to stress the gracious gift and God's desire to fully save God's people. Thus, the gradual progress to be made was acceptable so long as one was seeking, praying for, and expecting entire, instantaneous sanctification.

NEW BIRTH AS THE FIRST STEP

In the process of sanctification, the new birth is the first step. Being born again happens simultaneously with justification, but is logically distinct from justification because it is something God does in us rather than something that God does for us. He defines it as:

> that great change which God works in the soul when he brings it into life: when he raises it from the death of sin to the life of righteousness. It is the change wrought in the whole soul by the almighty Spirit of God when it is "created anew in Christ Jesus," when it is "renewed after the image of God," "in righteousness and true holiness," when the love of the world is changed into the love of God, pride into humility, passion into meekness; hatred, envy, malice, into a sincere, tender, disinterested love for all mankind. In a word, it is that change whereby the "earthly, sensual, devilish" mind is turned into "the mind which was in Christ."[16]

There is a strong analogy with natural birth. While sanctification is a long process, the new birth is relatively short. Previously he did not see, now he does. Previously he did not have knowledge of God, now he does. Previously he did not desire to hear God's words, now he does. Now he understands and feels the peace and love of God. Even the breathing of a newborn is analogous to the respiration of the born again—grace entering the believer's heart, and prayer and praise going back to heaven.[17] Wesley says that we should not ask for a clear description of how this happens. He interprets John 3:8 as Jesus' warning that human beings cannot know how the Spirit does this. Again, as with the doctrine of the Trinity, Wesley finds the Scripture being clear on the fact, but not the manner.

In "The Marks of the New Birth" Wesley discusses what specific changes God makes in the life of the believer. The first such mark is faith, because it is through faith that we are born again. He claims, as we have seen above, that power over outward sin is conjoined with saving faith and cannot be separated from it, "not for an hour."[18] Peace also comes with faith, the kind of happiness in God that might be present "whether they are in ease or in pain, in sickness or health, in abundance or want."[19] The second mark is hope, by which he means the assurance of present salvation or the witness of the spirit. Thereby those who mourn their sins are comforted, fulfilling the promise of Matthew 5:4.[20] The third and greatest mark is love of God and neighbor. Thus, one knows if one has been born again if these three marks are present.

As he describes these, it sounds as if the new birth is the same as sanctification. Rather, it is more correct to say that it is the entrance into sanctification. It is a part, not the whole:

> When we are born again, then our sanctification, our inward and outward holiness, begins. And thenceforward we are gradually to "grow up in him who is our head." This expression of the Apostle admirably illustrates the difference between one and the other, and farther points out the exact analogy there is between natural and spiritual things. A child is born of a woman in a moment, or at least in a very short time. Afterward he gradually and slowly grows till he attains the stature of a man. In like manner a child is born of God in a short time, if not in a moment. But it is by slow degrees that he afterward grows up to the measure of the full stature of Christ. The same relation therefore which there is between our natural birth and our growth there is also between our new birth and our sanctification.[21]

One of the many difficulties in this doctrine is Wesley's conviction that the new birth happens in a "very short time." His conviction that this is a gift from God and that God can do anything God pleases, allows the possibility that this might happen. But the ways in which the almost instantaneous changes are described make it appear routine that persons who are born again undergo radical change very quickly.

Another problem Wesley addresses is the relationship between the new birth and baptism. He says in the opening section of one sermon, "That these privileges, by the free mercy of God, are ordinarily annexed to baptism (which is thence termed by our Lord in the preceding verse the being 'born of water and of the Spirit') we know; but we would know what these privileges are."[22] In "The New Birth" he is at some pains to recognize first, that the church's liturgy presumes that infants are reborn in the sacrament of baptism. But for adults, it is clear that the sign of the sacrament sometimes is not directly linked to the thing signified, the rebirth.[23] In both "The New Birth" and "The Marks of the New Birth," Wesley argues that simply having been baptized does not make one a Christian. It is possible to sin away the grace given in that sacrament. Everyone needs to be born again to see the kingdom of heaven. This should be contrasted with the United Methodist Church's liturgy for baptism, which says clearly, "Through the Sacrament of Baptism we are initiated into Christ's holy church. We are incorporated into God's mighty acts of salvation and given new birth through water and the Spirit. All this is God's gift, offered to us without price."[24] The resolution "By Water and the Spirit" deals with this tension by teaching,

> Baptism is the sacramental sign of new life through and in Christ by the power of the Holy Spirit. . . . Baptism is the means of entry into new life in Christ (John 3:5; Titus 3:5), but new birth may not always coincide with the moment of the administration of water or the laying on of hands. Our awareness and acceptance of our redemption by Christ and new life in him may vary throughout our lives. But, in whatever way the reality of the new birth is experienced, it carries out the promises God made to us in our baptism.[25]

Hence, the Church teaches that baptism is a sign of the new birth and that God's sacramental promises are fulfilled by faith, whether that fulfillment comes simultaneously or at a later date.

John Newton's hymn "Amazing Grace" conveys the kind of change about which Wesley is speaking:

> Amazing grace! How sweet the sound
> that saved a wretch like me!
> I once was lost, but now am found;
> was blind, but now I see.[26]

A less well-known hymn, but one full of interesting implications, is Charles Wesley's re-telling of the encounter between Jacob and God in Genesis 32:24-32. During the struggle Wesley has Jacob saying he will not give up "till I thy name, thy nature know." He says, "Tell me if thy name is Love." At the crucial turning point he says, " 'Tis Love! 'tis Love! thou diedst for me . . . pure Universal Love thou art." Then comes the healing of Jacob's lameness and the new birth:

> Lame as I am, I take the prey,
> hell, earth, and sin with ease overcome;

I leap for joy, pursue my way,
and as a bounding hart fly home,
through all eternity to prove
thy nature, and thy name is Love.[27]

ASSURANCE AS A NORMAL MARK OF THE NEW BIRTH

One of the normal benefits of this early stage of sanctification is that the believer receives the gift of assurance. Wesley believes there is an objective ground for this because it is something that the Holy Spirit does in the believer's life. In "The Witness of the Spirit, II" he repeats the definition he had given twenty years earlier in the companion sermon:

> But perhaps one might say (desiring any who are taught of God to correct, soften, or strengthen the expression), by "the testimony of the Spirit" I mean an inward impression of the soul, whereby the Spirit of God immediately and directly witnesses to my spirit that I am a child of God, that "Jesus Christ hath loved me, and given himself for me"; that all my sins are blotted out, and I, even I, am reconciled to God.[28]

He expands on this definition to say that the inward impression can be accomplished in a variety of ways, and not necessarily or even usually by an audible voice. We are seeing again Wesley's appeal to the fact and not the manner. The believer knows she has been adopted as a daughter of God. How she received that information she may not know, but its presence is real and must have come from the Holy Spirit.

Wesley's reason for teaching this is the same as his warrant for the doctrine of Christian perfection: "the plain, natural meaning of the text."[29] He takes this to be the obvious meaning of Romans 8:16: "The Spirit itself beareth witness with our spirit, that we are the children of God."[30] Wesley explicitly says that this is not an appeal to experience. Doctrine is established properly on the basis of Scripture, and experience is only brought in to confirm what Scripture teaches. It so happens that, in this case, there is a great deal of experiential evidence to support this interpretation of Scripture, according to Wesley.[31]

What is at stake here is charting a course between formality and fanaticism (which he calls "enthusiasm"). On the one side, Wesley wants to find the power of religion that comes from a confidence in one's salvation. He believes that the experiences of persons who are assured of salvation are truly grounded in the objective operations of the Holy Spirit. On the other hand, he guards against "the wildness of enthusiasm" by claiming that the message of the Spirit is simply that of adoption. There are no grounds here for claims of the Spirit's giving persons other messages or commissions. In fact, the true witness of the spirit is known by the fact that the fruit of love, joy, and peace follow upon it.[32]

Fannie Crosby's hymn puts nineteenth-century words to this gift:

> Blessed assurance, Jesus is mine!
> O what a foretaste of glory divine!
> Heir of salvation, purchase of God,
> born of his Spirit, washed in his blood.[33]

REPENTANCE AFTER JUSTIFICATION

The path of sanctification is not always smooth and steady. In fact, inward sin still remains in the believer's heart and thus there is a struggle to overcome it. When one sins, a kind of repentance is necessary. This repentance is different from the repentance before justification:

> This implies no guilt, no sense of condemnation, no consciousness of the wrath of God. It does not suppose any doubt of the favour of God, or any "fear that hath torment." It is properly a conviction wrought by the Holy Ghost of the "sin" which still remains in our heart, of the φρόνεμα σαρκός, "the carnal mind," which "does still *remain*," as our Church speaks, "even in them that are regenerate" although it does no longer *reign*, it has not now dominion over them. . . . It is a conviction of the tendency of our heart to self-will, to atheism, or idolatry; and above all to unbelief, whereby in a thousand ways, and under a thousand pretences, we are ever "departing" more or less "from the living God."[34]

This repentance is the awareness of continuing sin. The believers have been born again and God is sanctifying them, but there is still a struggle against sin. The big difference here is the lack of condemnation. One is secure in one's relationship to God. Justification is real and is not in any way threatened. Yet, one is grieved over the remaining sin and knows oneself to still need God's forgiveness for this portion of one's life.

Wesley's concluding exhortation to "The Witness of the Spirit, II" is crucial to understanding that sometimes this gift of assurance does not come to believers. His two inferences, taken together, say that the fruit of the Spirit and the witness of the Spirit belong together. If one has the witness but not the fruit, one should not rest until the fruit appear. Conversely, if one has the fruit but not the witness, one should not rest until one gets that sense of assurance that one has been adopted as a child of God:

> If we are wise we shall be continually crying to God, until his Spirit cry in our heart, "Abba, Father!" This is the privilege of all the children of God, and without this we can never be assured that we are his children. Without this we cannot retain a steady peace, nor avoid perplexing doubts and fears. But when we have once received this "Spirit of adoption," that "peace which passes all understanding," and which expels all painful doubt and fear, will "keep our hearts and minds in Christ Jesus." And when this has brought forth its genuine fruit, all inward and outward holiness, it is undoubtedly the will of him that calleth us to give us always what he has once given. So that there is no need that we should ever more be deprived of either the testimony of God's Spirit or the testimony of our own, the consciousness of our walking in all righteousness and true holiness.[35]

In the normal course of the way of salvation, the gift of assurance comes soon after the new birth. Wesley nowhere says it is necessary for salvation. But it is a "privilege" that is to be earnestly desired and sought after.

HOLINESS AND HAPPINESS

Outler calls Wesley's linkage of holiness and happiness "one of Wesley's most consistent themes."[36] In another place he says, "in no less than thirty of his sermons Wesley rings the changes on the theme: *only the holy can ever be truly happy.*"[37] Holiness and happiness were part of God's original intention for humanity in the Garden.[38] As the image of God is restored in sanctification, humanity regains its happiness: "But true religion, or a heart right toward God and man, implies happiness as well as holiness. For it is not only righteousness, but also 'peace and joy in the Holy Ghost.'"[39] Happiness for Wesley is not the superficial sense of pleasure which the word sometimes connotes today. Rather, it is precisely happiness *in God*, which he then describes as peace and joy. When Wesley translated the Beatitudes, we have already noted that he used the word "happy" instead of blessed.[40] He makes the same translation point in his sermons on those texts.[41] His conclusion to the third sermon sums up all of the Beatitudes:

> Behold Christianity in its native form, as delivered by its great Author! This is the genuine religion of Jesus Christ. . . . What beauty appears in the whole! How just a symmetry! What exact proportion in every part! How desirable is the happiness here described! How venerable, how lovely the holiness! . . . This is the *spirit* of religion; the quintessence of it. These are indeed the *fundamentals* of Christianity.[42]

The image of God that is the goal of sanctification truly represents human fulfillment. It is holiness, happiness, righteousness, peace, and joy. It is God's intention for God's highest creation. It is what it means to be truly human.

THE WILDERNESS STATE AND HEAVINESS

The *Sermons* distinguish two different conditions that might occur during the process of sanctification. The wilderness state is equivalent to losing one's salvation. Heaviness is grief that comes because of the trials of life. Wesley suggests that there is a great difference between the two. While heaviness is to be expected, the darkness of the wilderness state is to be avoided at all costs.

The crucial difference between the two spiritual conditions is the presence or absence of faith, love, and joy. In the wilderness state, all three are absent. Those who are caught therein do not have the sure trust and confidence in God that justified them in the first place. Further, they do not love God or neighbor. Consequently, they cannot rejoice and they lack the sense of peace they once had. Further, they then lack power over sin and they sink into bondage. Since the "kingdom of God is . . . righteousness, and peace, and joy in the Holy Ghost,"[43] they have lost the kingdom that was in their hearts. Such a condition can be caused by sins of commission, sins of omission, inward sin, desire, spiritual sloth, ignorance, or temptation.[44] Believers should be aware that they can lose their salvation and backslide into unbelief. Such regression in the way of salvation is not necessary, and Wesley prescribes a number of remedies, each determined by the cause.

Heaviness is a condition that is much more to be expected in the Christian life than is the wilderness state. Working from 1 Peter 1:6, "Wherein ye greatly rejoice, though now for a season, if need be, ye are in heaviness through manifold temptations,"[45] Wesley argues the word for heaviness is better translated as "grieved." Many sources of this sorrow are possible, and all of them are compatible with a clear faith, hope, love, joy, and peace that are part of the Christian life. God permits these trials to attack God's people because such trials tend toward holiness. God does not will the trials. God's will is always for the good of God's children. But God permits the trials to happen knowing that the children will ultimately benefit from them.

Wesley describes the wilderness state as darkness. He says:

> Lastly, if darkness be occasioned by manifold, heavy, and unexpected temptations, the best way for removing and preventing this is—teach believers always to expect temptation; seeing they dwell in an evil world, among wicked, subtle, malicious spirits, and have an heart capable of all evil. Convince them that the whole work of sanctification is not (as they imagined) wrought at once; that when they first believe they are but as new-born babes, who are gradually to grow up, and may expect many storms before they come to the full stature of Christ. Above all let them be instructed, when the storm is upon them, not to reason with the devil, but to pray; to pour out their souls before God, and show him of their trouble.[46]

209

Thus, believers may be kept out of darkness. One method is to teach them to expect difficult times:

> We ought therefore, lastly, to watch and pray, and use our utmost endeavours to avoid falling into darkness. But we need not be solicitous how to avoid, so much as how to improve by heaviness. Our great care should be so to behave ourselves under it, so to wait upon the Lord therein, that it may fully answer all the design of his love in permitting it to come upon us; that it may be a means of increasing our faith, of confirming our hope, of perfecting us in all holiness.[47]

The point here is that progress in sanctification is uneven. So long as genuine faith remains, and from it continue to flow the hope, love, and power over outward sin that conjoin with that faith, the believer is still safe and secure with God. There will be times when things go well and the believer is growing rapidly in faith, hope, and love. There will be other times when "manifold temptations" occur and the person's Christian character is sorely tried. During such trials believers should figure out how to use them as an opportunity for further sanctification.

PERFECTION AS THE GOAL

The ultimate goal of salvation for each person is the restoration of the image of God. Thus, the process of sanctifying grace leads believers to grow toward the point where they are made fully righteous. That state of holiness has been variously described as maturity, perfection, "having the mind which was in Christ Jesus," and entire sanctification. Confession XI focuses on love as the criterion. When believers are "delivered from the power of sin" they can fulfill the Great Commandments of Matthew 22:37-39. When love so motivates the believer that all voluntary actions, both inward and outward, are motivated by the love demanded and promised by this commandment, then the moral image of God has been restored. Wesley believed this was possible in this life by God's grace.

However, there are some limitations and restrictions on what is meant by this doctrine of entire sanctification. It is not primarily concerned with outward sin. Wesley believes that a believer no longer committs outward sin after justification. He focuses on 1 John 3:9, "Whosoever is born of God doth not commit sin." He says of this verse,

> By "sin" I here understand outward sin, according to the plain, common acceptation of the word: an actual, voluntary "transgression of the law"; of the revealed, written law of God; of any commandment of God acknowledged to be such at the time that it is transgressed. But "whosoever is born of God," while he abideth in faith and love and in the spirit of prayer and thanksgiving, not only "doth not," but "cannot" thus "commit sin." So long as he thus believeth in God through Christ and loves him, and is pouring out his heart before him, he cannot voluntarily transgress any command of God, either by speaking or acting what he knows God hath forbidden—so long that "seed" which "remaineth in him" (that loving, praying, thankful faith) compels him to refrain from whatsoever he knows to be an abomination in the sight of God.[48]

When Wesley speaks of sin remaining in the heart but not reigning after justification, he means that remaining sin is not sufficiently strong to lead the person into outward sin.[49]

In "Christian Perfection," Wesley reiterates this by saying that the very least implied in Romans 6:1-18 is freedom from outward sin.[50] He bases his argument on Scripture, saying that only New Testament proofs would count against the plain, obvious meaning of 1 John 3:8-9. After considering several such biblical arguments, he says, "In conformity therefore both to the doctrine of St. John, and to the whole tenor of the New Testament, we fix this conclusion: 'A Christian is so far perfect as not to commit sin.'"[51] While this is the privilege of even "babes in Christ," yet there is a deeper sense of the word "sin" that only mature Christians are freed from. Evil thoughts and evil tempers will affect the newborn Christians, while only those who are "strong in the Lord" are freed from such inward sins.[52] He affirms that Jesus saves us "not only from outward sins, but also from the sins of their hearts; from evil thoughts and from evil tempers."[53] Because of 1 John 4:17, it is to be expected in this life and not merely in the world to come.[54] He treats these as the fulfillment of promises made in Deuteronomy 30:6 and Ezekiel

36:25. Thus, the process of sanctification is gradual freedom from inward sin.

In "Christian Perfection" Wesley acknowledges that there is no perfection that exempts the individual from sin in the broadest sense of the word. Above he defined sin as "an actual, voluntary 'transgression of the law'; of the revealed, written law of God; of any commandment of God acknowledged to be such at the time that it is transgressed."[55] This is the narrow sense of the word, and entire sanctification occurs when no such voluntary transgressions of known laws are committed. However, sin in the broadest sense of the word would cover any violation, whether voluntary or involuntary, of any law of God, whether known or unknown.

Under the broad definition of sin, there is no such thing as sinless perfection for four reasons. First, humanity is not perfect in knowledge. There are things about God (such as *how* the three are one in the Godhead) and things about the world, both in principle and in fact, of which humanity is ignorant. It appears from both Scripture and experience that this will always be so. Second, there is no freedom from mistake. Wesley argues that Christians do not make mistakes in things essential for salvation. But in all other matters, including the interpretation of Scripture, they regularly make mistakes. Third, no human beings can expect to be freed completely from infirmities. By this he means not immoral behaviors over which we have control, but "those which are properly termed 'bodily infirmities,' . . . all those inward or outward imperfections which are not of a moral nature."[56] Fourth, there is no freedom from temptation. In this last category, along with the previous one, Wesley treats the "wandering thoughts" that come into our mind which are not sinful in and of themselves, but can be occasions for sin if we let them be so.[57]

Why does Wesley teach such an uncompromising version of a controversial doctrine? The reason is simply that the Bible says so. He acknowledges that the word "perfect" bothers some; the claim that people can reach perfection bothers others. Wesley asks about such expressions,

> But are they not found in the oracles of God? If so, by what authority can any messenger of God lay them aside, even though all men should be offended? We have not so learned Christ; neither may we thus give place to the devil. Whatsoever God hath

spoken, that will we speak, whether men will hear or whether they will forbear: knowing that then alone can any minister of Christ be "pure from the blood of all men," when he hath "not shunned to declare unto them all the counsel of God."

We may not therefore lay these expressions aside, seeing they are the words of God, and not of man. But we may and ought to explain the meaning of them, that those who are sincere of heart may not err to the right hand or to the left from the mark of the prize of their high calling.[58]

One of Wesley's rules of interpreting Scripture is to "speak as the oracles of God."[59] Thus, Wesley took passages such as Matthew 5:48, Romans 14:17, Philippians 2:5, and Hebrews 12:14 with great seriousness.[60]

Other Christians can also claim to have taken these texts seriously, but Wesley's hermeneutics seeks two things. First, he is looking for the plain, obvious meaning of the text. Second, he has discerned the analogy of faith, which is a grand scheme of doctrine running through the whole of the Bible. That system of doctrine is the way of salvation, and it culminates in the entire sanctification of the believer.

Some of the problem is resolved if the two main ways in which the word "perfection" is used are distinguished. Randy Maddox points out that Wesley's understanding of perfection is not a static concept, but a dynamic one. Maddox distinguishes between "(1) a dynamic conception of perfection as ever-increasing maturity (like the goal of τελειότης in early Greek writers), and (2) a static conception of perfection as unsurpassable attainment (epitomized in the Latin model of Adam as *perfectus est*)."[61] One of the basic themes of Maddox's analysis of Wesley's theology is his integration of Eastern Christianity's therapeutic approach to salvation with Western Christianity's juridical approach.[62] However, Wesley's understanding of perfection is almost totally of the dynamic sort. For him there is no end to the process of growth, and there is no attainable perfection without mistakes, infirmities, ignorance, and temptation. Thus, the best way to interpret Wesley is to use the image of maturity.

Entire sanctification is a gift that will come to persons who continue to grow in the Christian life. It should, in the words of Confession XI, "be sought earnestly by every child of God." It is not however, necessary that everyone attain it. One should seek it "not as something that *must* be, or thou wilt go to hell, but as what *may* be, to lead thee to heaven. Look upon it as the most *desirable* gift which is in all the stores of the rich mercies of God."[63]

Charles Wesley's hymn "Love Divine, All Loves Excelling" gives support. God is here addressed by God's "reigning attribute," the one that defines God's nature most fully.[64] Stanzas two and four say,

> Breathe, O breathe thy loving Spirit
> into every troubled breast!
> Let us all in thee inherit;
> let us find that second rest.
> Take away our bent to sinning;
> Alpha and Omega be;
> end of faith, as its beginning,
> set our hearts at liberty. . . .
>
> Finish, then, thy new creation;
> pure and spotless let us be.
> Let us see thy great salvation
> perfectly restored in thee;
> changed from glory into glory,
> till in heaven we take our place,
> till we cast our crowns before thee,
> lost in wonder, love, and praise.[65]

Candidates for ordination as deacons and elders in The United Methodist Church are asked three questions with respect to this doctrine:

> Are you going on to perfection?
> Do you expect to be made perfect in love in this life?
> Are you earnestly striving after perfection in love?[66]

Several considerations from the above analysis are helpful in developing answers to these questions. First, if one is *not* going on to perfection, where *is* one going? The Wesleyan interpretation is that the goal of human life is to allow God's grace to shape us into the kind of mature human beings God intended us to be. Rather than seeking any goal espoused by the world, Christians seek to be filled with love of God and neighbor. Within United Methodist doctrine, this holiness is the highest form of human happiness. Recognizing sin as the chief obstacle to such love, persons use God's grace to heal their sin and shape them to become more and more like Christ.

Second, the Christian life is a process. Sanctification does not usually happen all at once, although United Methodist doctrine says that it might, since it is a gift from God. Most often God works in persons so that they are changed gradually from natural persons unaware of their sin, to convicted sinners, to justified believers, and finally to entirely sanctified persons. The process is often characterized by struggle and by spiritual highs and lows, but one never totally loses one's faith. Nevertheless, there is no state of grace to which one can attain, from which one cannot fall. There is always the need to watch and pray to keep from falling away from this life of grace.

Third, perfection in the twenty-first century is a much more complicated concept than it was in the eighteenth century, when many of these texts were written. Modern persons now have knowledge of modern psychology, which raises serious questions about human intentions and what constitutes voluntary actions. Persons also have benefit of the discipline of sociology and its understanding of systems and cultures, which often have moral implications. The relationship of social justice to Christian perfection, to be discussed in the next chapter, brings further complications. This leads to a much more complex understanding of sin and how human beings are often unintentionally involved in sinful behaviors. Nevertheless, focusing on Wesley's narrow definition of sin as "a voluntary transgression of a known law of God" allows one to voice the desire of fully hoping to get to the place where all actions are consciously motivated by love. The larger psychological and sociological contexts in which modern persons now live provide even more scope for the mature person to continue growing, even after entire sanctification is received.

The last question posed to ordinands could be put, "Are you earnestly trying to grow up?" Chapter 9 will discuss the means of grace as practices that shape persons' souls and lead them to maturity. Through prayer, Scripture, eucharist, worship, service to the poor, Christian conversation, fasting, and other means of grace we are striving to become better persons and more like Christ.

JUDGMENT, HEAVEN, AND HELL

Under "Basic Christian Affirmations" United Methodist doctrine offers an understanding of the reign of God. It says:

> We pray and work for the coming of God's realm and reign to the world and rejoice in the promise of everlasting life that overcomes death and the forces of evil.
>
> **With other Christians we recognize that the reign of God is both a present and future reality.** The church is called to be that place where the first signs of the reign of God are identified and acknowledged in the world. Wherever persons are being made new creatures in Christ, wherever the insights and resources of the gospel are brought to bear on the life of the world, God's reign is already effective in its healing and renewing power.
>
> We also look to the end time in which God's work will be fulfilled. This prospect gives us hope in our present actions as individuals and as the Church. This expectation saves us from resignation and motivates our continuing witness and service.[67]

There are many rich possibilities of expanding the idea of the reign of God into many other parts of Christian doctrine. As yet, those are not well developed in United Methodist doctrine.[68]

What is clearly dealt with in the other authoritative texts is the idea of a last judgment—heaven and hell. Confession XII says, "We believe all men stand under the righteous judgment of Jesus Christ, both now and in the last day. We believe in the resurrection of the dead; the righteous to life eternal and the wicked to endless condemnation."[69] Given what was said previously in the Confession of Faith about justification and sanctification, the word "righteous" should be interpreted as those who are "accounted righteous" by faith and who have continued in the path of sanctification.

Wesley's sermon "The Great Assize" concerns the end of the world. He brings together a number of biblical texts about the circumstances preceding the last judgment. There is no interest in a chronology here, no effort to pick a date when the world would end.[70] But at the beginning and at the end of the sermon Wesley discusses the earthquakes and other natural disasters predicted in Scripture and the destruction of the earth by fire. He is concerned about how such destruction is possible and speculates that there might be "abundant magazines of fire ready prepared"[71] that would make such a fiery end possible. But it is apparent in the conclusion of the sermon that Wesley's chief interest is in the judgment itself. He says that on the judgment day all persons will give an account of their works. He says:

> And in that day shall be discovered every inward working of every human soul: every appetite, passion, inclination, affection, with the various combinations of them, with every temper and disposition that constitute the whole complex character of each individual. So shall it be clearly and infallibly seen who was righteous, and who unrighteous; and in what degree every action or person or character was either good or evil.[72]

Wesley closes the sermon with a comparison between the trial court then sitting (which was the occasion for the sermon) and the final court. The latter will consider a person's whole life, not just a few actions; it will involve everyone, not just a few accused persons; and there will not be a lack of evidence, for all will be known. Wesley then uses the prospect of a last judgment to encourage his hearers to be holy persons. God wishes all to come to repentance, and thence to faith, and thence to the full image of God.[73]

The same sort of argument is employed in "The Good Steward." There Wesley makes a more extensive analysis of God's inquiry about how the individual has used soul, body, worldly goods, and talents. In this context he makes it clear that the last judgment does not come immediately upon a person's death, but at the end of time.[74] On this day an account of how we have used God's possessions (for all the earth belongs to God) must be rendered. Thus, "there is no employment of our time, no action or conversation, that is purely *indifferent*."[75] Further, there are no works of supererogation, since we can never do more than our duty.[76] This is the same teaching as that of Article XI.[77]

In "The Good Steward" the last judgment involves justification by works. After asking about one's use of soul, body, and worldly goods, Wesley says:

Thy Lord will farther inquire: "Hast thou been a wise and faithful steward with regard to the talents of a mixed nature which I lent thee? . . . Didst thou from thenceforth present thy soul and body, all thy thoughts, thy words, and actions, in one flame of love, as an holy sacrifice, glorifying me with thy body and thy spirit? Then "well done, good and faithful servant! [. . .] Enter thou into the joy of thy Lord!" And what will remain either to the faithful or unfaithful steward? Nothing but the execution of that sentence which has been passed by the righteous Judge; fixing thee in a state which admits of no change, through everlasting ages. It remains only that thou be rewarded to all eternity according to thy works.[78]

There are two justifications where we are accounted righteous. The first in this world is salvation by faith alone. However, if there is time and opportunity good works are necessary to ensure the continuance of faith. Saving faith works. Thus, at the final justification, believers are still saved by faith, but it is the kind of faith that has manifested itself in the works of piety and works of mercy that are so integral to the process of sanctification.[79]

United Methodist doctrine stresses the linkage between salvation in the world to come and salvation in the present world. It does not speculate on when the world will end or what heaven will look like. Rather, it trusts that God's judgment is coming and that we are called to live now with the grace that God has given us, so in the day of judgment we might stand.

Notes

1. Discipline, 69-70.

2. Sermon 43, "Scripture Way of Salvation," §III.3, *Works* 2:163-64.

3. Discipline, 66. Note that this is a contemporary statement not protected by the Restrictive Rules.

4. *Notes* Eph. 4:12-13.

5. See 1 Cor. 2:6, Phil. 3:15, Col. 1:38, Col. 4:12, James 1:4, and Eph. 4:13. At Phil. 3:12, the NRSV has "have reached the goal" where the KJV has "were already perfect." At Gal. 3:3, NRSV uses "ending" where the KJV uses "made perfect."

6. Sermon 40, "Christian Perfection," §II.1-2, *Works* 2:105.

7. Maddox 1994, 69.

8. *Notes* 1 John 2:16. Cf. Sermon 4, "Scriptural Christianity," §I.6, *Works* 1:163-64.

9. Sermon 13, "On Sin in Believers," §V.2, *Works* 1:333-34.

10. Sermon 19, "The Great Privilege of Those that are Born of God," §III.2, *Works* 1:442.

11. Outler says that Wesley uses the hyphen in the word "for emphasis" and

calls attention to the *Oxford English Dictionary*'s citation of this as a pioneer usage, *Works* 1:436, footnote 26.

12. Charles Wesley, "O Thou Who Camest From Above," UMH, 501.

13. Sermon 43, "The Scripture Way of Salvation," §§III.14-18, *Works* 2:167-69.

14. KJV.

15. Sermon 43, "The Scripture Way of Salvation," §III.18, *Works* 2:168-69.

16. Sermon 45, "The New Birth," §II.5, *Works* 2:193-94.

17. Sermon 45, "The New Birth," §II.4, *Works* 2:192-93.

18. Sermon 18, "The Marks of the New Birth," §I.4, *Works* 1:419.

19. Sermon 18, "The Marks of the New Birth," §I.7, *Works* 1:422.

20. Sermon 18, "The Marks of the New Birth," §II.5, *Works* 1:424.

21. Sermon 45, "The New Birth," §IV.3, *Works* 2:198.

22. Sermon 18, "The Marks of the New Birth," §1, *Works* 1:417.

23. Sermon 45, "The New Birth," §§IV.1-2, *Works* 2:196-97.

24. "The Baptismal Covenant I," UMH, 33.

25. BOR, 807.

26. John Newton, "Amazing Grace," UMH, 378.

27. Charles Wesley, "Come, O Thou Traveler Unknown," UMH, 387.

28. Sermon 11, "The Witness of the Spirit, II," §II.2, *Works* 1:287.

29. Sermon 11, "The Witness of the Spirit, II," §III.1, *Works* 1:288. See sermon 40, "Christian Perfection," §II.14, *Works* 2:111 for his appeal to the "plain, natural, obvious meaning."

30. KJV.

31. See Discipline, 46 for a contemporary statement of this doctrine.

32. Sermon 11, "The Witness of the Spirit, II," §V.2, *Works* 1:296.

33. Fannie J. Crosby, "Blessed Assurance," UMH, 369.

34. Sermon 43, "Scripture Way of Salvation," §III.6, *Works* 2:164-65.

35. Sermon 11, "The Witness of the Spirit, II," §V.4, *Works* 1:298.

36. Footnote 18, *Works* 1:185.

37. Footnote 28, *Works* 1:35.

38. Sermon 5, "Justification by Faith," §I.4, *Works* 1:184.

39. Sermon 7, "The Way to the Kingdom," §I.10, *Works* 1:223.

40. *Notes* Matt. 5:1-11.

41. Sermon 21, "Upon Our Lord's Sermon on the Mount, I," §I.2, *Works* 1:475, sermon 22, "Upon Our Lord's Sermon on the Mount, II," §I.1, *Works* 1:488,

42. Sermon 23, "Upon Our Lord's Sermon on the Mount, III," §IV, *Works* 1:530.

43. Rom. 14:17 KJV.

44. Sermon 46, "The Wilderness State," §§I.1-5, *Works* 2:205-8.

45. KJV.

46. Sermon 46, "The Wilderness State," §III.14, *Works* 2:220.

47. Sermon 47, "Heaviness Through Manifold Temptations," §V.4, *Works* 2:235.

48. Sermon 19, "The Great Privilege of Those that are Born of God," §II.2, *Works* 1:436.

49. Sermon 13, "On Sin in Believers," §III.8, *Works* 1:323.

50. Sermon 40, "Christian Perfection," §II.4, *Works* 2:106.

51. Sermon 40, "Christian Perfection," §II.20, *Works* 2:116.

52. Sermon 40, "Christian Perfection," §II.21, *Works* 2:117. Wesley quotes Eph. 6:10 here.

53. Sermon 40, "Christian Perfection," §II.27, *Works* 2:119.

54. Sermon 40, "Christian Perfection," §II.27, *Works* 2:119-20.

55. Sermon 19, "The Great Privilege of Those that are Born of God," §II.2, *Works* 1:436.

56. Sermon 40, "Christian Perfection," §I.7, *Works* 2:103.

57. Sermon 41, "Wandering Thoughts," §IV.7, *Works* 2:136.

58. Sermon 40, "Christian Perfection," §§2-3, *Works* 2:99-100.

59. For discussion of this and the other rules, see Jones, 110-14. The prime statement of the rule is *Notes* 1 Pet. 4:11.

60. Jones notes that an analysis of all 151 of Wesley's sermons shows the last three of these are among Wesley's nine most often quoted verses.

61. Maddox 1994, 180.

62. Maddox 1994, 141-46.

63. Sermon 42, "Satan's Devices," §II.3, *Works* 2:149.

64. *Notes* 1 John 4:8.

65. Charles Wesley, "Love Divine, All Loves Excelling," UMH, 384.

66. Discipline, 203-4.

67. Discipline, 44.

68. For significant help in using the concept of the reign or kingdom of God in understanding evangelism, see Abraham 1989 and Arias.

69. Discipline, 70.

70. See *Notes* on Revelation for his adoption of Bengal's chronology, but without Wesley's taking responsibility for it. He says in the preface to the book, "Every part of this I do not undertake to defend."

71. Sermon 15, "The Great Assize," §III.4, *Works* 1:369.

72. Sermon 15, "The Great Assize," §II.7, *Works* 1:363.

73. Sermon 15, "The Great Assize," §IV.5, *Works* 1:374.

74. Sermon 51, "The Good Steward," §III.1, *Works* 2:292.

75. Sermon 51, "The Good Steward," §IV.2, *Works* 2:297.

76. Sermon 51, "The Good Steward," §IV.3, *Works* 2:297.

77. Discipline, 62.

78. Sermon 51, "The Good Steward," §III.6, *Works* 2:296.

79. For discussions of this point, see Lindström 205-15, Deschner 177-81, and Maddox 1994, 171-72.

CHAPTER EIGHT

SOCIAL JUSTICE AS SANCTIFICATION

The practicality of United Methodist doctrine lies in part in its goal of correct practice of Christianity. The question of what constitutes correct practice is basically the question of sanctification. In one way, it relies on having the right character, "the mind which was in Christ" as Wesley frequently put it.[1] But even having the right character necessitates knowing what is the loving thing to do. As a start, one must follow the specific commandments of Scripture. However, many commandments are general, and Wesley argued that one must use reason and experience to determine how best to fulfill them in particular circumstances.[2] The General Rules were framed as *general* rules, some of which were prefaced by "such as."

In two important respects living a sanctified life in the twenty-first century is significantly more complex than it was in the eighteenth century. Since that time humanity's knowledge of social and political sciences has advanced immeasurably. Rather than taking a particular social or political structure as inevitable, it is now assumed that deep structural changes will occur and inquiries are made about the sorts of consequences associated with anticipated changes. We now know more about the way human societies are structured for both good and evil than was known in the period of time when the Articles, General Rules, *Sermons*, and *Notes* were being composed and edited.

Second, the technological changes that began with the Industrial Revolution have greatly increased humanity's capacity to affect each other and the environment. Ethical questions about nuclear weapons, environmental pollution, cloning, and the allocation of scarce resources arise in ways that were not possible in earlier times. While a number of significant moral principles are clearly applicable to these new situations, there are complexities that make the question, What should Christians do?, much more difficult than before.

Wesley was often found on the leading edge of applying Christian principles to the emerging awareness of social problems in the eighteenth century. While few of these analyses are found in the constitutional standards, they do contain two significant sources. Later United Methodist concern for social justice has grown naturally out of its earlier, Wesleyan roots.[3]

With regard to slavery, Wesley's comment on 1 Timothy 1:10 is compelling: "*Manstealers*—The worst of all thieves, in comparison of whom, highwaymen and housebreakers are innocent. What then are most traders in negroes, procurers of servants for America, and all who list soldiers by lies, tricks, or enticements?" Written in 1755, Wesley's comment is one of the earlier English protests against the social evil of slavery.[4]

Wesley's discussion of the morality of earning a living matters when considering the social implications of individual behavior. Christians are indeed to gain all they can, but there are limits on how they should do this. First, they cannot do so if it hurts their health: "Some employments are absolutely and totally unhealthy— as those which imply the dealing much with arsenic or other equally hurtful minerals, or the breathing an air tainted with steams of melting lead, which must at length destroy the firmest constitution."[5] Written in 1760, this counts as an early call for safe working conditions. Similarly, gaining money cannot hurt our minds or involve sinful activities.

These rules apply not only to the ways Christians treat themselves, but also to the ways they treat their neighbors. They cannot hurt a neighbor "in his substance." Selling goods below the market price, hiring away a neighbor's needed employees, and pawn-

broking are seen as violating this rule.[6] They cannot hurt a neighbor's body, and thus cannot ever sell "spirituous liquors," that is,
distilled alcoholic beverages. Though Wesley acknowledges a possible use in medicine, most of the manufacturers and sellers of these
liquors "murder his Majesty's subjects by wholesale."[7] But medical
practitioners who work for gain and not for the patient's quick cure
are equally guilty. We further cannot hurt their neighbor's soul.
Christians should cease all activities that lead others to sin.

Wesley's limitations on economic activity, while valuable in
and of themselves, lay the theological groundwork for the later
development of the Social Principles. The Preamble to the Social
Principles begins with an affirmation of faith in God and then
continues,

> We acknowledge our complete dependence upon God in birth,
> in life, in death, and in life eternal. Secure in God's love, we
> affirm the goodness of life and confess our many sins against
> God's will for us as we find it in Jesus Christ. We have not always
> been faithful stewards of all that has been committed to us by
> God the Creator. We have been reluctant followers of Jesus Christ
> in his mission to bring all persons into a community of love.
> Though called by the Holy Spirit to become new creatures in
> Christ, we have resisted the further call to become the people of
> God in our dealings with each other and the earth on which we
> live.[8]

The Social Principles teach how Christians should live as new creatures in this complex, modern world. These seek to extend
Christian witness not only to the ends of the earth, but also to "the
depths of our common life and work."[9] The denomination's mission statement acknowledges that part of making disciples of Jesus
Christ is to "send persons into the world to live lovingly and justly
as servants of Christ by healing the sick, feeding the hungry, caring
for the stranger, freeing the oppressed, and working to develop
social structures that are consistent with the gospel."[10] The actions
of pursuing social justice in the world are seen as integral to the
process that began with the proclamation of the gospel, and continues with the invitation into the Christian life and being nurtured
therein.

SOCIAL JUSTICE AS THE WILL OF GOD

United Methodist doctrine thus picks up many biblical themes relating to the well-being of the whole world. Sometimes references are made to the teaching of the prophets in the Old Testament.[11] However, it is the Kingdom (or Reign—the two terms are used interchangeably in United Methodist doctrine) of God that provides the strongest undergirding for the doctrine's understanding of how God's will is applied to all of creation.

Consonant with its practical nature, United Methodist doctrine does not refer to God's reign with much systematic exposition or biblical exegesis.[12] However, three key texts show how fundamental it is for United Methodist teaching. First, in the list of "Basic Christian Affirmations" it is claimed that a recognition of God's reign is central to Christian teaching:

> **With other Christians we recognize that the reign of God is both a present and future reality.** The church is called to be that place where the first signs of the reign of God are identified and acknowledged in the world. Wherever persons are being made new creatures in Christ, wherever the insights and resources of the gospel are brought to bear on the life of the world, God's reign is already effective in its healing and renewing power.[13]

New Testament study for the last century has noted how basic the idea of the reign of God is in the preaching of Jesus as recorded in the Synoptic Gospels.[14] God's reign is both "at hand" and coming, and we find ways in which that reign is made visible or real in the midst of this world. This statement includes both personal transformation and the transformation of the whole world as key signs of God's reign.

When United Methodist doctrine discusses its theological task, a number of crucial problems are delineated as needing special attention. It lists struggles for human dignity, liberation and fulfillment, the perils of nuclear destruction, terrorism, war, poverty, violence and injustice, racism, classism and sexism, and secularism.[15] What is important here is that this list is introduced by this sentence: "Daily we are presented with an array of concerns that challenge our proclamation of God's reign over all of human existence."[16] These problems, which could be listed by secular persons as difficulties currently being faced by human civilization, are given a theological location as threats to the reign of God.

The Church's mission statement also focuses on the reign of God. It says that the proclamation of "the good news of God's grace" thereby seeks "the fulfillment of God's reign and realm in the world."[17] The Church's mission is a response to the reign of God. Its fourfold process includes sending believers out "to live lovingly and justly as servants of Christ," which includes "working to develop social structures that are consistent with the gospel."[18]

These general statements make us mindful that God is aiming at nothing less than the salvation and renewal of all creation. That includes individual human beings, the social structures and institutions that compose human society, and the nonhuman creation. In its teaching the United Methodist Church offers a vision of how that activity of God can best be understood and what actions Christians should take to be a part of God's activity.

Perhaps the strongest ground for ministries of social justice lies in the broad nature of the General Rules themselves. The first two rules are truly general in that they call on Christians to manifest their identity as recipients of God's grace, to avoid evil of every kind, and to do good to all in as many ways as possible. There are no limits on either rule. Thus, when one is aware that high levels of consumption preclude sacrificial giving for the basic needs of others, then the General Rules require curtailment of the former and increase of the latter. When careful analysis then shows that certain government programs help the poor and other programs hurt the poor, the General Rules provide the basis for a radical Christian response in the political arena for the cause of justice in the name of Christ.

SOCIAL JUSTICE AND INDIVIDUAL SANCTIFICATION

In many parts of Protestant Christianity there are forms of privatized Christianity that focus on the salvation of the individual at the expense of social justice. In other places ministries of social justice have become the primary form of Christian witness to the exclusion of evangelistic efforts aimed at individuals.[19] One of the main theses of this study is that United Methodist doctrine holds both of these concerns simultaneously and views them as interdependent:

> Our struggles for human dignity and social reform have been a response to God's demand for love, mercy, and justice in the light of the Kingdom. We proclaim no *personal gospel* that fails to express itself in relevant social concerns; we proclaim no *social gospel* that does not include the personal transformation of sinners.
>
> It is our conviction that the good news of the Kingdom must judge, redeem, and reform the sinful social structures of our time.
>
> *The Book of Discipline* and the General Rules convey the expectation of discipline within the experience of individuals and the life of the Church. Such discipline assumes accountability to the community of faith by those who claim that community's support.[20]

Over a long period of time, the specific teachings of the church have changed to meet specific situations and new challenges. In some areas, the church has repented of its past mistakes and become aware of better ways that Christians should address social issues. But the basic principle that the church must be involved in ministries aimed at both individual transformation and social justice is clear and basic to United Methodist doctrine.

THE SOCIAL PRINCIPLES AS A BODY OF TEACHING

STRUCTURE

The Social Principles have six sections preceded by a preface and preamble, and followed by "Our Social Creed." The Preface details United Methodism's history of concern for social justice and describes the nature of the Social Principles. The Preamble and the opening paragraphs of each of the six main sections discuss the theological principles that underlie the whole document. Each section then discusses United Methodist teaching on particular topics. The Social Creed is a brief attempt at recapitulating some of the main teachings in a form that can be used liturgically by an entire congregation. The concluding sentence suggests that it be used frequently in worship services.

The topics of the six sections are intended to be comprehensive teaching about the whole of creation. The first section talks about humanity's relationship to the natural world. The following five sections discuss various aspects of Christian community. "The Nurturing Community" discusses issues related to family life, sexuality, birth, and death. "The Social Community" considers how persons are treated in social settings. "The Economic Community" looks at issues of property, work, corporations, and other forms of economic activity. "The Political Community" discusses governmental issues, including basic freedoms and crime. "The World Community" looks at international issues.

For good reason these categories are not discrete; each section has aspects that overlap with other sections. Topics such as "sustainable agriculture" and "rural life" are treated in the social section, and family farms are treated in the economic section. Such interrelationships are unavoidable because so many of these issues are deeply intertwined.

Four Characteristics

The Preamble to the Social Principles notes, "The United Methodist Church has a long history of concern for social justice."[21] Among its predecessor denominations, The Methodist Episcopal Church in 1908 became the first to adopt a social creed.[22] Both The Methodist Church and The Evangelical United Brethren Church had statements at the time of their union in 1968. The 1968 General Conference formed a commission to write a new statement that was considered, revised, and adopted at the 1972 General Conference.[23] Since that time, each General Conference has amended the statement with regard to particular issues. However, large segments as well as the overall structure remain unchanged since the 1972 statement. Four significant aspects of the Social Principles give a sense of its general character.

Theological Grounding

The Preamble and the introductory paragraphs of each of the six sections give the theological rationale underlying the principles in the document. The Preamble affirms faith in the triune God and acknowledges dependence upon God and God's love. It then says,

> Secure in God's love, we affirm the goodness of life and confess our many sins against God's will for us as we find it in Jesus Christ. We have not always been faithful stewards of all that has been committed to us by God the Creator. We have been reluctant followers of Jesus Christ in his mission to bring all persons into a community of love. Though called by the Holy Spirit to become new creatures in Christ, we have resisted the further call to become the people of God in our dealings with each other and the earth on which we live.[24]

Thus, all of the specific principles in the following sections are each put in the context of faith in God, our sinful rebellion against God's will, and the guiding work of the Holy Spirit helping God's people to become fully what God has called us to be. The connection between the Social Principles and the overall structure of the way of salvation contained in United Methodist doctrine becomes apparent.

Within the individual sections the relationship between the theological principles and specific conclusions is less clear. General theological principles are clearly given for each section. The theological principle underlying the statements in "The Nurturing Community" emphasizes human fulfillment. It says,

> The community provides the potential for nurturing human beings into the fullness of their humanity. We believe we have a responsibility to innovate, sponsor, and evaluate new forms of community that will encourage development of the fullest potential in individuals. Primary for us is the gospel understanding that all persons are important—because they are human beings created by God and loved through and by Jesus Christ and not because they have merited significance.[25]

The theological principles of God's universal love, God's desire for the fulfillment of each person, and the role that the community plays in nurturing such growth are clearly expressed here. Partly because of the way in which the text has been revised in the midst of heated controversies over the last twenty-eight years, the connections between the theological rationale and specific positions is sometimes unclear. In this section, the statement then jumps from these principles to the claim that "divorce does not preclude a new marriage," "sexual relations are only clearly affirmed in the marriage bond," and "although we do not condone the practice of homosexuality and consider this practice incompatible with Christian teaching, we affirm that God's grace is available to all."[26] These passages have been among the most hotly debated and contested portions of ¶161. As Allen notes, different understandings of the nature of God's love and the shape of human fulfillment lead to very different conclusions on divorce, remarriage, premarital sex, and homosexual practice.[27] A more explicit connection between the doctrinal standards and the specific positions advocated would make the theological grounding of the Social Principles more clear.

Comprehensive Statements

Thomas Frank reviews the Social Principles and calls them "comprehensive statements encompassing many dimensions of human life."[28] Despite criticisms that they are too broad, he says, "Yet the Principles implicitly claim that no area of life is outside God's care and therefore none is outside the church's witness to God's intentions for the world. This places the church fully in contact with the 'common life and work' of human beings everywhere."[29] The Principles are clearly comprehensive in their framework, and Frank's interpretation of their intent is correct. The document is intended to apply to all universally. The same principles must be followed regardless of which country or society is being discussed.[30] While the Social Principles cannot address every specific issue, they seek to bring the gospel to bear on all of the major categories of social life. Within these categories, it addresses the specific issues that are most pressing at the time. They are comprehensive in seeking to address all aspects of Christian witness about God's intention for the creation. In specifics, however, they tend to give attention to the issues seen as most significant for the contemporary situation. Thus, since 1972 new sections have been added covering such topics as energy resource utilization, food safety, sexual harassment, sustainable agriculture, media violence and Christian values, and corporate responsibility. As new situations and issues have arisen, or new insights have been achieved, new principles have been added.

Social Issues

The issues dealt with in this document apply most directly to considerations of how a community should order its life. First and foremost, it addresses those issues which apply to the structure of human community. Concerns about pollution, health care, racism, alcohol and drug use, labor relations, and war all must be addressed to entities larger than the individual. The proposed solutions address policies to be pursued and actions to be taken by societies in their various manifestations. In some cases, these are governments of cities, states, and nations. In other cases, the agents being addressed are corporations, institutions, or other organized groups. In some instances the agents are not specified, and a general term like "society" is used to convey that all persons, both individually and collectively, should follow a certain course of action.

The distinction between "personal" issues and "social" issues is not always clear. Indeed, specific actions are advocated for individuals to take in many of these areas. Abstinence from alcohol and tobacco, having sexual intercourse only within marriage, treating pets and farm animals humanely, and limiting personal consumption are all steps that an individual can take to follow God's will more closely. On other issues—such as participating in recycling programs, civil disobedience to unjust laws, or advocacy for affirmative action to remedy racism and sexism—individual actions can be seen as contributing to social and political movements with much larger consequences.

Emphasis on Human Rights

Each of the six substantive sections has at least one reference to someone's rights. The language about rights is most prevalent in the section on the social community, which also provides theological grounding for the concept. It argues that, in God's sight, all persons are equally valuable: "We therefore work toward societies in which each person's value is recognized, maintained, and strengthened."[31] The rights that are bestowed on, or withheld from, certain persons by a society indicate "the relative esteem" in which those persons are held. In some places these are collectively referred to as "human and civil rights."[32] The statement also encompasses the assertion of specific rights: housing, education, employment, medical care, legal redress for grievances, physical protection,[33] right to know the content of foods,[34] right to full participation in the church,[35] right to organize for collective bargaining,[36] right to a job at a living wage,[37] right to possess property, right to earn a living by tilling the soil,[38] right to free and fair elections, freedom of speech, religion, assembly, communications media, petition for redress of grievances without fear of reprisal, right to privacy, guaranteed rights to adequate food, clothing, shelter, education, health care,[39] and the right and duty of all nations to determine their own destiny.[40]

The resolution "Globalization and Its Impact on Human Dignity and Human Rights" gives a theological rationale for supporting the struggle for human rights, grounding it in human dignity, which "is the image of God in each human being."[41] However, other options such as talking about covenant and the reign of God might be considered as alternatives or supplementary approaches. In the sections on abortion and on dying (two issues where in American culture there is a great deal of talk about rights) there is no mention of the rights of various individuals involved, though within sizable segments of American culture the rights of the individual are believed to matter a great deal. Yet, language based on human rights is a common ethical approach in interfaith dialogues and international deliberations. By taking a stand in support of human rights, United Methodist doctrine indicates that Christian moral values intersect with the moral values of non-Christian groups.

THE MESSAGE OF THE SOCIAL PRINCIPLES AND RESOLUTIONS

The vision that the Social Principles and BOR hold is clearly stated in the opening paragraph of the Section VI, "The World Community." It says, "We commit ourselves as a Church to the achievement of a world community that is a fellowship of persons who honestly love one another. We pledge ourselves to seek the meaning of the gospel in all issues that divide people and threaten the growth of world community."[42] In terms of the way of salvation described in the doctrinal standards, the Social Principles are guidelines for sanctified living that moves toward a restored and sanctified creation.

In this body of principles, the importance of love, justice, liberation, and human fulfillment are clear. In a sense, the first two of the General Rules—"doing no harm, by avoiding evil of every kind, especially that which is most generally practiced," and "doing good; by being in every kind merciful after their power; as they have opportunity, doing good of every possible sort, and, as far as possible, to all"[43]—have been expanded to cover a wider range of moral issues than were considered in the eighteenth century. Yet, the underlying purpose is to respond to the love of God and God's gracious gift of the Kingdom by being faithful witnesses to God's intention for all of creation, "to the depths of our common life and work." The principles advocated on seven key issues can illustrate this general theme.

Environmental Justice

Both the Social Principles and the BOR are clear that we face an ecological crisis. Pollution, waste disposal, global warming, extinction of animal species, and overpopulation are among the signs to which these texts point us. The resolution "Environmental Justice for a Sustainable Future" suggests that we have misinterpreted Genesis 1:28 and forgotten that God's covenant is with all creation.[44] It focuses on the concept of "sustainability" as the key "to achieve social, economic, and ecological justice for all of creation."[45] Specific steps regarding the atmosphere, earth, water, and energy are outlined along with action ideas for many different groups within the United Methodist Church.

Sexism

The BOR notes that "sexism continues to be a pervasive and systemic force within our church and our society" and it "deprives the church and society of the opportunity to use the skills and talents that women have."[46] The Social Principles address this issue in sev-

eral places, saying "we affirm with Scripture the common humanity of male and female, both having equal worth in the eyes of
God."[47] Within the social community, it strongly affirms the rights
of women to equal treatment and advocates the elimination of sex-
role stereotypes. Affirmative action is supported.[48] The resolution
"The Status of Women" grounds this position theologically in the
practice of Jesus, who resisted the cultural patterns of male preference and dominance current in his time. Appealing to love for God
and neighbor as "the central theme of Jesus' teaching," it says, "To
regard another as an inferior is to break the covenant of love; denying equality demeans, perpetuates injustice, and falls short of the
example of Jesus and the early church."[49] The resolution goes on to
address concerns about the status of women in many different cultures. As United Methodists sing the third stanza of "In Christ
There Is No East or West," they find:

> In Christ is neither Jew nor Greek,
> and neither slave nor free;
> both male and female heirs are made,
> and all are kin to me.[50]

Nowhere does United Methodist doctrine deal with the exegetical issues that allow Scripture to be used to exclude women from
ordained ministry and leadership in the church and to argue for the
superiority of men over women. However, the position of the
United Methodist Church in favor of women's equality is clear, and
the appeal to Matthew 22:34-40 and the inclusive practice of Jesus
indicate some possible ways to deal with those biblical passages
that have been used to perpetuate the exclusion and subordination
of women.

Racism

As noted above, the United Methodist concern with racism goes
back to Wesley's effort to witness against slavery in the eighteenth
century. The Methodist Episcopal Church split over the issue of slavery and gave rise to three predominantly black Methodist denominations and others who broke off because they disagreed with the

denomination's teachings or practices. For many years segregation was practiced in the denomination, including the formation of separate annual conferences and a jurisdiction for African Americans. Since 1968, the United Methodist Church has had the following language as part of its constitution: "In The United Methodist Church no conference or other organizational unit of the Church shall be structured so as to exclude any member or any constituent body of the Church because of race, color, national origin, status, or economic condition."[51] Similar language exists to ensure inclusiveness in worship, programming, and membership.

The Social Principles define racism and distinguish between personal racism and institutional racism. They then say, "Racism plagues and cripples our growth in Christ, inasmuch as it is antithetical to the gospel itself. White people are unfairly granted privileges and benefits that are denied to persons of color. Therefore, we recognize racism as sin and affirm the ultimate and temporal worth of all persons."[52] Of the many evils addressed in the Social Principles, only racism is specifically labeled as sin.[53]

The resolution "A Charter for Racial Justice Policies in an Interdependent Global Community" lists eight beliefs that theologically ground the Church's opposition to racism, beginning with the belief "that God is the Creator of all people and all are God's children in one family"; and "that racism is a rejection of the teachings of Jesus Christ."[54] It then says the church is committed in word and deed "to struggle for the rights and the self-determination of every person and group of persons." This is followed by eight steps to be taken by the denomination as a whole and by its congregations and members.[55]

"Racism—A Violation of Human Rights" gives extended consideration to the pervasiveness of racism around the world and its interactions with other systemic evils. Among its recommendations is the call for the United Methodist Church "to support public and corporate policies designed to eliminate racism and to redress its past and present effects."[56]

ALCOHOL AND (OTHER) DRUG ABUSE

Among the immoral practices specifically prohibited in the General Rules is drunkenness and the consumption or sale of "spirituous liquors" ("unless in cases of extreme necessity").[57] The Social Principles go farther and affirm abstinence from alcohol and all illegal drugs. It is said that the use of these drugs "is a major factor in crime, disease, death, and family dysfunction."[58] The resolution "Drug and Alcohol Concerns" says "The United Methodist Church bases its recommendation of abstinence on critical appraisal of the personal and societal costs in the use of alcohol."[59] The relationship between the recommended position of abstinence, the General Rules restriction to distilled liquor, and the Bible's references to wine are not clarified. The moral ramifications of using other drugs, including tobacco, marijuana, and legal pharmaceuticals, are also discussed in the Social Principles. The benefits of therapeutic drug use are also noted.

MATERIALISM AND POVERTY

Wesley's sermons "The Use of Money" and "The Good Steward" lay the groundwork for United Methodist concern about how Christians should treat the material goods they receive. Wesley's three rules, "gain all you can, save all you can, give all you can," are an easy way to remember his approach.[60] "The Good Steward" makes clear that all are accountable to God for the proper use of our souls, bodies, and worldly goods.[61] The Social Principles teach the importance of work that contributes to the common good and that is done in safe conditions. Consumption that serves to enhance the quality of life without exploiting persons or hurting the environment is discussed.[62]

The Social Principles also address the issue of poverty. They say the Church "do[es] not hold poor people morally responsible for their economic state," and suggests a number of policies that might alleviate the problem.[63] The resolution "Principles of Welfare Reform" grounds this concern in "a divine mandate to side with and protect the poor."[64] It notes the connections between poverty and "biased assumptions about race, gender, and class that feed hostile social stereotypes about people living in poverty and suspicions that people with perspectives other than our own are either indifferent or insincere."[65] It then lists seven principles of welfare reform. The hymn "Here I Am, Lord" gives voice to God's concern:

I, the Lord of wind and flame,
I will tend the poor and lame,
I will set a feast for them.
My hand will save.
Finest bread I will provide
till their hearts be satisfied.
I will give my life to them.
Whom shall I send?[66]

The refrain "Here I am Lord, Is it I Lord? I have heard you calling
in the night. I will go Lord, if you lead me, I will hold your people
in my heart" gives voice to the Christian's desire to be a part of
God's ministry with the materially least fortunate of God's human
creatures.

WAR AND PEACE

In the Social Principles, issues of war and peace are treated most
fully in ¶¶ 164G and 165C. In both places war is condemned and
peaceful means of settling international disputes are urged. The
resolution "The United Methodist Church and Peace" notes the
interrelationships between disarmament, democracy and freedom,
strengthening the United Nations, just systems of world trade and
economic development, and ending military conscription. It says
all of these must "be dealt with concurrently in a quest for lasting
peace in a world community."[67] At the same time another resolution "honors, supports, and upholds in our prayers those men and
women who serve in our armed services."[68] The hymn "Let There
Be Peace on Earth" gives vocal expression to this desire as does
another hymn which asks God to "cure thy children's warring
madness."[69]

GLOBAL CULTURAL DIVERSITY

The Social Principles witness to God's plan that the world
should be a community of persons who "honestly love one
another." They emphasize that no one nation is the ideal, saying,

"As individuals are affirmed by God in their diversity, so are nations and cultures. We recognize that no nation or culture is absolutely just and right in its treatment of its own people, nor is any nation totally without regard for the welfare of its citizens."[70] This affirmation of diversity seeks to acknowledge that God is at work in all of the nations. The hymn "This Is My Song" professes a love for one's own country but acknowledges that God is God of all the nations, singing "a song of peace for their land and for mine."[71] The resolution "Globalization and Its Impact on Human Dignity and Human Rights" calls for a "counter-globalization" that will bring a culture of peace with justice in visible and tangible ways. "We are challenged to globalize an ethos that repects and protects human life with human rights so that all "may have life, and have it abundantly" (John 10:10*b*) as God intends."[72]

THE GOAL OF SANCTIFICATION

One of Charles Wesley's hymns gives voice to the desire for sanctification. Justified believers are given a purpose in their lives, which is making their souls ready for heaven. Seen from the perspective of the twenty-first century, this hymn's charge to serve the present age includes being a part of God's action for universal justice and human fulfillment.

> A charge to keep I have,
> a God to glorify,
> a never-dying soul to save,
> and fit it for the sky.
>
> To serve the present age,
> my calling to fulfill;
> O may it all my powers engage
> to do my Master's will!
>
> Arm me with jealous care,
> as in thy sight to live,
> and oh, thy servant, Lord, prepare
> a strict account to give!

Help me to watch and pray,
and on thyself rely,
assured, if I my trust betray,
I shall for ever die.[73]

Notes

1. Even though it is outside of United Methodist doctrine, Wesley's *Character of a Methodist* is a helpful summary of how he saw this side of sanctification. See *Works* 9:31-46.

2. See Sermon 37, "The Nature of Enthusiasm," §24, *Works* 2:55. For a discussion of how reason supplements Scripture, see Jones, 77-78.

3. See Marquardt for an insightful and thorough analysis of Wesley's position on these issues. Jennings and Smith both have important points to make on economics and slavery respectively.

4. His protests become more public and focused with his 1774 publication of *Thoughts Upon Slavery, Works* (J) 11:59-79.

5. Sermon 50, "The Use of Money," §I.1, *Works* 2:269.

6. Ibid., §I.3, *Works* 2:271.

7. Ibid., §I.4.

8. Discipline, 96.

9. Discipline, 96.

10. Discipline, 88.

11. See for example, BOR, 282, 286, 292, 501, 503, 509, and 518.

12. One should note Wesley's writings outside of the Standards Sermons that are helpful here: Sermon 59, "God's Love to Fallen Man," *Works* 2:422-35, Sermon 62, "The End of Christ's Coming," *Works* 2:471-84, and Sermon 63, "The General Spread of the Gospel," *Works* 2:485-99.

13. Discipline, 44.

14. Abraham 1989, 21-23. Klaiber, 29-74.

15. Discipline, 83.

16. Discipline, 83.

17. Discipline, 87.

18. Discipline, 88.

19. For a description of the development of this phenomenon within white, Protestant, North American Christianity around the beginning of the twentieth century, see Schmidt and Marsden.

20. Discipline, 49.

21. Discipline, 95.

22. For the historical context, see Hopkins and Handy.

23. For a brief accounting of the process, see Allen.

24. Discipline, 96.

25. Discipline, 98.

26. Discipline, 100-101.

27. Allen, 35.

28. Frank, 137.

29. Ibid. The quote is from the Preamble, Discipline, 96.

30. Frank 137, suggests they are "American in orientation." The selection of issues addressed may well emphasize those most currently debated in the United States. Other issues, such as plural marriages, that are pressing in other countries are ignored. However, the formulation of solutions clearly intends that the same principles be applied in every cultural situation. Thus, if the Church teaches that something is wrong for the United States, it is wrong in every place where the morally relevant conditions are the same.

31. Discipline, 104.

32. Discipline, 101.

33. Discipline, 104.

34. Discipline, 98.

35. Discipline, 112.

36. Discipline, 113.

37. Discipline, 114.

38. Discipline, 116.

39. Discipline, 116.

40. Discipline, 120.

41. BOR, 711-12.

42. Discipline, 120.

43. Discipline, 73.

44. BOR, 77-78.

45. BOR, 79.

46. BOR, 159.

47. Discipline, 100.

48. Discipline, 106.

49. BOR, 460.

50. UMH, 548. This stanza, written by Laurence Hull Stookey in 1987, was substituted for a stanza in the 1913 hymn by John Oxenham that used noninclusive language.

51. Discipline, 22.

52. Discipline, 104.

53. The word "sins" also appears in the preamble and in "Our Social Creed," but, except for ¶162A, it is not otherwise used in the Social Principles.

54. BOR, 383.

55. BOR, 383-84.

56. BOR, 399.

57. Discipline, 73.

58. Discipline, 107.

59. BOR, 200.

60. Sermon 50, "The Use of Money," *Works* 2:263-80.

61. Sermon 51, "The Good Steward," *Works* 2:281-98.

62. Discipline, 114.

63. Discipline, 115.

64. BOR, 379.

65. BOR, 380.

66. "Here I Am, Lord," Daniel Schutte, UMH, 593.
67. BOR, 788.
68. BOR, 634.
69. UMH, 431, 577.
70. Discipline, 120.
71. UMH, 437.
72. BOR, 711.
73. UMH, 413.

CHAPTER NINE

MEANS OF GRACE

MEANS OF GRACE IN THE CHRISTIAN LIFE

In the previous six chapters we have examined United Methodist teaching on the triune God, the authority of Scripture, anthropology, and the way of salvation. The point has repeatedly been made that true religion, the religion of Jesus Christ, has as its end the restoration of all God's creation to the state God originally intended. For humanity, this means moving toward having "the same mind . . . that was in Christ Jesus,"[1] the perfect love that fills the soul and thereby guides all our intentional words, thoughts, and deeds. This salvation is a gift from God, given by grace, and accepted by faith.

In United Methodist doctrine it is crucial to understand that this goal of religion governs everything else. Religion will describe a variety of practices that allow individuals and communities to experience God's grace, be transformed by it, and be nurtured toward the goal. But Wesley contends that all of these means are subordinate to the end. He notes that what the world calls "religion" corresponds to the practices mandated by the General Rules. Doing good, avoiding evil, attending worship, and partaking in the sacraments are all part of the outside, formal aspect of religion. Of the person who "hungers after God," Wesley says,

> He wants a religion of a nobler kind, a religion higher and deeper than this. He can no more feed on this poor, shallow, formal thing,

than he can "fill his belly with the east wind." True, he is careful to abstain from the very appearance of evil. He is zealous of good works. He attends all the ordinances of God. But all this is not what he longs for. This is only the outside of that religion which he insatiably hungers after. The knowledge of God in Christ Jesus; "the life that is hid with Christ in God"; the being "joined unto the Lord in one Spirit"; the having "fellowship with the Father and the Son"; the "walking in the light as God is in the light"; the being "purified even as he is pure"—this is the religion, the righteousness he thirsts after. Nor can he rest till he thus rests in God.[2]

These practices are means to the end, not the end itself. In another place Wesley says that the "weightier matters of the law," "faith, mercy, and love of God; holiness of heart; heaven opened in the soul" are the main things.[3]

Wesley's context must be kept in mind when evaluating these statements. He is preaching to a nominally Christian nation where morality and the "ordinances of God" were generally agreed upon in principle. However, they were not being practiced at all by some persons, and were being practiced as ends in themselves by many others. Hence Wesley points to the goal of religion, which is holiness of heart and life. His message emphasizes that it comes by grace through faith. But even that faith is a result of human cooperation with God's grace, which initiates the whole way of salvation.

The crucial issue then is how God reaches people with this grace. Prevenient grace is given to everyone, so that is not the issue. For those who seek justifying and sanctifying grace, where do they find it? God is sovereign and thus can offer grace to human beings in an unlimited variety of ways. It is possible to construe creation itself as a means of God's saving grace, at least insofar as God's self-revelation is a gracious act. Thus, when persons draw close to God through experiences of natural beauty or scientific wonder they can describe God's grace as touching their lives. Psalm 8, Romans 1:20, and stanzas 1 and 2 of the hymn "How Great Thou Art"[4] all acknowledge that God's creation is a means of knowing God and experiencing God's grace.

Wesley believes that God has ordained certain ways in which human beings can reliably receive God's grace. People who are seeking salvation may find it in a variety of ways. But the best way to experience God's mercy, forgiveness, and love is to use the normal ways God has established. He writes that those who are pure in heart see God in all things. He continues,

> But in a more especial manner they see God in his ordinances. Whether they appear in the great congregation to "pay him the honour due unto his name, and worship him in the beauty of holiness"; or "enter into their closets" and there pour out their souls before their "Father which is in secret"; whether they search the oracles of God, or hear the ambassadors of Christ proclaiming glad tidings of salvation; or by eating of that bread and drinking of that cup "show forth his death till he come" in the clouds of heaven. In all these his appointed ways they find such a near approach as cannot be expressed. They see him, as it were, face to face, and "talk with him as a man talking with his friend"—a fit preparation for those mansions above wherein they shall "see him as he is."[5]

These ordinances are called the means of grace. While Wesley emphasizes that these means of grace were not ends in themselves, he still emphasizes that they should be used. In the same section where he points to the "weightier matters of the law," he tells his reader that one should follow these ordinances.[6]

The place where Wesley most clearly discusses this matter is in the sermon "The Means of Grace."[7] Wesley starts with a text from Malachi 3:7, "Ye are gone away from mine ordinances, and have not kept them." The sermon is not an exposition of the situation that Malachi originally addressed, but instead asks the question whether there are any ordinances in the Christian dispensation. Wesley notes that while many had abused the ordinances, seeing them as ends in themselves and not using them in the right way, there were also those who now despised the ordinances as a kind of overreaction against the former group. Wesley's purpose in this sermon is to suggest a middle way. To define his subject he says, "By 'means of grace' I understand outward signs, words, or actions ordained of God, and appointed for this end—to be the *ordinary* channels whereby he might convey to men preventing, justifying, or sanctifying grace."[8] He uses this terminology because of its usage in the Christian church, particularly the Catechism in the

BCP of the Church of England where a sacrament is described as "an outward sign of inward *grace,* and a *means* whereby we receive the same."[9] He lists the three chief means of grace as prayer, searching the Scripture, and receiving the Lord's Supper. At the end of the sermon he describes how God ordinarily uses these means to bring sinners to salvation. Something awakens them, they listen to sermons, search the Scripture, talk about the things of God, pray, partake of the Lord's Supper, and continue doing all of these things until they reach salvation.[10]

Wesley's treatment of the Lord's Supper comes under the category of the means of grace. He does not list baptism in the places where the means of grace are discussed, but two possible reasons account for that.[11] First, Wesley could presume that most of his hearers were baptized. Thus, the issue for them was the relationship between baptism and the new birth that he strongly advocated.[12] Henry Knight suggests, "The most obvious reason for these omissions is practical: baptism was a onetime initiatory event, and thus had no further role to play in the ongoing life of the Christian."[13]

Second, Wesley could presume the existence of the Church of England as the main context for his work. Most of his hearers were baptized members of the established church, however much they practiced. Others were associated with Dissenting congregations. His movement was not a church in and of itself, but was a society within the Church of England that did not seek to compete with its mother church's liturgical and sacramental activities.[14]

The United Methodist Church understands the church to be a means of grace. As will be shown below, the definitions of the church given in the Articles and Confession are directly related to liturgical activities. The Resolution "By Water and the Spirit" makes this clear:

> Divine grace is made available and effective in human lives through a variety of means or "channels," as Wesley called them. While God is radically free to work in many ways, the church has been given by God the special responsibility and privilege of being the body of Christ which carries forth God's purpose of redeeming the world. Wesley recognized the church itself as a means of grace—a grace-filled and grace-sharing community of faithful people.[15]

Thus, while the church does not show up on any of Wesley's lists as a means of grace, it should be construed as the pre-eminent means that God has established in order to accomplish God's purposes. All of Wesley's teaching about the means of grace presumes that the church itself is the channel through which most of those means, and certainly the sacraments, come to people. Grace is in no way limited to the church, and yet the church is what God has chosen as the ordinary way in which to convey grace to the world.

It is useful to understand that Wesley calls these means of grace "instituted" because they were commanded by Christ.[16] Words like "appointed," "ordained," and "ordinance" are frequently used in the *Sermons* and *Notes* to indicate that some Christian practices are given by Christ as ordinary channels through which, if they are used rightly, human beings can dependably receive God's grace. Using them *rightly* is important, but so is *using* them.

At the end of the sermon "The Means of Grace" Wesley condemns the idea that any of the means are powerful in and of themselves. He says,

> There is no *power* in this. It is in itself a poor, dead, empty thing: separate from God, it is a dry leaf, a shadow. Neither is there any *merit* in my using this, nothing intrinsically pleasing to God, nothing whereby I deserve any favour at his hands, no, not a drop of water to cool my tongue. But because God bids, therefore I do; because he directs me to wait in this way, therefore here I wait for his free mercy, whereof cometh my salvation.
>
> Settle this in your heart, that the *opus operatum*, the mere work done, profiteth nothing; that there is no *power* to save but in the Spirit of God, no *merit* but in the blood of Christ; that consequently even what God ordains conveys no grace to the soul if you trust not in him alone. On the other hand, he that does truly trust in him cannot fall short of the grace of God, even though he were cut off from every outward ordinance, though he were shut up in the centre of the earth.[17]

Gayle Carlton Felton says that Wesley "drew a sharp distinction between two parts of the sacrament—the outward or human act and the inward or change wrought by God."[18] Though the two ordinarily go together, they do not always do so.

There is a deep tension here between a high sacramental view of the means of grace and a more evangelical understanding. Colin

Williams finds this a "creative tension between the Catholic and Protestant views of the Church and the Sacraments which is of great importance in the present ecumenical struggle."[19] Whether this tension is described as "creative" or "unresolved" depends on how the coherence of the Church's teaching on these matters is perceived. The strongest link between the two is to understand salvation as a process that, under normal circumstances, requires all the means of grace. Suzanne Johnson says, "Formation is not a state to be attained, but rather a dynamic relationship with God to be sustained."[20]

THE CHURCH

One of the least well-defined areas of United Methodist doctrine is its ecclesiology. United Methodists view themselves as a church, holding the same status as the other churches that are part of the body of Christ. Yet, the tensions between the Catholic and Protestant parts of its heritage, between its Anglican doctrinal roots and experience as a missional society, and between its concern for correct doctrine and the pragmatic focus on results all lead to a mixture of views in tension with each other. However, an approach identified by Karen Westerfield Tucker reveals a degree of consistency in United Methodist ecclesiology. In analyzing Wesley's liturgical revisions for the "Sunday Service" sent to the United States in 1784, she concludes,

> Wesley conveyed the expectation that there would be a certain "ethos" characteristic of Methodist worship: an organized, coherent, simple—and variable—form; freedom of expression as warranted by the movement of the Spirit, the particular occasion or event, and the context of the worshipers; the articulation of concern for the needy which leads to intercessory prayer, discipleship, and service; and active participation of the congregation in song and prayer.[21]

This is a very pragmatic approach to worship and the sacraments. It is in some ways structured and sacramentally centered, while in other ways unstructured and homiletically centered. It is the pragmatic concern for saving souls in the particular context that allows for liturgical adaptation. In a similar way, United Methodist ecclesiology and understanding of the means of grace is practical. From a firm base in a traditional Anglican approach, the Church makes adaptations to enhance its mission.

THE NATURE OF THE CHURCH

The first place where this tension shows up is in the different senses of the word "church" used in the constitutional standards. Article XIII restricts its definition to the *visible* church: "The visible church of Christ is a congregation of faithful men in which the pure Word of God is preached, and the Sacraments duly administered according to Christ's ordinance, in all those things that of necessity are requisite to the same."[22] This is a definition that focuses on the church as a means of grace. According to this sense the church has three marks. First, it is a body of faithful persons.[23] The church is composed of those who have responded in faith to God's saving invitation. Second, it is marked by its preaching of the "pure Word of God." This has reference to the church's doctrine and its foundation in the Scriptures as the determiners of the church's preaching. Third, the church is marked by its sacramental life of administering baptism and the Lord's Supper. Sacraments are clearly defined as ordained by Christ.

Confession V makes the same point but in a different way. It does not use the delimiting word "visible" but makes a number of claims about the church as a whole:

> We believe the Christian Church is the community of all true believers under the Lordship of Christ. We believe it is one, holy, apostolic and catholic. It is the redemptive fellowship in which the Word of God is preached by men divinely called, and the sacraments are duly administered according to Christ's own appointment. Under the discipline of the Holy Spirit the Church exists for the maintenance of worship, the edification of believers and the redemption of the world.[24]

All of these characteristics are applied to the Christian church. Like Article XIII, Confession V emphasizes preaching the Word of God and proper administration of the sacraments. In addition, however, the four marks of the church from the third section of the Nicene Creed are applied.[25] Furthermore, Confession V asserts that the church's mission is worship, edification, and the redemption of the world.

When taken together, Article XIII and Confession V are best understood to be speaking of the "Church universal, which is one Body in Christ" of which the United Methodist Church understands itself to be a part. That church's unity is a gift from God, a gift not yet fully realized. However, when United Methodists accept the baptism and church membership of other Christians, they witness to the deeper unity in the body of Christ. In discussing the unity and holiness of the church, Bicknell and Carpenter describe each of them as "a gift, an achievement and a promise."[26] Both of these marks come from God and are integrally related to the church's identity as the Body of Christ. Just as Christ is one and yet has many parts, the one body that is the church also has many parts that are the various denominations. Just as God is holy, belonging to God confers a kind of holiness as well. However, these marks are imperfectly achieved here on earth, and we must look forward to the time when God will make all things new and restore God's church to its true reality. It is in this sense that United Methodists pray in the last sentence of the Great Thanksgiving in the liturgy for "A Service of Word and Table": "Through your Son Jesus Christ, with the Holy Spirit in your holy church, all honor and glory is yours, almighty Father, now and forever."[27] Holiness and unity are only imperfectly realized at this time, but they are still present and real.

The Church is also catholic. This word is so widely misunderstood that in the UMH it is given a footnote defining it as "universal."[28] Two important parts of United Methodist ecclesiology are rooted in this concept. Both serve as the topics of paragraphs in the Church's Constitution.

Paragraph 4 describes the inclusiveness of The United Methodist Church. It says,

> All persons without regard to race, color, national origin, status, or economic condition, shall be eligible to attend its worship services, participate in its programs, receive the sacraments, upon baptism be admitted as baptized members, and upon taking vows declaring the Christian faith, become professing members

in any local church in the connection. In The United Methodist Church no conference or other organizational unit of the Church shall be structured so as to exclude any member or any constituent body of the Church because of race, color, national origin, status, or economic condition.[29]

In this sense, catholicity implies that the Church embraces human beings from a wide variety of groups. Catholic in the sense of universal means that many of the ways in which persons define themselves as groups are not barriers to membership in the Church. Only the vows of baptism and Church membership exclude persons from the Church.

In a second sense, catholicity also means ecumenism. Paragraph 5 says,

> As part of the church universal, The United Methodist Church believes that the Lord of the church is calling Christians everywhere to strive toward unity; and therefore it will seek, and work for, unity at all levels of church life: through world relationships with other Methodist churches and united churches related to The Methodist Church or The Evangelical United Brethren Church, through councils of churches, and through plans of union and covenantal relationships with churches of Methodist or other denominational traditions.[30]

Wesley's sermon "Catholic Spirit" lays the groundwork for ecumenical relations.[31] All those whose "heart is right" belong together in one church. The Discipline further states that "Christian unity is not an option; it is a gift to be received and expressed."[32] This is amplified liturgically in the United Methodist practice of recognizing the baptism of other Christian denominations, and also recognizing the ordination of ministers from those churches. Ecumenism is not the same as interfaith encounters. In those areas we are called to be both neighbors and witnesses with persons from other religions. But in our relations with Christians from other churches, we recognize them as brothers and sisters in the Lord and seek to make our unity more fully visible.

Toward the end of better ecumenical relations, the Church passed a resolution in 1970 (subsequently reaffirmed) concerning the interpretation of the anti-Roman Catholic Articles in the Articles of Religion. Articles XIV, XV, XVI, XVIII, XIX, XX, and XXI attack certain practices and beliefs associated with Roman Catholicism such as purgatory, use of language not understood by the people, transubstantiation, and clerical celibacy. The key phrase in the resolution says, "We declare it our official intent henceforth to interpret all our Articles, Confession, and other 'standards of doctrine' in consonance with our best ecumenical insights and judgment, as these develop in the light of the Resolution of the 1968 General Conference on 'The Methodist Church and the Cause of Christian Unity.' "[33] The import of this statement should be kept in perspective. Because resolutions are of lesser authority than constitutional standards of doctrine, it cannot be said that the position represented by the Articles against these Roman Catholic doctrines has been changed. Rather, we should recognize that Roman Catholic teaching has changed considerably since 1784, and that what Wesley and the Church of England were condemning may no longer and perhaps may never have been Roman Catholic teaching. In recognizing the Roman Catholic Church as a legitimate Church, United Methodists are prepared to engage in dialogue to understand each other better and to grow closer to full communion. The same holds true for all of the other ecumenical partners. A long history of relationships with the predominantly black Methodist Churches—African Methodist Episcopal, African Methodist Episcopal Zion, and Christian Methodist Episcopal— has led to the formation of the Commission on Pan-Methodist Cooperation, and this concern for dialogue is supported by official resolutions.[34] The work of the World Methodist Council unites the various Wesleyan bodies for fellowship and shared ministry.[35] Similarly, it endorses United Methodist participation in the Consultation on Church Union, the National Council of Churches, and the World Council of Churches.[36]

ORDAINED MINISTRY

United Methodism understands that there are three types of ministry in the Christian church. The first is most basic. Christian ministry generally is "the expression of the mind and mission of Christ by a community of Christians that demonstrates a common life of gratitude and devotion, witness and service, celebration and discipleship. All Christians are called through their baptism to this ministry of servanthood in the world to the glory of God and for human fulfillment."[37] This ministry is one all Christians share by virtue of their baptism. Being conformed to Christ means sharing in Christ's ministry. God demands that persons love God with everything that they have (Matt. 22:37), which includes loving their neighbors as themselves (Matt. 22:39) and presenting their bodies as living sacrifices to God (Rom. 12:1). In this sense, all Christians are ministers. United Methodist doctrine understands this as a servant ministry that has both great privilege and great obligation. The privilege is a deeply spiritual relationship with God; the obligation is holy living in the world.[38]

Some are set apart within this community of ministers for leadership in the Church. In continuity with the ministry of the Apostles, the Church recognizes that the Holy Spirit has gifted and called certain persons to ministries of Service, Word, Sacrament, and Order.[39] There are two orders:

> Those who respond to God's call to lead in service and to equip others for this ministry through teaching, proclamation, and worship and who assist elders in the administration of the sacraments are ordained deacons. Those whose leadership in service includes preaching and teaching the Word of God, administration of the sacraments, ordering the Church for its mission and service, and administration of the *Discipline* of the Church are ordained as elders.[40]

Deacons and elders are accountable to the annual conference, of which they are members, as well as to the bishop and district superintendents.

Laypersons are sometimes appointed as pastors of local congregations. They are licensed for pastoral ministry, and are then given pastoral authority while they are appointed to a particular charge.[41] The anomalies of giving laypersons sacramental authority are not dealt with because of the pragmatic need to get pastoral leadership to places where it is not possible to send an elder. It is typical of United Methodism's practical approach to its doctrine that a knowledgeable interpreter evaluates the adequacy of "any ordering of ministry" in terms of "its effectiveness in fulfilling the mission."[42]

Ordination is not a sacrament, and yet ordination for the same order is not repeatable. It thus seems to have a sacramental character analogous to baptism, and yet United Methodists are not sure what difference it makes. Whether and in what ways ordination is a means of grace is not clear. The same is true of the consecration of bishops and the commissioning of probationary members of the conference.

MISSION

Five other marks are important to United Methodist ecclesiology. First and foremost is its sense of mission. The Church's mission statement has a clear, one-sentence formulation: "The mission of the Church is to make disciples of Jesus Christ."[43] The rationale that follows grounds this sense of mission in God's gracious action through covenant with Abraham, the ministry, death and resurrection of Jesus, and the Spirit's continuing work in the world. This mission statement then claims that mission is central to the life of the Church: "Whenever United Methodism has had a clear sense of mission, God has used our Church to save persons, heal relationships, transform social structures, and spread scriptural holiness, thereby changing the world. In order to be truly alive, we embrace Jesus' mandate to make disciples of all peoples."[44] The process for carrying out mission indicates that many different aspects of the church's life, including evangelism, worship, nurture, education, and justice ministries, are all component parts.

This is directly related to the whole structure of United Methodist doctrine and its practical concern for salvation. Thomas Frank says of its "distinctive ecclesiology,"

> Among many notable features, the UMC is structured first and foremost for mission. By tradition and polity it is set up to invite people to Christian faith and life, to provide them the disciplines of Christian discipleship, and to send them into their communities as catalysts of a loving and just society. United Methodist clergy itinerate as missionaries in local places, and local churches are organized as mission outposts.[45]

Methodism's practical approach means that many different parts of its ecclesiology are viewed primarily in the light of its mission.

It is an apostolic ecclesiology in the sense of being sent into the world to serve God there.

ITINERANCY

Related to this missional sense is the work of the Church's ministers who are understood to be itinerant. The itinerant system is the appointment of elders to their fields of labor by the bishop.[46] The bishop has the sole right to make such appointments, and they

> are to be made with the consideration of the gifts and evidence of God's grace of those appointed, to the needs, characteristics, and opportunities of congregations and institutions, and with faithfulness to the commitment to an open itinerancy. Open itinerancy means appointments are made without regard to race, ethnic origin, gender, color, disability, marital status, or age, except for the provisions of mandatory retirement.[47]

This should be construed as the deployment of human resources for the sake of the Church's mission. Bishops are required to consult local churches and elders, but as advisory only.

CONFERENCE

At about the same time as ordination as a deacon or elder, the person also is voted into full membership of an annual conference. Just as laypersons are members of local congregations, so the clergy are members of their conference. The Conference has two orders, as well as an optional fellowship of local pastors. Diaconal ministers and deaconesses may also meet together. The deacons and elders are bound in a special covenant with each other.[48] When the conference meets, the ordained have special responsibilities for admission of new persons into ordination and conference membership, the maintenance of standards, and the discipline of behavior and doctrine. The annual conference session has the right to decide all matters not related to matters of ordination and clergy discipline. Such a session has equal numbers of lay and clergy members.

The purpose of the annual conference is "to make disciples for Jesus Christ by equipping its local churches for ministry and by providing a connection for ministry beyond the local church; all to the glory of God."[49] The clergy and laity of the Church deliberate about how best to serve God in a network of conferences. The "conciliar principle"[50] means that the General Conference is the ultimate authority in the Church, with Jurisdictional, Central, Annual, District, and Charge Conferences playing important roles in more restricted geographic areas. Power is thus given to the members of these conferences. It is presumed that these are missional entities whose purpose is to discern God's will and provide for the Church's faithful and effective missional response.[51]

EPISCOPACY

Methodism's understanding of episcopacy is an important part of its ecclesiology. The Church protects its episcopal form of government in the same way it protects its constitutional standards of doctrine. The third Restrictive Rule says, "The General Conference shall not change or alter any part or rule of our government so as to do away with episcopacy or destroy the plan of our itinerant general superintendency."[52] United Methodist doctrine argues that from apostolic times persons have been ordained who have had the task of superintending the ministry of the church. Bishops are not a third order. They are elders elected to the task of ordering the life of the Church.[53] General supervision is done, in part by individual bishops who often serve as officers of general agencies, and by the Council of Bishops collectively.[54]

CONNECTION

The United Methodist Church calls its form of polity connectionalism. It is not purely episcopal, nor is it congregational. Rather, it is a "web of interactive relationships." The Discipline continues, saying,

> We are connected by sharing a common tradition of faith, including our Doctrinal Standards and General Rules (¶103); by

sharing together a constitutional polity, including a leadership of general superintendency; by sharing a common mission, which we seek to carry out by working together in and through conferences that reflect the inclusive and missional character of our fellowship; by sharing a common ethos that characterizes our distinctive way of doing things.[55]

An additional feature not mentioned in the above list is that all United Methodist property is held in trust for the connection. While legal ownership may be vested in local church trustees or in the directors of a corporation, the property is subject to the rules of the United Methodist Book of Discipline because it is for the benefit of the whole Church. Yet the whole Church is not a legal entity.

THE CHURCH AS A MEANS OF GRACE

United Methodist doctrine views the church as a means of grace. The sacraments, the ministry of the word, and other practices connect persons with God's grace in ways that are not available outside the church. These are not the only ways in which God gives grace to persons. After all, prevenient grace is given to persons whether or not the church is present in their lives at all. But where the church is present, God's grace is available in more explicit ways. With mission at the heart of its life, the United Methodist Church understands the church to be sent into the world to bear witness to the reign of God there.

Many of the particular organizational forms the United Methodist Church has chosen throughout its history should be understood as devoted to maximizing its effectiveness in this mission. Conference, episcopacy, itinerancy, and ordination as deacons and elders are all prudential means of grace. No church is required to have any of these. Yet United Methodists have found them beneficial to their mission and to be genuine means of grace both for themselves and for those whom they serve. Each of these, when faithfully used and received, can be a channel for God's grace. Bishops can serve as the leaders of a missionary team, deploying resources of laity, deacons, and elders where their gifts and graces can best be used for mission. Itinerancy as a system of deploying missionary elders gives the Church maximum flexibility to meet emerging opportunities. The ordained are leaders of congregations. By teaching, preaching, serving, enabling, organizing, and caring they help their congregations witness faithfully and effectively. Laity are also leaders of congregations in partnership with the clergy, and they carry their witness into the world in ways often not available to clergy. In businesses, schools, families, and neighborhoods they are missionaries where often the gospel most needs to be heard and lived. Conferences confer and their agencies carry out mission on behalf of the connection, both enabling local congregations and doing on their behalf what no single congregation could accomplish.

All of these forms of United Methodist polity can convey God's grace. Sometimes they are corrupted and ineffective. Yet, like other prudential means of grace, history shows they have often been used by God to great effect in many different places.

SACRAMENTS

Some key phrases in the constitutional standards provide the basis for how United Methodism understands the sacraments. First, Article XVI stresses that the sacraments are "certain signs of grace, and God's good will toward us, by which he doth work invisibly in us, and doth not only quicken, but also strengthen and confirm, our faith in him."[56] Confession VI says that sacraments are "symbols and pledges" but are also "means of grace by which God works invisibly in us, quickening, strengthening and confirming our faith in him."[57] Thus baptism and the Lord's Supper are indeed outward signs of the inward grace the Christian has experienced and is experiencing. But in each of these sign-acts God is also the actor who uses the sacrament as a channel for the grace God seeks to give to the person. Exactly how this transpires is unknown. But Scripture, tradition, and experience teach that these are truly means of God's grace. Perhaps Charles Wesley's words in the hymn "O the Depth of Love Divine" express it best:

> How can spirits heavenward rise,
> by earthly matter fed,

drink herewith divine supplies
and eat immortal bread?
Ask the Father's wisdom how:
Christ who did the means ordain;
angels round our altars bow
to search it out, in vain.

Sure and real is the grace,
the manner be unknown;
only meet us in thy ways
and perfect us in one.
Let us taste the heavenly powers,
Lord, we ask for nothing more.
Thine to bless, 'tis only ours
to wonder and adore.[58]

The resolution "By Water and the Spirit" clarifies United Methodist teaching about the sacraments. It says,

> The ritual action of a sacrament does not merely point to God's presence in the world, but also participates in it and becomes a vehicle for conveying that reality. God's presence in the sacraments is real, but it must be accepted by human faith if it is to transform human lives. The sacraments do not convey grace either magically or irrevocably, but they are powerful channels through which God has chosen to make grace available to us.[59]

The constitutional standards also indicate that sacraments are ordained by Christ. Article XVI stipulates that confirmation, penance, orders, matrimony, and extreme unction are not sacraments because "they have not any visible sign or ceremony ordained of God."[60] Christ did not command these for his followers, even though some of them may be "states of life allowed in the Scriptures." Baptism and the Lord's Supper are positively commanded by Christ for all of his disciples. The other instituted means of grace—prayer, searching the Scriptures, and fasting—are also commanded by Christ, but they lack a "sign or ceremony."

While Wesley saw the means of grace as lacking power in and of themselves, neither did they depend on the goodness or character of the minister for their validity. Rather, their validity rests on God, who appointed the means and has promised to be present in them. Wesley says,

> Again, unto them, unto false prophets, undeniably such, is frequently committed (O grief to speak! for surely these things ought not so to be) the administration of the sacraments also. To direct men, therefore, not to hear them would be in effect to cut them off from the ordinance of God. But this we dare not do, considering the validity of the ordinance doth not depend on the goodness of him that administers, but on the faithfulness of him that ordained it; who will and doth meet us in his appointed ways.[61]

BAPTISM

Article XVII maintains this sacramental perspective by saying that baptism is not only a "sign of profession" but also a "sign of regeneration or the new birth."[62] Confession VI is clear only on baptism's character as a "representation of the new birth and a mark of Christian discipleship." Taken together, there is no contradiction between the two, but the Confession is more reticent on the issue of baptismal regeneration.

The Church's liturgy is helpful with what is going on in the sacrament. It says, "Through the Sacrament of Baptism we are initiated into Christ's holy church. We are incorporated into God's mighty acts of salvation and given new birth through water and the Spirit. All this is God's gift, offered to us without price."[63]

"By Water and the Spirit" expands on these statements. First, it claims that baptism is "by water and the Spirit." It is God's action in the lives of human beings. It says, "Working in the lives of people before, during, and after their baptisms, the Spirit is the effective agent of salvation. God bestows upon baptized persons the presence of the Holy Spirit, marks them with an identifying seal as God's own, and implants in their hearts the first installment of their inheritance as sons and daughters of God."[64] Water is the symbol and applying it in the name of the triune God is the sign-act that God uses to convey grace. There is also laying on of hands to invoke the presence of the Holy Spirit in the person's life.

Baptism is also incorporation into the body of Christ. Wesley says in his note on Acts 5:11 that the New Testament church is composed of persons "called by the gospel, grafted into Christ by baptism."[65] Hence, baptized persons are counted as members of the church and in the rite of baptism the local congregation promises to support their continued growth in discipleship.[66] In the United Methodist view, baptism is into the body of Christ and not just the United Methodist Church. Membership in the United Methodist Church requires the additional question of loyalty and support for this particular part of the universal church.

Baptism is also seen as forgiveness for sin. Water is seen as the key symbol for cleansing. "By Water and the Spirit" says,

> This reconciliation is made possible through the atonement of Christ and made real in our lives by the work of the Holy Spirit. We respond by confessing and repenting of our sin, and affirming our faith that Jesus Christ has accomplished all that is necessary for our salvation. Faith is the necessary condition for justification; in baptism, that faith is professed.[67]

The baptismal liturgy includes a prayer that the Holy Spirit "might bless this gift of water and those who receive it, to wash away their sin and clothe them in righteousness throughout their lives, that, dying and being raised with Christ, they may share in his final victory."[68] To ask whether the sacrament is necessary for justification is to ask the wrong question. Strictly speaking, baptism is not required in all cases, yet all persons seeking God's forgiveness will seek baptism if there is time and opportunity.

Since baptism is primarily God's action, it is unrepeatable.[69] God is faithful, and whatever the person does after baptism God will not back away from God's promise. When a person sins away the grace of baptism, or denies the faith, that individual becomes a lost member of the family. Yet, that person remains a member of the family and does not need baptism again to be incorporated into the church. Such an occasion may call for a reaffirmation of baptism, a ritual for which is included in the UMH and BOW.[70]

Baptism and the New Birth

"By Water and the Spirit" summarizes Wesley's views of the dual necessity for baptism and conversion. On the one hand he taught that even infant baptism is generally accompanied by the new birth. On the other, he taught that persons usually sinned away the grace received in this sacrament and stood in need of conversion as adults.[71] Given that the vast majority of his hearers had already been baptized and were nominally Christian, Wesley put the greatest stress in the standard sermons on the need for being born again. He contends that sometimes persons who are baptized as adults and thus "born of water" are not at that same time "born of the Spirit." He cites Matthew 12:33 that "a tree is known by its fruits," and says that some persons "who were children of the devil before they were baptized continue the same after baptism. . . . they continue servants of sin, without any pretence either to inward or outward holiness."[72]

His primary concern is to urge people to be born again. He does not doubt that his readers were born again when baptized. But he presumes they have sinned away that grace and now stand in need of conversion.[73] He says:

> Lean no more on the staff of that broken reed, that ye *were* born again in baptism. Who denies that ye were then made "children of God, and heirs of the kingdom of heaven"? But notwithstanding this, ye are now children of the devil; therefore ye must be born again. And let not Satan put it into your heart to cavil at a word, when the thing is clear. Ye have heard what are the marks of the children of God; all ye who have them not on your souls, baptized or unbaptized, must needs receive them, or without doubt ye will perish everlastingly. And if ye have been baptized, your only hope is this: that those who were made the children of God by baptism, but are now the children of the devil, may yet again receive "power to become the sons of God"; that they may receive again what they have lost, even the "Spirit of adoption, crying in their hearts, Abba, Father!"[74]

Wesley continued to emphasize both infant baptismal regeneration and the new birth of adult conversion throughout his ministry. Such a position makes sense if the sacraments are seen as ordained means of grace, and then personal practice is adjusted to the goal of transforming persons in justification and sanctification.

Modes of Baptism

Wesley regarded the proper mode of baptism as a matter of opinion on which Christians could disagree without breaking fellowship. As we have seen, though, catholic spirit is not indifference to important matters, and Wesley was persuaded that "infants ought to be baptized, and that this may be done either by dipping or sprinkling."[75] In the *Notes* Wesley makes a number of relevant points. He argues that the Greek word for baptism, applied at Mark 7:4 to dishes and couches, could mean either dipping or sprinkling. Immersion is one of the ancient practices,[76] but in discussing John the Baptist's work in the river Jordan, there were so many people present they could not possibly be dipped. Wesley says, "It seems, therefore, that they stood in ranks on the edge of the river; and that John, passing along before them, cast water on their heads or faces; by which means he might baptize many thousands in a day."[77] "By Water and the Spirit" shows us that United Methodists may administer baptism by sprinkling, pouring, or immersion. "However it is administered, water should be utilized with enough generosity to enhance our appreciation of its symbolic meanings."[78] Mark Stamm suggests, "The congregation should be able to see the water and hear it as well. In far too many baptisms the fact that water has been used at all must be accepted by faith alone."[79] Water is a powerful symbol of grace at work.

Infant Baptism

While Article XVII affirms the baptism of young children, Confession VI offers two reasons for this practice. First, they are "under the atonement of Christ." Second, they are "heirs of the Kingdom of God."[80] However, ¶225 restates these reasons, noting for the second one that "Jesus explicitly included the children in his kingdom." The Discipline thus says that the pastor "shall earnestly exhort all Christian parents or guardians to present their children to the Lord in baptism at an early age."[81] Wesley's comment on the baptism of Lydia and her family is instructive. He says, "Who can believe, that in so many families there was no infant? or, that the Jews who were so long accustomed to circumcise their children, would not now devote them to God by baptism?"[82] Though there is a strong preference for infant baptism in United Methodist doctrine, there is also an expression of respect for the opinions of those who differ from the Wesleyan understanding of the sacrament.[83] The Church's doctrine also acknowledges, "While the baptism of infants is appropriate for Christian families, the increasingly

261

minority status of the church in contemporary society demands more attention to evangelizing, nurturing, and baptizing adult converts."[84] The words of Ruth Duck's hymn brings together a number of these ideas:

> Wash, O God, our sons and daughters,
> where your cleansing waters flow.
> Number them among your people;
> bless as Christ blessed long ago.
> Weave them garments bright and sparkling;
> compass them with love and light.
> Fill, anoint them; send your Spirit,
> holy dove and heart's delight. . . .
>
> O how deep your holy wisdom!
> Unimagined, all your ways!
> To your name be glory, honor!
> With our lives we worship, praise!
> We your people stand before you,
> water-washed and Spirit-born.
> By your grace, our lives we offer.
> Recreate us; God, transform![85]

Baptism is cleansing from sin, incorporation into God's people the church, anointing with the Holy Spirit, a time of new birth, and transformation for service—all by God's grace.

Lord's Supper

Typical of the practical approach of United Methodist doctrine is its focus on the effects of the sacrament rather than clarity of the sacrament's definition. Certain Roman Catholic teachings and practices are condemned, but no fully developed eucharistic doctrine is taught in their place. Within United Methodism there is plenty of scope for a variety of theological reflections on this subject.

Both John and Charles Wesley have a great deal to say about the Eucharist. Their work taken as a whole could augment the

Church's authoritative doctrine further. Several excellent studies of their thought form a helpful introduction to Wesleyan understandings of the nature of the Lord's Supper and the related issues. Specifically, Maddox's *Responsible Grace*, Knight's *Presence of God in the Christian Life*, Borgen's *John Wesley on the Sacraments*, Rattenbury's *Eucharistic Hymns of John and Charles Wesley*, and Wainwright's essay "The Sacraments in Wesleyan Perspective" are excellent studies in Wesleyan theology. Because their subject matter is the theology of the two brothers, they rely heavily on Charles's hymns and John's publication of borrowed materials. Particularly helpful are the sermon "On the Duty of Constant Communion" and John Wesley's edited version of Daniel Brevint's *On the Christian Sacrament and Sacrifice* (published as the preface to *Hymns on the Lord's Supper* in 1745). Most scholars find that the Wesleys held a doctrine of the real presence of Christ in the Eucharist, whether receptionism or virtualism. But none of the evidence for such a conclusion is contained in the authoritative doctrine of the United Methodist Church.

As a Means of Grace

The clearest teaching of United Methodist doctrine is that the Lord's Supper is a means whereby God conveys prevenient, justifying, and sanctifying grace to persons.[86] Article XVIII says, "to such as rightly, worthily, and with faith receive the same, the bread which we break is a partaking of the body of Christ; and likewise the cup of blessing is a partaking of the blood of Christ."[87] Article VI says believers receive the body and blood "in a spiritual manner."[88]

In "The Means of Grace" Wesley is at some pains to show that Christ commanded us to partake of the sacrament. He says,

> Here then the direction first given by our Lord is expressly repeated by the Apostle: "Let him eat," "let him drink" ἐσθιέτω, πινέτω— both in the imperative mood); words not implying a bare permission only, but a clear explicit command; a command to all those either who already are filled with peace and joy in believing, or who can truly say, "The remembrance of our sins is grievous unto us; the burden of them is intolerable."[89]

Wesley interprets the petition for daily bread in the Lord's Prayer to refer to physical bread, spiritual bread, and the sacramental bread as the "grand channel" for God's grace.[90] The Lord's Supper is then a way for persons to be saved. When "a stupid, senseless wretch" is awakened and finds the way of salvation through prayer and searching the Scriptures, there comes a time when the Lord's Supper is a means of grace. Wesley says,

> But here he observes others go up to "the table of the Lord." He considers, Christ has said, "Do this." How is it that I do not? I am too great a sinner. I am not fit. I am not worthy. After struggling with these scruples a while, he breaks through. And thus he continues in God's way—in hearing, reading, meditating, praying, and partaking of the Lord's Supper—till God, in the manner that pleases him, speaks to his heart, "Thy faith hath saved thee; go in peace."[91]

Confession VI uses other terms that provide starting points for theological reflection about the Eucharist. It is a "representation of our redemption, a memorial of the sufferings and death of Christ, and a token of love and union which Christians have with Christ and with one another."[92] Holy Communion is a polyvalent event with many aspects. Each of these has its place in a complete description of the sacrament.[93]

Not Transubstantiation

With regard to exactly how the elements convey God's grace, United Methodist doctrine is unclear. It is deliberately so in the hymn "O the Depth of Love Divine" where the claim that the "manner be unknown" is juxtaposed with the claim that "sure and real is the grace."[94] Much of the theological argument about the nature of the Eucharist has focused on Jesus' words at the Last Supper. Wesley's comments there continually point out that the language is "figurative," by which he means it is not to be taken literally.[95]

United Methodist doctrine, with some of its doctrinal roots in the English Reformation, has a number of articles that condemn certain Roman Catholic doctrines and practices as they were understood then. Roman Catholic teaching and Methodist understandings have evolved in significant ways since the Council of Trent and the writing of the Articles, and it is possible that there is more common ground than first appears.

Nevertheless, Article XVIII tells us that in the Lord's Supper the substance of bread and wine do not change. This understanding of transubstantiation "is repugnant to the plain words of Scripture, overthroweth the nature of a sacrament, and hath given occasion to many superstitions."[96] Neither is the sacrament a new offering of Christ, because Christ died once as a "perfect redemption, propitiation, and satisfaction for all the sins of the whole world, both original and actual."[97] Both the bread and the cup are to be given to the people. When Article XVIII says, "The Sacrament of the Lord's Supper was not by Christ's ordinance reserved, carried about, lifted up, or worshipped," it is not clearly prohibiting such practices, but indicating that they are not scripturally based. As Article XVI says, the sacraments are meant to be used.[98]

This, then, leaves open a variety of interpretations of the nature of the Lord's Supper. Consubstantiation, memorialism, virtualism, and receptionism are among the possibilities allowed for here. The liturgy for Holy Communion is equally open to a variety of interpretations. When the minister prays, "Pour out your Holy Spirit on us gathered here, and on these gifts of bread and wine. Make them be for us the body and blood of Christ, that we may be for the world the body of Christ, redeemed by his blood,"[99] a variety of interpretations are possible.

The Open Table

Mark Stamm notes that the "open table" is an oral tradition in United Methodism that is not mentioned in the Church's doctrinal statements. He says, "While the assumptions inherent in that phrase *open Table*, are profoundly true on the one hand, they can be misleading (even false) if we fail to understand them in light of our traditional words for inviting people to the Lord's Table."[100] The recently approved constitutional amendment on inclusiveness has a bearing on who is admitted to the sacrament of holy communion. The new text of ¶4 reads,

> The United Methodist Church is a part of the church universal, which is one Body in Christ. The United Methodist Church acknowledges that all persons are of sacred worth. All persons, without regard to race, color, national origin, status, or economic

condition, shall be eligible to attend its worship services, participate in its programs, receive the sacraments, upon baptism be
admitted as baptized members, and upon taking vows declaring
the Christian faith, become professing members in any local
church in the connection.

There are no prerequisites to receiving holy communion other than
what is contained in the liturgy itself. In the liturgy the invitation
says, "Christ our Lord invites to his table all who love him, who
earnestly repent of their sin and seek to live in peace with one
another."[101] In "A Service of Word and Table IV" the invitation is,
"Ye that do truly and earnestly repent of your sins, and are in love
and charity with your neighbors, and intend to lead a new life, following the commandments of God, and walking from henceforth
in his holy ways: Draw near with faith, and take this Holy
Sacrament to your comfort."[102] These two basically invite those
who are Christians to come and participate in the sacrament. There
is no mention of baptism, nor is there mention of membership in
any church, and definitely not a restriction to belonging to the
United Methodist Church. No age is specified. If one can agree to
the conditions of the invitation, the table is open.

OTHER INSTITUTED MEANS

Three other instituted means of grace commanded by Christ are
mentioned in the doctrines of the United Methodist Church:
prayer, Scripture, and fasting. While these are not sacraments, their
use is not optional. Because Christ commanded them they are to be
followed both for the sake of obedience to the Lord and because of
the benefits they bring to the persons who faithfully use them.

PRAYER

Wesley begins his discussion of prayer in the sermon "The
Means of Grace" by emphasizing that it was commanded by
Christ. Quoting Matthew 7:7-8 he says, "Here we are in the plainest
manner directed to ask in order to, or as a *means* of, receiving; to

seek in order to find the grace of God, the pearl of great price; and to knock, to continue asking and seeking, if we would enter into his kingdom."[103] Wesley believes prayer to be part of an ongoing relationship between the believer and God. "Prayer is the lifting up of the heart to God."[104] Without the relationship, the words mean nothing. Prayer is communication, and the one praying is more often changed:

> So that the end of your praying is not to inform God, as though he knew not your wants already; but rather to inform yourselves, to fix the sense of those wants more deeply in your hearts, and the sense of your continual dependence on him who only is able to supply all your wants. It is not so much to move God—who is always more ready to give than you to ask—as to move yourselves, that you may be willing and ready to receive the good things he has prepared for you.[105]

His analysis of the Lord's Prayer then indicates some of the components prayer can and should have: relationship, praise, and petition.

The General Rules mandate that members of the Church should "attend upon all the ordinances of God." Among these are "The public worship of God" and "family and private prayer."[106]

Scripture

In chapter 3 we examined the role of Scripture as an authority in matters of faith. Similar to the discussion of causative authority there, it is also true that the Bible is a means of grace for those seeking the Lord. The commandment Wesley quotes here is John 5:39. He says,

> Our Lord's direction with regard to the use of this means is likewise plain and clear. "Search the Scriptures," saith he to the unbelieving Jews, "for [. . .] they [. . .] testify of me." And for this very end did he direct them to search the Scriptures, that they might *believe in him.*
>
> The objection that this is not a command, but only an assertion that they did "search the Scriptures," is shamelessly false. I desire

those who urge it to let us know how a command can be more clearly expressed than in those terms, Ἐρευνᾶτε τὰς γραφάς. It is as peremptory as so many words can make it.[107]

Wesley is correct in the possible translation that the words will bear. *Ereunate* can either be present indicative or present imperative. However, the context shows that the indicative form is the best translation. While this particular foundation may be shaky, the idea that the Scriptures have authority for Christians is both found in the New Testament and the early church. Christ's own example of frequently quoting Old Testament passages shows by example the role that Scripture played for him, at least as the Gospel writers understood it. Wesley's note on Colossians 3:16 indicates how the Scripture can enter a person's whole being. He says, "*Let the word of Christ*—So the apostle calls the whole scripture, and thereby asserts the divinity of his Master. *Dwell*—Not make a short stay, or an occasional visit, but take up its stated residence. *Richly*—In the largest measure, and with the greatest efficacy; so as to fill and govern the whole soul." The language of Wesley's own sermons is saturated with scriptural phrases, making apparent, one senses, that this living in the biblical world was very much a reality for him.

Wesley understands "searching the Scriptures" in a broad sense in this sermon. It includes hearing, reading, and meditating. Thus, listening to sermons, reading the Bible privately, hearing the Scriptures read publicly, and thinking about the meaning of the words are all included. In the General Rules, "the ministry of the Word, either read or expounded" is listed separately, perhaps to give it greater emphasis and avoid misunderstanding.[108]

FASTING

Fasting is listed in the General Rules, but not as one of the "chief" means of grace in the sermon of that title.[109] One of the longest discussions of the practice comes in "Upon Our Lord's Sermon on the Mount, VII."[110] In this sermon Wesley offers six reasons for fasting. First, people who are emotionally focused on some great thing often forget to eat, and so naturally fast when contemplating their sin. Second, sometimes sin involves abuse of food and so they abstain from the items that caused them to be intemperate. Third, experience shows that "fullness of bread increased not only care-lessness and levity of spirit but also foolish and unholy desires, yea, unclean and vile affections." Too much food can lead to lust and sensuality. Fourth (although Wesley says not to lay too much stress on this reason), some holy persons believe in punishing themselves for their past sins. Then he says,

> A fifth and more weighty reason for fasting is that it is an help to prayer; particularly when we set apart larger portions of time for private prayer. Then especially it is that God is often pleased to lift up the souls of his servants above all the things of earth, and sometimes to rap them up, as it were, into the third heaven. And it is chiefly as it is an help to prayer that it has so frequently been found a means in the hand of God of confirming and increasing not one virtue, not chastity only (as some have idly imagined, without any ground either from Scripture, reason, or experience), but also seriousness of spirit, earnestness, sensibility, and tenderness of conscience; deadness to the world, and conse-quently the love of God and every holy and heavenly affection.[111]

A sixth reason is that God has commanded it and will reward those who practice it.

The BOW talks about fasting in the context of Lenten obser-vance. It says that Lent was a time of spiritual preparation for Easter, and an occasion for preparing persons for baptism and rec-onciling those who had committed serious sins. Through these practices "the whole congregation was reminded of the mercy and forgiveness proclaimed in the gospel of Jesus Christ and the need we all have to renew our faith."[112] The following invitation to "prayer, fasting and self-denial" indicates that fasting is a practice that contributes to the believer's spiritual formation.

All of these means of grace, plus the prudential ones discovered by the church at various times and various places, constitute the ways in which God continues to give God's people the grace they need. In the discussion of "Basic Christian Affirmations" there is a statement about the wholeness of the Christian life and the role that the means of grace play in it. The Discipline says:

We share the Christian belief that God's redemptive love is realized in human life by the activity of the Holy Spirit, both in

personal experience and in the community of believers. This community is the church, which the Spirit has brought into existence for the healing of the nations.

Through faith in Jesus Christ we are forgiven, reconciled to God, and transformed as people of the new covenant.

"Life in the Spirit" involves diligent use of the means of grace such as praying, fasting, attending upon the sacraments, and inward searching in solitude. It also encompasses the communal life of the church in worship, mission, evangelism, service, and social witness.[113]

Notes

1. Phil. 2:5.

2. Sermon 22, "Upon Our Lord's Sermon on the Mount, II," §II.4, *Works* 1:497.

3. Sermon 33, "Upon Our Lord's Sermon on the Mount, XIII," §III.3, *Works* 1:695.

4. UMH, 77.

5. Sermon 23, "Upon Our Lord's Sermon on the Mount, III," §I.8, *Works* 1:514.

6. Sermon 33, "Upon Our Lord's Sermon on the Mount, XIII," §III.3, *Works* 1:695.

7. Sermon 16, "The Means of Grace," *Works* 1:376-97.

8. Sermon 16, "The Means of Grace," §II.1, *Works* 1:381.

9. Sermon 16, "The Means of Grace," §II.1, *Works* 1:381.

10. Sermon 16, "The Means of Grace," §V.1, *Works* 1:393-94.

11. There has been a great deal of scholarly writing regarding the Wesleys' views of baptism. Conspicuously missing from the list of "chief means" is the sacrament of baptism. Such an omission is remarkable and points to the confusion about Wesley's position. Holland entitles his first chapter "The Riddle of Wesley's Baptismal Beliefs." Felton, 48 concludes her chapter on Wesley by suggesting that many students of his thought have failed "to take some of his essential distinctions fully into account." For further discussions see Knight, Borgen, Williams, and Maddox 1994. Because these works are studies either of the Wesley views or the practices of early Methodism, they use the full range of publications from both John and Charles Wesley, most of which are not included in authoritative United Methodist doctrine as outlined in chapter 1 above.

12. However, Holland, 102 suggests that Wesley administered the sacrament of baptism frequently, noting that in an eight-year period at the end of his ministry he baptized fifty-seven persons on forty-seven occasions. This is a remarkable number for a man without assignment as a parish priest.

13. Knight, 178. Randy Maddox agrees with this assessment. See Maddox 1994, 222.

14. See Baker 2000 for the best discussion of the developments over Wesley's lifetime.

15. BOR, 803.

16. The distinction between instituted and prudential means of grace is made explicit in "The Large Minutes." "Minutes of Several Conversations Between the

Rev. Mr. Wesley and Others From the Year 1744, to the Year 1789," *Works* (J) 8:322-24.

17. Sermon 16, "The Means of Grace," §V.4, *Works* 1:396.

18. Felton, 33. See Sermon 45, "The New Birth," §IV.1, *Works* 2:196.

19. Williams, 121. On 116 he labels the parts of the same tension "ecclesiastical" and "evangelical."

20. Johnson, 25.

21. Tucker, 30.

22. Discipline, 62.

23. The continuing use of noninclusive language in the constitutional standards is a significant problem. However, understanding the usage of words like "men" at the time they were written allows for the clear conclusion that both men and women are meant to be included in the definition. However, finding a way to express the same thought in twenty-first century language would be helpful in all of the constitutional standards.

24. Discipline, 67-68. Note that a slightly modified version of these words serves as the opening paragraph of the Constitution, Discipline, 21.

25. UMH, 880.

26. Bicknell and Carpenter, 245.

27. UMH, 10, 14.

28. UMH, 35, 41, 46, 51, 880, 881, 882.

29. Discipline, 22 as amended. As of the writing of this book, the full text was available at http://www.gbod.org/worship/default.asp?act=reader&item_id=2251.

30. Discipline, 23.

31. Sermon 39, "Catholic Spirit," *Works* 2:79-95.

32. Discipline, 84.

33. BOR, 238.

34. BOR, 233-35.

35. BOR, 233.

36. BOR, 229-33.

37. Discipline, 89.

38. Discipline, 91.

39. Discipline, 191.

40. Discipline, 183. Within the UMC today there are persons who were consecrated as diaconal ministers. Persons are no longer being consecrated for that role. There is currently an "Office of Deaconess" for which persons are commissioned.

41. Discipline, 232.

42. Harnish, 148.

43. Discipline, 87. I wrote the first draft of this statement for submission to a group called "The Aldersgate Covenant." In that draft the mission was described in the same way that the Methodist Episcopal Church had characterized the mission in 1784: "to reform the continent and to spread scriptural holiness across these lands." (*Minutes of Several Conversations . . . Composing a form of Discipline for . . . the Methodist Episcopal Church in America*, 1785, 4.) Gary Mueller and Michael Cartwright were the first to see the draft, and object that the terms were obscure

and that biblical language would be better. They proposed "to make disciples for Jesus Christ." The 1996 General Conference eventually changed the word "for" to "of" and approved a revised statement.

44. Discipline, 88.

45. Frank, 32.

46. Discipline, 215.

47. Discipline, 289.

48. Discipline, 201, 209.

49. Discipline, 331.

50. Discipline, v, 76.

51. Frank, 251 notes "Annual conferences have grown by circumstance and necessity to a complex state that is part revival meeting, part educational forum, part promotional rally, part business meeting, part community of worship." See Richey 1996 for an excellent historical survey.

52. Discipline, 27.

53. Discipline, 267.

54. Kirby, 239 argues that history has seen "the original commitment of American Methodism to an itinerant general superintendency being transformed by degrees into acceptance of a diocesan episcopacy." While he has persuasively chronicled the changes over time, some might argue that bishops remain itinerant in much the same way as elders do, namely they are subject to reassignment within a geographic region by the proper authorities. Given that the United Methodist practice of episcopacy has changed significantly over the years, the Church's commitment to some form of episcopal government has not.

55. Discipline, 90. For an extended and generally helpful discussion of United Methodist polity, see Frank.

56. Discipline, 63.

57. Discipline, 68.

58. Charles Wesley, UMH, 627.

59. BOR, 803-4.

60. Discipline, 63.

61. Sermon 32, "Upon Our Lord's Sermon on the Mount, XII," §III.8, *Works* 1:682-83.

62. Discipline, 63.

63. UMH, 33.

64. BOR, 805.

65. *Notes* Acts 5:11. See also Wesley's "Treatise on Baptism" *Works* (J) 10:188-201.

66. UMH, 35, 40, 44, 48-49.

67. BOR, 807.

68. UMH, 36, 42.

69. BOR, 810.

70. UMH, 50-53.

71. BOR, 798.

72. Sermon 45, "The New Birth," §IV.2, *Works* 2:197-98.

73. Martyn Atkins suggests that this view may have been unique to Wesley at that time. Further research is needed to determine it was original with him or borrowed from someone else.

74. Sermon 18, "The Marks of the New Birth," §IV.5, *Works* 1:430.

75. Sermon 39, "Catholic Spirit," §II.2, *Works* 2:90.

76. *Notes* Col. 2:12.

77. *Notes* Matt. 3:6.

78. BOR, 806.

79. Stamm, 60.

80. Discipline, 68.

81. Discipline, 133.

82. *Notes* Acts 16:15. See also Wesley's *Thoughts Upon Infant Baptism.*

83. BOR, 810.

84. BOR, 808.

85. Ruth Duck, UMH, 605.

86. Sermon 16, "The Means of Grace," §II.1, *Works* 1:381.

87. Discipline, 64.

88. Discipline, 68.

89. Sermon 16, "The Means of Grace," §III.11, *Works* 1:389. In Sermon 101, "On the Duty of Constant Communion," §II.3, *Works* 3:431, he says, "Perhaps you will say, 'God does not command me to do this *as often as I can*'; that is, the words 'as often as you can' are not added in this particular place. What then? Are we not to obey every command of God as often as we can? Are not all the promises of God made to those, and those only, who 'give all diligence'; that is, to those who do all they can to obey his commandments? Our power is the one rule of our duty. Whatever we can do, that we ought. With respect either to this or any other command, he that when he may obey it if he will does not, will have no place in the kingdom of heaven."

90. Sermon 26, "Upon Our Lord's Sermon on the Mount, VI," §III.11, *Works* 1:584-85.

91. Sermon 16, "The Means of Grace," §V.1, *Works* 1:394.

92. Discipline, 68.

93. *The United Methodist Hymnal* with the liturgies for Communion was published in 1989. *The United Methodist Book of Worship* was published in 1992. In 1996 the General Conference passed a resolution still in effect, ordering "that the words 'The pure, unfermented juice of the grape shall be used during the service of Holy Communion' be added beneath the headings 'A Service of Word and Table I,' 'A Service of Word and Table II,' and 'A Service of Word and Table III,' " BOR, 838. At such time as there is a revision or reprinting of the ritual, these words will be added.

94. UMH, 627.

95. *Notes* Luke 22:19. See also Mark 14:24, Matt. 26:26, 1 Cor. 10:16, 1 Cor. 11:24.

96. Discipline, 64.

97. Discipline, 64.

98. Discipline, 63.

99. UMH, 10, 14.

100. Stamm, 68.

101. UMH, 7, 12.

102. UMH, 26.

103. Sermon 16, "The Means of Grace," §III.1, *Works* 1:384.

104. Sermon 26, "Upon Our Lord's Sermon on the Mount, VI," §II.1, 1:575.

105. Sermon 26, "Upon Our Lord's Sermon on the Mount, VI," §II.5, 1:577.

106. Discipline, 74.

107. Sermon 16, "The Means of Grace," §III.7, *Works* 1:387.

108. For a fuller treatment of Wesley's conception and use of Scripture, see Jones. For a discussion of searching the Scriptures as a means of grace, see Knight, 148-59.

109. Among the questions asked of a candidate for ordination is "Will you recommend fasting or abstinence, both by precept and example?" Discipline, 204, 214.

110. The following discussion is taken from Sermon 27, "Upon our Lord's Sermon on the Mount, VII," §§II.1-12, *Works* 1:597-604.

111. Sermon 27, "Upon our Lord's Sermon on the Mount, VII," §II.6, *Works* 1:600.

112. BOW, 322.

113. Discipline, 43.

PART III

THE GOAL OF DOCTRINE

CHAPTER TEN

PREACHING AND MAINTAINING UNITED METHODIST DOCTRINE

According to the teaching of The United Methodist Church, the "religion of the heart" is the goal of Christian doctrine: "This alone is religion, truly so called: this alone is in the sight of God of great price. The Apostle sums it all up in three particulars—'righteousness, and peace, and joy in the Holy Ghost.'"[1] At times Wesley's sermons deride the importance of orthodoxy, claiming that it cannot be the essence of true religion. Yet, orthodoxy and belonging to the church "blessed with the purest doctrine, the most primitive liturgy, [and] the most apostolical form of government . . . are doubtless so many reasons for praising God, as they may be so many helps to holiness."[2] Holiness is the goal. Correct doctrine tends toward holiness, all other things being equal.

The goal of doctrine is to bring about that true religion which is the salvation offered to all people. Thus, United Methodist doctrine spends much more time on those topics most directly related to the practice of Christianity by believers. Measured by the bulk of its various sections, it is more concerned with soteriology than Christology, and more focused on ethical issues than the end times.

One might argue that this practical focus was possible for Wesley precisely because he could presume the structure of Anglican doctrine and liturgy, to which he had no serious objections. His burning issue was how genuine Christianity could be established in the world. For him, this was primarily asking how people could be saved. Most of his published work was directed toward clarifying those issues.

One way to formulate the question about doctrine today is to rephrase one of the questions that is asked of candidates for ordination as elder in the United Methodist Church: How will you preach and maintain our doctrines?[3] Maintenance of doctrine should be understood with reference to the whole of one's ministry. Thus, to maintain doctrine is to exercise one's work as a leader in the Christian community so that the doctrine of the faith shapes the community and the lives of its members. Preaching these doctrines, then, forms one important aspect of maintenance.

MAINTAINING UNITED METHODIST DOCTRINE

In his published letter to Conyers Middleton written in 1749, Wesley distinguishes between Christianity as a principle in the soul and Christianity as a system of doctrine. They are related, because the doctrine does three things: it describes Christian character, it promises that one can attain it, and it shows how one can attain it.[4] This is Wesley's way of summarizing an important relationship between Christian doctrine and the Christian life.

DOCTRINE DESCRIBES A FORM OF LIFE

Throughout this study we have seen that United Methodist doctrine treats the normal topics found in Christian teaching. There are doctrines of God, Christ, Holy Spirit, Scripture, salvation, ecclesiology, and eschatology. One of the features that distinguishes the teaching of this Church from other branches of the Christian church is its focus on salvation. God's saving grace is the central theme of this teaching. Hence, consideration of other doctrines is sometimes more abbreviated than is the case elsewhere. Further, other topics are usually considered in light of their impact on salvation as a present reality. For example, there is no extended discussion of the last judgment, heaven, or hell. There is no concern with setting a date for the second coming of Christ, unless one construes the *Notes* on Revelation with more emphasis than Wesley himself was willing to put on them. When matters of the end of the world are discussed, it is usually with the concern of how the prospect of a final accounting for our actions should motivate us to make better use of God's grace to work out our salvation here and now. Even in contemporary statements of United Methodist doctrine, the concern with the reign of God is expressed in statements about personal and social holiness.

Thus, United Methodist doctrine is practical, in part, because it focuses on the practice of the Christian faith and avoids what it understands to be speculative and less central to questions of practice. What is central to Christian practice? Whatever most closely pertains to the activities of God's saving grace. God's saving grace is bringing persons from sin through repentance and justification to sanctification, and ultimately to entire sanctification. What aids in that process is central. What is less important to that process is less central.

Thus, United Methodist doctrine describes a form of life. It has a description of the human condition. Human beings are creatures made in God's image who have sinned and broken the relationship God intended. God loves them and is preveniently active in their lives, seeking to repair the damage sin has wrought. Christ died to redeem all of humanity, thereby making possible the offer of salvation that God has extended to everyone.

This description of the human situation is directly tied to a prescription. God is calling everyone to repent, believe, and obey. God's prevenient, justifying, and sanctifying grace make all of this possible. While God's grace is available in many different ways, God has ordained the church, its sacraments, and its other practices as ways in which individuals might avail themselves of God's grace. While salvation is an individual matter, it always involves life in community.

Obedience to God thus means faithfully following the way of salvation, which points to the restoration of one's self as a daughter or son of God. Daughters and sons of God live lives shaped by certain specific practices. They perform works of mercy such as caring for the poor and those in need. They are concerned for justice in society and seek to participate in God's liberating activity in the world. They avoid evil, which means that they take note of how people are breaking God's laws and they are careful not to engage in such behavior.

At the same time, God's children are involved in works of piety. They worship God regularly. They engage in public and private prayer. They read the Bible and study the writings of Christian teachers. They engage in Christian conference with others in order to watch over one another and help one another make progress in the way of salvation. They are baptized either as infants or at the time of justification, and they receive the Lord's Supper at every opportunity. They are faithful and strong participants in the church that they believe is most biblical. While they are strong in their own Christian convictions, they are careful to recognize other Christians as brothers and sisters in the Lord, even when they disagree on matters of opinion.

Within specific Christian congregations, then, the form of life can be further specified. Christianity must be contextualized, and so different expressions of United Methodism have different practices because culture varies. Worship looks different in East Texas than it does among the street people of San Francisco, than it does among the new converts in Moscow, than it does in Zimbabwe. Such variations should not simply be tolerated, but instead positively encouraged in order to make concrete the guiding principles of the denomination's doctrine. Similarly, the social justice issues that are addressed in each of the above-named places will be different because the human need is different and God's saving grace is doing different things in response to that need.

Ministry Enables and Nurtures Christian Life

One of Wesley's "Rules of a Helper" says, "You have nothing to do but to save souls. Therefore spend and be spent in this work."[5] The same could be said of United Methodist clergy today, provided one has a Wesleyan understanding of all that is included in the process of "saving souls." The practice of ordained ministry involves the transformation of persons, communities, and all of human society to be more closely conformed to God's intention for them.

The mission statement of the United Methodist Church[6] makes it clear that all of the various ministries of the church are included as part of one organic process. For far too long Christians have selected one part of the mission and neglected others. Persons committed to evangelism have opposed ministries of social justice and vice versa. Persons committed to social justice have de-emphasized ministries of spiritual formation and worship. Persons involved in education ministries have seen their work as a good substitute for evangelism. Yet, when viewed from the perspective of the person going along the way of salvation, the ministries of the church all form an important connection as components of one, integrated way of life.

The relationship between doctrine and this way of life is dialectical. Doctrine is the teaching that arises out of this way of life, and in turn shapes it. In the course of living out the faith, questions arise that need careful, authoritative answers. As the Church answers the questions, it then shapes and reforms its practices in accordance with the doctrine. As new practices give rise to new questions and new answers, its doctrine is reformed, too.

Worship

Worship is central to the Christian life. It can be defined as "the adoration and service of God through Christ in the power of the Holy Spirit within the body of Christ."[7] Romans 12:1 describes the Christian life, urging the disciples "to present your bodies as a living sacrifice, holy and acceptable to God, which is your spiritual worship."[8] While all of life is worship in this sense, the Christian community gathers for worship services to offer praise and service to God through prayer, song, preaching, sacraments, and celebration. Because Christianity is essentially a social religion, Christians gather for worship services as a community.[9]

Doctrine relates to worship in a variety of ways. The very motivation for worship comes from an understanding of who God is and what humanity's relationship to God should be. What is said during worship is an expression of the church's doctrine, and doctrine is a formalized way of explaining what is done in worship. If we offer prayers to one God, but then name that God as Father, Son, and Holy Spirit, we clearly need to understand why there can be one God in three persons. If we thank God for God's mighty acts of salvation and then eat bread and wine together saying that we are partaking of the body and blood of Christ, then the doctrine helps the church understand the meaning and purpose of its action. If the church addresses God in both feminine and masculine terms and refers to human beings with gender inclusive pronouns, then it is being faithful to its deepest and best understandings of God and humanity. Indeed, doctrine tells the church both why it is doing these things, and when it is doing them appropriately or inappropriately.

In United Methodist doctrine worship is one of the most important activities of a Christian. It is in worship as a means of grace that a person might be awakened to his need for forgiveness and be led to repentance. It is in worship that a person might be brought to saving faith in Christ. It is in worship that a person might receive sanctifying grace. The General Rules require that for all those who are serious about salvation, "attending upon the ordinances of God" is a necessary practice. There is something deeply wrong about persons who claim to be Christians and are physically able to attend, and do not worship with their congregation on a regular, weekly basis.

Evangelism

Given this understanding that the will of God is to restore sinners to the image of God, part of the church's ministry is to engage in evangelism. Evangelism is not defined in the authoritative texts, but might be construed as comprising the first two steps in the process of making disciples:

> We make disciples as we:
> —proclaim the gospel, seek, welcome and gather persons into the body of Christ;
> —lead persons to commit their lives to God through baptism and profession of faith in Jesus Christ.[10]

Evangelism is best understood as that ministry of initiating persons into the Christian life. Local congregations do this in a wide variety of ways, but the first step is the congregation's decision to be missionary—to reach out to those who are not already part of the body of Christ. The gospel must be proclaimed in ways that will convince persons of their sin and lead them to repent. Every person is loved by God enough for God to demand they quit destroying themselves, each other, and the world. The healing solution, as understood by United Methodist doctrine, is reception of God's saving grace by faith, incorporation into the church, and transforming service in the world.

What is the content of the message that is proclaimed? Again, the dialectical relationship with Christian doctrine is important. Christian doctrine specifies the content of the gospel, which must be shared. The practice of ministry in evangelistic situations not only contextualizes the message, but also raises new questions that must be answered.

Education and Formation

Part of initiation into the Christian life is the intellectual understanding of all that is involved in becoming a Christian. Thus, the educational task is already begun when the sinner learns who God is, what God's expectations are, and how to become the person God is calling that person to be. There is an intellectual component to the process of initiation.[11] The third step in the mission process is

> We make disciples as we: . . .
>   —nurture persons in Christian living through worship, the sacraments, spiritual disciplines, and other means of grace, such as Wesley's Christian conferencing.[12]

This part of the process of sanctification is education in the broadest sense of the word. In fact, it is best to think of it not simply as intellectual growth, but the formation of a whole person through Christian practices. Part of this is learning to love God with one's mind, and learning more about Christian things. Bible study, discussion groups, reading books on theology, and other educational practices help persons grow in their faith and more deeply understand the Christian way of life.[13] This kind of intellectual formation should be conjoined with other practices that include private prayer, worship, fasting, ministry with the poor, accountability groups, and other means of grace. Some of these practices are instituted means of grace, meaning that God has commanded we follow them.[14] Worship, the Lord's Supper, prayer, Scripture reading, fasting, and ministry with the poor are all required Christian practices. Wesley called the other means of grace "prudential," because they are judgments based not directly on Scripture but on reason and experience as how best to implement Scripture's more general commands. Thus Sunday school might be a means of grace to some, but not to others. Those who do not attend Sunday school, however, might be asked about better or more effective ways in which they are in touch with God's grace to form their minds and hearts.

In the current North American context, however, renewed attention to teaching Christian doctrine to believers is essential. North American Protestant churches in general and The United Methodist Church in particular face a situation where fewer and fewer of their members know the basics of the faith. There are more and more religious options competing with them in the marketplace of ideas. At one time there was a kind of Protestant establishment that allowed churches to presume that their members would understand the basics of the faith. Now, with the influence of television and other forms of information, and the departure of explicit Christian teaching from public forums like public schools, the church must take its own ministry of catechesis for converts and education for believers very seriously.[15]

Justice Ministries

The fourth step in the process of the Church's mission is once again focused on those outside the community.

> We make disciples as we: . . .
> —send persons into the world to live lovingly and justly as servants of Christ by healing the sick, feeding the hungry, caring for the stranger, freeing the oppressed, and working to develop social structures that are consistent with the gospel.[16]

United Methodist doctrine stipulates that the more persons have the mind which was in Christ Jesus, the more they act "lovingly and justly" in the world. We are stewards of all God has given us, and we shall some day be called to account for our stewardship. With the increasing resources and knowledge available to use, one would think that the human capacity to love others would have increased dramatically. As patterns of oppression become clear, the Christian obligation to be involved in the corresponding acts of liberation become equally apparent. The Social Principles indicate the many different ways in which the Church perceives that God is working to save not only individuals, but also societies and the nonhuman creation as well.

Engaging in ministries of social justice is part of sanctification. The issues involved are often complex and Christians may disagree about what the best course of action is. Humans are liable to make mistakes in many ways. But the basic principle, that Christians as individuals and the church as a community are both to be involved in furthering justice in the world, is absolutely clear.

Holistic Practice

These various aspects of ministry could have been described differently in this chapter. In particular, practices of education and spiritual formation could have been listed individually. More attention should have been paid to pastoral counseling and its relationship to spiritual formation and spiritual disciplines. The crucial point is to see all of them together in a dialectical relationship with Christian doctrine. Taken together, they constitute a holistic practice of enabling and nurturing the Christian life.

There are two different ways in which these practices should cohere. First, they should not compete, but mutually reinforce each other. Doctrine helps us perceive the way in which all of these are part of one process—the way of salvation. Thus, worship has evangelistic aspects as does ministry with the poor. Bible study assists the congregation's authentic worship, and evangelism provides persons with the born-again spirit that leads them to engage in demonstrations against injustice. Upon closer analysis, the lines between these various ministries appear quite fuzzy, with each of them involving all of the others in various ways.

Second, individual practices retain their Christian identity by reference to their place in the whole. Sometimes these practices get sidetracked and lose their focus. Ministries of social justice become simply ways of engaging in politics without a christological and evangelistic focus. Evangelism can become pie-in-the-sky-when-you-die, thereby deserving religion's Marxist label as the opiate of the people. Study groups can focus less on learning the Bible than gossiping about the latest rumors in the congregation. All of these practices retain their purpose and their place as *Christian* practices when they have reference to the gospel and are serving a function within the way of salvation. Doctrine then becomes the reference point by which we measure whether a practice has retained its integrity or not.

At the same time, the totality of the Church's practice needs to be measured against its doctrine as well. There is always more to do than the resources will allow at any one time and place. Choices will be made about which aspects of the mission are more or less important. A clear apprehension of the Christian way of life embedded in its doctrine will help keep the Church's priorities straight. If a congregation has become an inwardly focused club of privilege, ignoring the needs for justice expressed by persons of a different race who live in its neighborhood, it has clearly failed to understand its own missionary nature. If a congregation does not engage in a well-focused and carefully planned ministry of evangelism, it does not understand how the gospel is meant to be heard by all persons. If a congregation accepts persons into membership and does not educate and form them through spiritual disciplines, it is leaving those members outside the means of grace. Christian practice is holistic. All the aspects of the way of salvation need to be part of the Church's ministry.

But at the same time there are many opportunities to spend inordinate amounts of time and money on small things that are far away from the main thing. Congregations engage in major arguments over the color of the new carpet in the sanctuary, the size of the parsonage, and the placement of the coffeepot in the new building. It would be far better to give that same amount of energy to consideration of (and yes, arguments about, for people do argue about what is important to them) which evangelistic strategy will work the best and which issue of social justice is most pressing in their community. All of the above issues, including parsonages and coffeepots, can be important issues. The crucial point is to see them in relation to the overall mission of the church and to give them only the attention, time, and resources they deserve in relation to other aspects of the mission.

With a clear understanding of the whole of Christian teaching, one can ask which ministries must be included in the life of a congregation, and how they should best be carried out so that the church can be faithful stewards of the gifts God has given them. When doctrine shapes the church's ministries and when the priorities in the doctrine determine the priorities with the church's ministries, then the church is maintaining doctrine. At the same time, seeing doctrine and the ministries of the church as integrally related will then provide a context for the shaping and reformulation of the church's doctrine.

PREACHING UNITED METHODIST DOCTRINE

Candidates for ordination as elder are asked if they will preach the doctrines of the Church. On a superficial level one might construe this as a commitment to preach an instructional sermon on each of the topics covered in traditional summaries of Christian doctrine. A minister might preach a sermon on each article of the Nicene Creed, or a twenty-five-week series on the Articles of Religion and the Confession of Faith, or one might take the eight chapters in part 2 of this study and devote a sermon to each one at least once a year.

There is a place for such doctrinal sermons in the life of a congregation. For congregations that follow the liturgical year, Christ the King Sunday is an important time for Christology, All Saints Day for ecclesiology, Christmas for incarnation, Good Friday for atonement, Easter for Resurrection, and Pentecost for inclusiveness and eschatology. Other calendar days, like Martin Luther King, Jr.'s birthday in the United States, are important occasions for addressing injustices like racism and poverty. World Communion Sunday might be a time for talking about the catholicity of the church. Confirmation Sunday might be the occasion when the specific claims of the Nicene Creed are addressed. In the current state of the church, the sermon is one of the few opportunities where such issues can be addressed before the whole congregation. Done poorly, sermons that aim solely to inculcate doctrinal information may be boring and ineffective in achieving their aim. Such approaches can be superficial in their understanding of preaching and their understanding of the role doctrine should play in preaching.

DOCTRINE AS PART OF THE PREACHER'S CONTEXT

Fred Craddock suggests that the sermon has to be experienced by its hearers in several contexts. He is convinced that "preaching is both words and the Word":

> Rather, the preacher takes the words provided by culture and tradition, selects from among them those that have the qualities of clarity, vitality, and appropriateness, arranges them so as to convey the truth and evoke interest, pronounces them according to the best accepted usage, and offers them to God in the sermon. It is God who fashions words into the Word.[17]

Thus, one of the contexts in which the sermon is experienced is the theological context. Craddock summarizes the relationship between theology and preaching in three statements. First, they exist in a "relationship of mutuality." Second, "theology prompts preaching to treat subjects of importance and avoid trivia." His third point relates to theology's focus on concepts and the sermon's use of "more concrete and graphic vocabulary." He says, "Theology stands by to ask if the language of the sermon could be recast into a concept or concepts, not because concepts are more appropriate for the pulpit, but because, when framed as theological concepts, the words of our sermons prove their sound substance and good intent."[18] Craddock's three statements are essentially correct. For this study, they become very helpful if one changes the subject from theology to doctrine.[19]

There is a sense in which doctrine is fulfilled in preaching. If the United Methodist Church as a community of believers has determined that the way of salvation is an important expression of the word of God, its preachers should be using sermons to convey that message. The whole scope of United Methodist doctrine, with its center in God's saving grace, helps the preacher decide which topics are most important and which are trivial. Further, Craddock's last point about the concepts of doctrine could be expanded with reference to doctrine as the grammar of the Church's witness. By using such concepts as justification and sanctification, the preacher is training up her community into a language intimately connected with the United Methodist understanding of the Christian way of life.

Further, the Church's doctrine defines the boundaries of acceptable preaching. The preacher speaks both for and to the community.[20] The preacher's message ought to be recognizable by the community as the faith of the Church on the basis of Scripture. This is true even in prophetic denunciation of the Church's sinful practices. But what if a United Methodist preacher told a congregation that Jesus was not the incarnate Son of God and that, as just another wise human being, Jesus should be respected in the same way as Socrates, Buddha, and Muhammad. Such a preacher would have broken his or her commitment to preach the doctrines of the Church he or she represents. Thus, doctrine norms preaching.

Doctrine also helps shape a theology of preaching. What is the sermon's purpose? The rich resources of United Methodist doctrine can help a preacher see many different purposes. The doctrine of prevenient grace means that God is already at work in the world before Christians ever name what God is doing. Mary Hilkert calls this "preaching as the art of naming grace." She says,

> God's presence is mediated in and through creation and human history, but that mystery remains hidden and untapped unless it is brought to word. The proclamation of the word and the celebration of the sacraments (Augustine's "visible words") bring the depth dimension of reality—grace—to recognition and thus effective power.[21]

She is clear that recognizing that depth dimension requires a faith tradition with the language to both identify God's presence and name it. Christian doctrine helps us realize that a person's search for meaning in life is in reality the response to God's wooing through prevenient grace.

Most important for United Methodist doctrine, though, preaching is about inviting persons into the reality of God's saving grace. Doctrinally sophisticated sermons use narrative, poetry, questions, exposition, teaching, denunciation, and many other techniques to become means of that convincing, justifying, and sanctifying grace. In this sense, preaching doctrine is all about saving souls.

DOCTRINE AND SCRIPTURAL INTERPRETATION

Preaching's relationship to the Word of God is complex, and how that Word is related to Scripture is equally complex. Without pre-empting any of the significant interpretations of that proper relationship, it should be said that doctrine has a bearing on how we interpret Scripture to discern God's Word for a particular time and place. In whatever way that the Bible informs preaching, how one reads the Bible will be an important part of how the sermon is prepared.

David Kelsey's point, that calling a text "scripture" inherently means one attributes a kind of wholeness to it, is very important.[22] Doctrine provides a hermeneutical framework that arises out of Scripture but then interprets Scripture. United Methodists discern God's saving grace as the central theme of the text. Thus, when a text appears to teach predestination, the Church says, "No, you are misunderstanding the whole message of Scripture." When the Scripture appears to limit women's full participation in the leadership of the Church, United Methodists say, "No, the whole Scripture authorizes such participation." When persons argue that the church should not engage in politics, United Methodists say, "No, God is God of the whole world, and the Scripture as a whole supports our political engagement."

DOCTRINE AS THE FRAMEWORK OF A BODY OF SERMONS

Ministry cannot be judged by one day of work, and preaching should not be judged by one sermon. Instead, preaching United Methodist doctrine ought to be evaluated over a long period of preaching to the same congregation. Whether the minister follows the lectionary or discerns the needs of the community and then selects the texts in response to those needs, the preacher should seek to convey the basic truths of the gospel to the people in appropriate ways over time.

Thus, over several years of preaching there ought to be many occasions when the doctrines of original sin, actual sin, repentance, justification, the new birth, witness of the Spirit, and Christian perfection are all addressed. God's grace and God's gift of faith ought to be frequent topics. Specific ways in which Christians should respond in works of mercy and works of piety ought to be mentioned. Explanations of the means of grace, whether Scripture, eucharist, baptism, fasting, justice ministries, or other activities should be given and participation in them encouraged.

Pastoral judgments need to be made about how this is best done. Homiletical judgments should be made about how best to communicate the good news. But communicating the topics of United Methodist doctrine are an important way in which the gospel is offered and understood by people who need to hear it. How these topics are preached is a contextually based pastoral judgment. That they are preached in some manner on a regular basis is an obligation of ordination.

PREACHING DOCTRINE IN CONTEXT

Craddock also notes that preaching, for the most part, occurs in a pastoral context, which ought to influence it in significant ways.[23] Recent trends in theology, particularly those of liberation theologies, have helped raise awareness that the cultural context in which Christians live is and should be an important factor in the way they bear witness. One might argue that the act of preaching is one important way in which doctrine is contextualized. Eunjoo Kim says about her own community,

> The internal and external conditions of Asian American congregations, which were explored in the previous chapter, reveal that one of the major tasks of Asian American homiletics is to develop a new theological perspective for preaching from the particular experience of Asian American congregations. . . .
>
> Asian American congregations are waiting for contextually relevant theological responses to these questions. They expect that sermons they hear every Sunday to reflect critically on their particular life experience and to provide them with a theological direction for their spiritual lives.[24]

In fact, the same could be said for every particular congregation whether in Angola, Norway, Ohio, or Oregon. Preaching United Methodist doctrine to African Americans experiencing racism can be different from preaching the same doctrine to upper-class white people who live in the same city. Even though the message is fundamentally the same, the many elements of how it is conveyed and where the emphases are placed could be very different and appropriately so.

The doctrine of incarnation means *in principle* that the gospel must be inculturated into new contexts. There is one gospel. But even the Scripture has its multiple versions written from multiple perspectives, and the church today must accept that plurality. However, there are limits to that plurality imposed by the canon of Scripture itself and by a particular church's doctrinal rendering of the Scripture's message.

DISSENTING FROM DOCTRINE

It is quite probable that a United Methodist minister in good standing as deacon or elder could read the authoritative texts of United Methodist doctrine and find something with which to disagree. How does one dissent responsibly from the official teachings of the Church one has vowed to support? Four theses bear on this question.

First, theological exploration is a necessary part of the Christian life because only through such exploration can individuals and the whole church grow in their faith and understanding. United Methodist doctrine affirms the theological task as part of the Church's mission. The theological task is critical, constructive, individual, communal, contextual, incarnational, and practical.[25] This exploration and inquiry is the task of every Christian, whether lay or ordained, whether a professional theologian or not. Such inquiry fulfills many functions, not least of which is "the testing, renewal, elaboration, and application of our doctrinal perspective in carrying out our calling 'to spread scriptural holiness over these lands.'"[26]

Because the teaching of the Church is a historical, dynamic process taking place in changing contexts, theological exploration will sometimes find places where the Church's authoritative texts need to be changed. Sometimes they are wrong. Sometimes they are expressed poorly. Sometimes they are internally inconsistent.

Sometimes they are silent on important issues that need to be addressed. In all of these cases responsible members of the community should seek ways to alter the Church's official teaching. Because the General Conference speaks for The United Methodist Church, suggested changes should be presented to the General Conference for consideration. The political process of discerning the will of God and the faith of the whole Church is often a complex and untidy series of events. Formation of organized groups, publication of books, pamphlets, magazines and videos, demonstrations at meetings, and many other ways have been used to give input into the process. All of these are important and appropriate ways of expressing dissent from the teachings of the Church. From such dissenting opinions new doctrines or new expressions of old doctrines sometimes result.

Second, the most helpful form of dissent and the easiest way to argue for a change, is to appeal from a lower level of teaching to a higher level or to point out contradictions between different parts. One might appeal even from the doctrinal standards to the authority of Scripture. One might suggest, for example, that infant baptism is really unbiblical and that it inhibits the spread of the gospel. A new and fresh reading of Scripture might suggest that we should change Article XVII and Confession VI. One might also suggest that, given the teachings of Vatican II, we should change the Articles of Religion that condemn certain teachings because both we and the Catholic Church now understand them better and in similar ways. Similar arguments could be mounted for a better revision of our doctrines about the church, the sacraments, and other matters in the Articles and Confession.

Third, the doctrinal statements of the Church need to be updated from time to time. As the Holy Spirit guides the Church's discernment of the truth, there are times that new aspects of the gospel become clear and the Church must share that with the world. At other times, mistakes need to be corrected or old truths need to be stated in new, more contemporary ways. As language evolves, the use of words that are several centuries old may obscure the message rather than communicate it. Specifically, the noninclusive language of the Articles, Confession, *Sermons*, and *Notes* represents a barrier to communicating the genuine gospel of Jesus Christ in the twenty-first century.

It would be logical, then, that General Conference appoint an official committee to lead the Church in discerning how best to revise our constitutional doctrinal standards and statements. This happens in minor ways at every General Conference, but twice in the last thirty years General Conference made major revisions. In both cases the decision was made not to seek amendments to the constitutional standards. Given the current changes in language, the progress of ecumenical dialogues, and the importance of doctrinal reinvigoration, I believe that the next major revision must involve the difficult process of amending those texts protected by the Restrictive Rules. While there are dangers and difficulties in such an enterprise, the goals of doctrinal integrity and reinvigoration require the effort.

Fourth, if dissent from doctrine involves disagreement with something very close to the center of the Church's teaching and attempts to get the Church to change its teaching fail, then a responsible person will surrender his or her conference relationship and leave the Church. Rather than preach a unitarian understanding of God, theories of white supremacy, or other doctrines contrary to the core teachings of the Church, persons of integrity will come to the conclusion that they do not belong as a representative of the United Methodist Church and should in good conscience join another religion. There are certain beliefs like the Trinity and God's love for persons of all races that are so central to the United Methodist understanding of the gospel that fundamental disagreement with them requires the breaking of fellowship. This is the spiritual basis for the chargeable offense in ¶2702, "dissemination of doctrines contrary to the established standards of doctrine of The United Methodist Church."[27] In cases where doctrinal dissent is so fundamental and yet the dissenter will not voluntarily leave the Church, the Church must protect the integrity of its own witness by removing the person from its fellowship.

The difficulty here lies in deciding which issues are so central that they require breaking fellowship and which are not. One clue is that the chargeable offense is disagreement not with contemporary statements of doctrine, but with the doctrinal standards. Another important indicator is the whole structure of United Methodist doctrine itself. If the center of United Methodist doctrine is God's saving grace, then those parts of the doctrinal standards that are peripheral to that general theme are of less importance. One might disagree with Wesley's understanding of how quickly the new birth happens. Such an opinion, in Wesley's words, is "compatible with love to Christ, and a work of grace" and ought to be covered by our catholic spirit.[28] In fact, one might argue that Wesley's teaching in the sermons "The New Birth" and "The Marks of the New Birth" is internally inconsistent on that point. Such doctrinal dissent is helpful when it works within the framework of United Methodist doctrine and appeals from the periphery of the Church's teaching to its center.

DOCTRINAL REINVIGORATION

Since 1972 the various editions of *The Book of Discipline* have said something very close to the following: "The United Methodist Church stands continually in need of doctrinal reinvigoration for the sake of authentic renewal, fruitful evangelism, and ecumenical dialogue. In this light, the recovery and updating of our distinctive doctrinal heritage—catholic, evangelical, and reformed—is essential."[29] During the last thirty years, how has the process of "doctrinal reinvigoration" gone? The vision that Albert Outler and his study committee put forth in 1972 has borne fruit. There have been a number of major doctrinal conversations and controversies over pluralism, the authority of Scripture, inclusive language, the mission of the Church, baptism, and Church membership. It has been recognized that the debate over homosexual practice, while itself a doctrinal matter, has deeper roots in different understandings of ecclesiology and the authority of Scripture. Numerous books, articles, pamphlets, and speeches have helped United Methodists clarify their understandings of these matters. Persons preparing for ordination now must take a class in United Methodist doctrine. The publication of Disciple Bible Study by the United Methodist Publishing House has provided a way for laypersons to read Scripture through the lens of Wesleyan doctrine. The Walk to Emmaus movement organized by the General Board of Discipleship has taught many persons a deeper appreciation for Holy Communion, as well as the language of prevenient, justifying, and sanctifying grace. More recently the Christian Believer program has begun to teach people to think about the doctrine of the Church. As one can see, there has been a renewed interest in doctrine in the United Methodist Church since 1972.

However, the task is far from complete. It is my hope that this study will contribute to the ongoing process of doctrinal reinvigoration by clarifying the shape and central theme of the teaching of the UMC. Doctrine is not an end in itself. Rather, it is a necessary part of the church's witness and mission in the world. At the end of his life Wesley was troubled about the future of the movement he had led for over five decades. There were many dangers, but one of them was abandoning the truth of the gospel. His warning should ring in our ears:

> I am not afraid that the people called Methodists should ever cease to exist either in Europe or America. But I am afraid lest they should only exist as a dead sect, having the form of religion without the power. And this undoubtedly will be the case unless they hold fast both the doctrine, spirit, and discipline with which they first set out.[30]

Notes

1. "The Way to the Kingdom," §I.6-7, *Works* 1:221.

2. "Upon Our Lord's Sermon on the Mount, XIII," §III.1, *Works* 1:694.

3. Discipline, 214.

4. Letter to Conyers Middleton, *Works* (J) 10:72. See Knight and Saliers 36-38 for a brief discussion of this.

5. "Minutes of Several Conversations Between the Rev. Mr. Wesley and Others," *Works* (J) 8:310. This document is often called "The Large Minutes" and was the precursor to the "Doctrines and Discipline of the Methodist Episcopal Church."

6. Discipline, 87-89.

7. I am indebted to a conversation with my colleague Mark Stamm for this definition.

8. NRSV.

9. Sermon 24, "Upon Our Lord's Sermon on the Mount, IV," §I.1, *Works* 1:533.

10. Discipline, 88.

11. For a description of six components to evangelism as initiation, see Abraham 1989.

12. Discipline, 88.

13. See Wood 1994 for an essay that could describe the Christian life, as well as study in a seminary.

14. "Minutes of Several Conversations Between the Rev. Mr. Wesley and Others," *Works* (J) 8:322-24.

15. See Abraham 1995 for his call for a new catechumenate.

16. Discipline, 88.

17. Craddock, 18-19.

18. Craddock, 47-50.

19. Craddock says that "the Scriptures are normative in the life of the church" (27) but does not discuss the preacher's relationship to the larger community and the other authoritative teachings of the church that is represented. There is some discussion of tradition, but none of the present authoritative context in which preachers stand. Craddock's omission is not surprising given the poor understanding of the relationship between doctrine and theology, and the weak ecclesiological commitments of North American Protestants.

20. Craddock, 26.

21. Hilkert, 47.

22. Kelsey, 106.

23. Craddock, 39.

24. Kim, 48.

25. Discipline, 75-76.

26. Discipline, 75.

27. Discipline, 696.

28. Wesley's Journal for May 14, 1765. "You have admirably well expressed what I mean by an opinion, contradistinguished from an essential doctrine. Whatever is 'compatible with love to Christ, and a work of grace' I term an *opinion*. And certainly the holding particular election and final perseverance is compatible with these." *Works* 21:509.

29. Discipline, 59. See the first statement in *The Book of Discipline of The United Methodist Church, 1972,* 49.

30. "Thoughts Upon Methodism," *Works* 9:527.

SELECTED BIBLIOGRAPHY

Abraham, William J.
    1989   *The Logic of Evangelism*. Grand Rapids, Mich.: Eerdmans.
    1995   *Waking From Doctrinal Amnesia: the Healing of Doctrine in the United Methodist Church*. Nashville: Abingdon.

Allen, Joseph L.
    1974   "Some Reflections on the 1972 Social Principles Statement," *Perkins Journal*, 28:1 (Fall, 1974):28-36.

Arias, Mortimer.
    1984   *Announcing the Reign of God: Evangelization and the Subversive Memory of Jesus*. Philadelphia: Fortress.

Atkins, Martyn.
    2001   "John Wesley's Baptismal Legacy." Unpublished manuscript.

Baird, William.
    1992   *History of New Testament Research. Volume One: From Deism to Tübingen*. Minneapolis: Fortress.

Baker, Frank.
    1966   "The Doctrines in the Discipline: A Study of the Forgotten Theological Presuppositions of American Methodism." *Duke Divinity School Review* 31 (Winter): 39-55.
    2000   *John Wesley and the Church of England*. 2nd edn. Rpt. of 1970 edn. with new preface. London: Epworth.

Behney, J. Bruce and Paul H. Eller.
    1979   *The History of the Evangelical United Brethren Church*. Ed. Kenneth W. Krueger. Nashville: Abingdon.

Bicknell, E. J. and H. J. Carpenter.
    1955   *A Theological Introduction to the Thirty-nine Articles of the Church of England*. 3rd rev. ed. London: Longmans, Green and Co.

The Book of Common Prayer, and Administration of the Sacraments . . . According to the Use of the Church of England.
    1710   Oxford: University Printers.
             Borgen, Ole E.
    1972   *John Wesley on the Sacraments: A Theological Study*. Nashville and New York: Abingdon.

Brockway, Allan R.
>
> 1972 "A Struggle for the Faith of the Church." *Engage.* 4:9 (June):28-48.

Burwash, Nathanael, ed.
>
> 1982 *Wesley's Doctrinal Standards. Part 1. The Sermons, with Introductions, Analysis and Notes.* 1881. Rpt. Salem, Ohio: Schmul Publishing Co.

Campbell, Dennis M., William B. Lawrence, and Russell E. Richey, eds.
>
> 1999 *United Methodism and American Culture.* Vol. 3. *Doctrines and Discipline.* Nashville: Abingdon.

Campbell, Ted A.
>
> 1991a *John Wesley and Christian Antiquity: Religious Vision and Cultural Change.* Kingswood Books. Nashville: Abingdon.
>
> 1991b " 'The Wesleyan Quadrilateral': The Story of a Modern Methodist Myth." In Thomas A. Langford, *Doctrine and Theology in The United Methodist Church.* Kingswood Books. Nashville: Abingdon, 154-61.
>
> 1999 *Methodist Doctrine: The Essentials.* Nashville: Abingdon.
>
> 2000 " 'Pure, Unbounded Love': Doctrine About God in Historic Wesleyan Communities." In M. Douglas Meeks, ed. *Trinity, Community and Power: Mapping Trajectories in Wesleyan Theology.* Kingswood Books. Nashville: Abingdon.

Carder, Kenneth L.
>
> 1996 *Living Our Beliefs.* Nashville: Discipleship Resources.

Charry, Ellen T.
>
> 1997 *By the Renewing of Your Minds: The Pastoral Function of Christian Doctrine.* New York and Oxford: Oxford Univ. Press.

Christian, William A., Sr.
>
> 1987 *Doctrines of Religious Communities: A Philosophical Study.* Yale Univ. Press: New Haven and London.

Cobb, John.
>
> 1995 *Grace and Responsibility: A Wesleyan Theology for Today.* Nashville: Abingdon.

Collins, Kenneth J.
>
> 1986 "John Wesley and the Means of Grace." *Drew Gateway* 56:3:26-33.
>
> 1997 *The Scripture Way of Salvation: The Heart of John Wesley's Theology.* Nashville: Abingdon.

The Compact Edition of the Oxford English Dictionary.
>
> 1971 2 vols. Oxford: Oxford Univ. Press.

Craddock, Fred B.
>
> 1985 *Preaching.* Nashville: Abingdon.

Dabney, D. Lyle.
>
> 2001 "Unfinished Business: John Wesley and Friedrich Schleiermacher on the Doctrine of the Holy Spirit." www.wesleyanstudies.org, posted 2 March 2001.

De George, Richard.
>
> 1985 *The Nature and Limits of Authority.* Lawrence, Kan.: University Press of Kansas.

Deschner, John.
  1985   *Wesley's Christology: An Interpretation.* Rpt. of 1960 edn. Dallas: Southern Methodist University Press.
Felton, Gayle Carlton.
  1992   *This Gift of Water: The Practice and Theology of Baptism Among Methodists in America.* Nashville: Abingdon.
Frank, Thomas Edward.
  1997   *Polity, Practice, and the Mission of The United Methodist Church.* Nashville: Abingdon.
Frei, Hans W.
  1974   *The Eclipse of Biblical Narrative: A Study in Eighteenth and Nineteenth Century Hermeneutics.* New Haven and London: Yale Univ. Press.
Green, Tyrrell.
  1896   *The Thirty-nine Articles and The Age of the Reformation: An Historical and Doctrinal Exposition in the Light of Contemporary Documents.* London: Wells Gardner, Darton and Co.
Gunter, W. Stephen.
  1989   *The Limits of Love Divine: John Wesley's Response to Antinomianism and Enthusiasm.* Kingswood Books. Nashville: Abingdon.
Gunter, W. Stephen, Scott J. Jones, Ted A. Campbell, Rebekah L. Miles, and Randy L. Maddox.
  1997   *Wesley and the Quadrilateral: Renewing the Conversation.* Nashville: Abingdon.
Handy, Robert T., ed.
  1966   *The Social Gospel in America, 1870–1920: Gladden, Ely, Rauschenbusch.* Library of Protestant Thought. New York: Oxford Univ. Press.
Harnish, John E.
  2000   *The Orders of Ministry in The United Methodist Church.* Nashville: Abingdon.
Heitzenrater, Richard P.
  1991a "At Full Liberty: Doctrinal Standards in Early American Methodism." In Thomas A. Langford, ed. *Doctrine and Theology in the United Methodist Church.* Kingswood Books. Nashville: Abingdon, 109-124.
  1991b "In Search of Continuity and Consensus: The Road to the 1988 Doctrinal Statement." In Thomas A. Langford, ed. *Doctrine and Theology in the United Methodist Church.* Kingswood Books. Nashville: Abingdon, 93-108. Partial reprint in Richey, Rowe and Schmidt, 699-706.
  1995   *Wesley and the People Called Methodists.* Nashville: Abingdon.
Hickman, Hoyt L.
  1997   "The Theology of the Lord's Supper in the New United Methodist Ritual." *Quarterly Review* 17:4 (Winter):361-76.
Hilkert, Mary Catherine.
  1997   *Naming Grace: Preaching and the Sacramental Imagination.* New York: Continuum.

Holland, Bernard G.
 1970 *Baptism in Early Methodism*. London: Epworth.
Hopkins, Charles Howard.
 1940 *The Social Gospel in American Protestantism, 1865–1915*. New Haven, Conn.: Yale Univ. Press and London: Oxford Univ. Press.
Hunter, George.
 1996 *Church for the Unchurched*. Nashville: Abingdon.
Hütter, Reinhard.
 2000 *Suffering Divine Things: Theology as Church Practice*. Trans. Doug Stott. Grand Rapids, Mich.: Eerdmans.
In Search of Unity: A Conversation with Recommendations for the Unity of The United Methodist Church.
 1998 New York: General Commission on Christian Unity and Interreligious Concerns. http://www.gccuic-umc.org/web/printedresources.htm. Partial reprint in Richey, Rowe and Schmidt, 699-706.
Jennings, Theodore W., Jr.
 1985 "Theology as the Construction of Doctrine" in *The Vocation of the Theologian*, ed. Theodore W. Jennings, Jr. Philadelphia: Fortress.
 1990 *Good News to the Poor: John Wesley's Evangelical Economics*. Nashville: Abingdon.
Johnson, Suzanne.
 1987 "John Wesley on the Duty of Constant Communion: The Eucharist as a Means of Grace for Today." In *Wesleyan Spirituality in Contemporary Theological Education*. Nashville: Division of Ordained Ministry, General Board of Higher Education and Ministry, The United Methodist Church., 25-46.
Jones, Scott J.
 1995 *John Wesley's Conception and Use of Scripture*. Kingswood Books. Nashville: Abingdon.
Judicial Council of The United Methodist Church.
 2001 http://www.umc.org/churchlibrary/judicial/decisions.htm.
Kelsey, David H.
 1975 *The Uses of Scripture in Recent Theology*. Philadelphia: Fortress.
Kim, Eunjoo Mary.
 1999 *Preaching the Presence of God: A Homiletic from an Asian American Perspective*. Valley Forge, Pa.: Judson.
Kirby, James E.
 2000 *The Episcopacy in American Methodism*. Kingswood Books. Nashville: Abingdon.
Kirby, James E., Russell E. Richey, and Kenneth E. Rowe.
 1996 *The Methodists*. Denominations in America, Number 8. Westport Conn. and London: Greenwood Press.
Klaiber, Walter.
 1997 *Call and Response: Biblical Foundations of a Theology of Evangelism*. Trans. Howard Perry-Trauthig and James A. Dwyer. Nashville: Abingdon. Orig. pub. as *Ruf und Antwort: Biblische Grundlagen einer Theologie der*

Evangelisation. Stuttgart: Christliches Verlagshaus GmbH and Neukirchen-Vluyn, Germany: Neukirchener Verlag, 1990.

Knight, Henry H.

1992 *The Presence of God in the Christian Life: John Wesley and the Means of Grace.* Pietist and Wesleyan Studies, No. 3. Metuchen, N.J. and London: Scarecrow Press.

Knight, Henry H. and Don Saliers.

1999 *The Conversation Matters: Why United Methodists Should Talk With One Another.* Nashville: Abingdon.

Langford, Thomas A.

1983 *Practical Divinity: Theology in the Wesleyan Tradition.* Nashville: Abingdon.

1991a *Doctrine and Theology in The United Methodist Church.* Kingswood Books. Nashville: Abingdon.

1991b "Conciliar Theology: A Report" in *Doctrine and Theology in The United Methodist Church.* Kingswood Books. Nashville: Abingdon, 176-85.

Lindbeck, George A.

1984 *The Nature of Doctrine: Religion and Theology in a Postliberal Age.* Philadelphia: Westminster.

1989 "Response to Bruce Marshall." *The Thomist.* 53:403-406.

Lindström, Harald.

1950 *Wesley and Sanctification: A Study in the Doctrine of Salvation.* London: Epworth.

Luby, Daniel Joseph.

1984 "The Perceptibility of Grace in the Theology of John Wesley: A Roman Catholic Consideration." Ph.D. Diss., Pontificia Studiorum Universitas A.S. Thoma Aq. In Urbe.

Maddox, Randy L.

1988 "John Wesley—Practical Theologian?" *Wesleyan Theological Journal* 23 (Spring-Fall):122-147.

1990 "The Recovery of Theology as a Practical Discipline." *Theological Studies* 51:650-672.

1991 "Practical Theology: A Discipline in Search of a Definition." *Perspectives in Religious Studies* 18 (Summer):159-169.

1992 "Opinion, Religion and 'Catholic Spirit': John Wesley on Theological Integrity," *Asbury Theological Journal* 47 (Spring):63-87.

1994 *Responsible Grace: John Wesley's Practical Theology.* Kingswood Books. Nashville: Abingdon.

Madsen, Norman P.

1987 "The Articles of Religion: Should We Take Them Seriously Today?" *Circuit Rider* (February):17-18.

Marquardt, Manfred.

1992 *John Wesley's Social Ethics: Praxis and Principles.* Trans. John E. Steely and W. Stephen Gunter. Nashville: Abingdon.

Marsden, George M.

1980 *Fundamentalism and American Culture: The Shaping of Twentieth-Century Evangelicalism, 1870–1925.* Oxford: Oxford University Press.

Marshall, Bruce D.
   1989   "Aquinas as Postliberal Theologian." *The Thomist* 53:353-402.
Matthews, Rex Dale.
   1986   "'Religion and Reason Joined': A Study in the Theology of John Wesley." Ph.D. Dissertation, Harvard University.
McGrath, Alister E.
   1990   *The Genesis of Doctrine: A Study in the Foundations of Doctrinal Criticism.* Oxford: Basil Blackwell.
Meadows, Philip R.
   2001   "The 'Discipline' of Theology: Making Methodism Less Methodological." *Wesleyan Theological Journal* 36:2 (Fall):50-87.
Oden, Thomas C.
   1988   *Doctrinal Standards in the Wesleyan Tradition.* Francis Asbury Press. Grand Rapids, Mich.: Zondervan.
   1991   "What Are 'Established Standards of Doctrine'? A Response to Richard Heitzenrater." In Thomas A. Langford, ed. *Doctrine and Theology in the United Methodist Church.* Kingswood Books. Nashville: Abingdon, 125-42.
Ogletree, Thomas.
   1991   "In Quest of a Common Faith: The Theological Task of United Methodists." In Thomas A. Langford, ed. *Doctrine and Theology in the United Methodist Church.* Kingswood Books. Nashville: Abingdon, 168-75.
O'Malley, J. Steven.
   1987   "A Distinctive German-American Credo: The United Brethren Confession of Faith." *The Asbury Theological Journal* 42:1 (Spring):51-63.
   1999   "The Distinctive Witness of the Evangelical United Brethren Confession of Faith in Comparison with the Methodist Articles of Religion." In Campbell, Lawrence, and Richey, eds., *United Methodism and American Culture.* Vol. 3. *Doctrines and Discipline.* Nashville: Abingdon, 55-76.
Outler, Albert C.
   1991   "Introduction to the Report of the 1968–72 Theological Study Commission." In Thomas A. Langford, ed. *Doctrine and Theology in the United Methodist Church.* Kingswood Books. Nashville: Abingdon, 20-25.
Pelikan, Jaroslav.
   1971   *The Christian Tradition: A History of the Development of Doctrine.* Vol. 1 *The Emergence of the Catholic Tradition (100-600).* Chicago and London: Univ. of Chicago Press.
Rattenbury, J. Ernest.
   1948   *The Eucharistic Hymns of John and Charles Wesley.* London: Epworth.
Reventlow, Henning Graf.
   1985   *The Authority of the Bible and the Rise of the Modern World.* Trans. John Bowden. Philadelphia: Fortress.

Richey, Russell E.
  1991   "History in the Discipline." In Thomas A. Langford, *Doctrine and Theology in the United Methodist Church.* Kingswood Books. Nashville: Abingdon, 190-202.
  1995   "The Legacy of Francis Asbury: The Teaching Office in Episcopal Methodism." *Quarterly Review* 15 (Summer), 145-174.
  1996   *The Methodist Conference in America: A History.* Kingswood Books. Nashville: Abingdon.
Richey, Russell E., Kenneth E. Rowe, Jean Miller Schmidt, eds.
  2000   *The Methodist Experience in America: A Sourcebook.* Nashville: Abingdon.
Rieger, Joerg.
  1997   "The Means of Grace, John Wesley, and the Theological Dilemma of the Church Today." *Quarterly Review* 17:4 (Winter):377-393.
Runyon, Ted.
  1998   *The New Creation: John Wesley's Theology Today.* Nashville: Abingdon Press.
Schaff, Philip, ed.
  1931   *The Creeds of Christendom: With a History and Critical Notes.* 3 vols. 6th edn. Rev. David S. Schaff. Rpt. 1998. Grand Rapids, Mich.: Baker Books.
Schmidt, Jean Miller.
  1991   *Souls or the Social Order: The Two-Party System in American Protestantism.* Brooklyn, N.Y. : Carlson.
Smith, Warren Thomas.
  1986   *John Wesley and Slavery.* Nashville: Abingdon.
Stamm, Mark W.
  2001   *Sacraments and Discipleship: Understanding Baptism and the Lord's Supper in a United Methodist Context.* Nashville: Discipleship Resources.
Starkey, Lycurgus M., Jr.
  1962   *The Work of the Holy Spirit: A Study in Wesleyan Theology.* New York and Nashville: Abingdon.
Stein, K. James.
  1988   "Doctrine, Theology, and Life in the Foundational Documents of the United Methodist Church." *Quarterly Review* 8:3 (Fall):42-62.
Strehle, Stephen.
  1989   "The Extent of the Atonement and the Synod of Dort." *Westminster Theological Journal* 51 (Spring): 1-23.
Sugden, Edward H., ed.
  1955   *Wesley's Standard Sermons.* 4th annotated edn. 2 vols. London: Epworth.
The United Methodist Book of Worship.
  1992   Nashville: The United Methodist Publishing House.
The United Methodist Hymnal: Book of United Methodist Worship.
  1989   Nashville: The United Methodist Publishing House.

Thorsen, Donald A.D.
　　1990　*The Wesleyan Quadrilateral: Scripture, Tradition, Reason & Experience as a Model of Evangelical Theology.* Grand Rapids, Mich.: Zondervan.
Tucker, Karen B. Westerfield.
　　1996　"Form and Freedom: John Wesley's Legacy for Methodist Worship." In Karen B. Westerfield Tucker, ed. *The Sunday Service of the Methodists: Twentieth-Century Worship in Worldwide Methodism: Studies in Honor of James F. White.* Kingswood Books. Nashville: Abingdon.
Wainwright, Geoffrey.
　　1988　"The Sacraments in Wesleyan Perspective." *Doxology* 5:5-20.
　　1990　"Why Wesley Was a Trinitarian." *Drew Gateway* 59 (Spring):26-43.
　　2001　"Wesley's Trinitarian Hermeneutics." Unpublished MS.
Wesley, John.
　　1751　*Thoughts Upon Infant Baptism, Extracted from a Late Writer.* Bristol: Felix Farley.
　　1755　*Explanatory Notes Upon the New Testament.* London: William Bowyer, 1755. Various reprints, including http://wesley.nnu.edu.
　　1921　*Wesley's Standard Sermons.* Ed. Edward H. Sugden. 2 vols. London: Epworth.
　　1872　*The Works of John Wesley, A.M.* Edited by Thomas Jackson. 14 vols. London: Wesleyan Conference Office, 1872. Reprint, Grand Rapids, Mich.: Zondervan, [1958–59].
　　1975-　*The Works of John Wesley.* Ed. Frank Baker and Richard P. Heitzenrater. Vols. 7, 11, 25 and 26: The Oxford Edition, Oxford: Clarendon, 1975–83. All other vols. Bicentennial Edition, Nashville: Abingdon, 1984– .
Wheeler, Henry.
　　1908　*History and Exposition of the Twenty-Five Articles.* New York: Eaton and Mains.
Williams, Colin.
　　1960　*John Wesley's Theology Today.* New York and Nashville: Abingdon.
Wood, Charles M.
　　1985　*Vision and Discernment: An Orientation in Theological Study.* Atlanta, Ga.: Scholars Press.
　　1994　*An Invitation to Theological Study.* Valley Forge, Pa.: Trinity Press.
　　1996　"Scripture, Authenticity and Truth." *Journal of Religion* 76 (April): 189-205.
　　1998　"Methodist Doctrine: An Understanding." *Quarterly Review* 18 (Summer):167-82.
Yrigoyen, Charles, Jr.
　　2001　*Belief Matters: United Methodism's Doctrinal Standards.* Nashville: Abingdon.

LIST OF VERSIONS CITED AND ABBREVIATIONS

Wesley's works are cited, whenever possible, in the Bicentennial Edition of *The Works of John Wesley*. If the relevant volumes have not yet been published, then older editions are used. To facilitate the use of multiple editions, I have cited section number as provided by Wesley in some writings, notably the *Sermons*. References to the *Explanatory Notes Upon the New Testament* will be given only by book, chapter, and verse since most editions are not paginated. Citations from the Bible are from the New Revised Standard Version unless otherwise noted. Books of the Bible are abbreviated following *The Society of Biblical Literature Handbook of Style*. Citations from the Greek New Testament are from the United Bible Societies' 4th revised edition, 1993.

The following abbreviations will be used to refer to these editions and other frequently cited works:

Article(s)   "The Articles of Religion of The Methodist Church," in *The Book of Discipline of The United Methodist Church, 2000*, 59-65. The roman numeral following the word "Article" or "Articles" indicates to which of the articles reference is being made.

BOR   *The Book of Resolutions of The United Methodist Church, 2000*. Nashville: The United Methodist Publishing House, 2000.

BOW   *The United Methodist Book of Worship*. Nashville: The United Methodist Publishing House, 1992.

Confession   "The Confession of Faith of the Evangelical United Brethren Church," in *The Book of Discipline of The United Methodist Church, 2000*, 66-71. The word "Confession" followed by a roman numeral indicates to which article of the Confession reference is being made.

D&T   Thomas A. Langford. *Doctrine and Theology in The United Methodist Church*. Kingswood Books. Nashville: Abingdon, 1991.

Discipline   *The Book of Discipline of The United Methodist Church, 2000*. Nashville: The United Methodist Publishing House, 2000. Citations from this source will be by page number unless specifically marked with a "¶".

Journal   *The Journal and Diaries of John Wesley*. Ed. Richard P. Heitzenrater. Vols. 18-23 in *Works*.

KJV   King James Version of the Bible.

NIV   New International Version of the Bible.

Notes   John Wesley's *Explanatory Notes Upon the New Testament*. London: William Bowyer, 1755. Various reprints.

NRSV   New Revised Standard Version of the Bible.

Resolutions   *The Book of Resolutions of The United Methodist Church, 2000*. Nashville: The United Methodist Publishing House, 2000.

Sermons	The fifty-three "standard sermons" of John Wesley. They are numbers 1-53 in Vols. 1 and 2 of *Works*, edited by Albert C. Outler.
Sugden	*Wesley's Standard Sermons.* Ed. Edward H. Sugden. 2 vols. London: Epworth, 1921.
UMH	*The United Methodist Hymnal: Book of United Methodist Worship.* Nashville: United Methodist Publishing House, 1989. Numbers cited here are either page numbers (v-x, 1-56, 906-962) or numbered items such as hymns, prayers and affirmations (57-904).
Wesley	When used without further qualification, this term refers to John Wesley.
Works	*The Works of John Wesley.* Bicentennial Edition. Ed. Frank Baker and Richard P. Heitzenrater. Nashville: Abingdon, 1984– . Vols. 7, 11, 25, and 26 were originally published by Clarendon Press, Oxford under the name "Oxford Edition."
Works (J)	*The Works of John Wesley.* [Ed. Thomas Jackson]. 14 vols. London: Wesleyan Conference Office, 1872. Reprint. Grand Rapids, Mich.: Zondervan, 1958.

INDEX